PRAISE FROM ACROSS THE NATION
FOR THE JOBBANK SERIES...

"If you are looking for a job ... before you go to the newspapers and the help-wanted ads, listen to Bob Adams, publisher of *The Metropolitan New York JobBank*."
-Tom Brokaw, *NBC*

"Help on the job hunt ... Anyone who is job-hunting in the New York area can find a lot of useful ideas in a new paperback called *The Metropolitan New York JobBank* ..."
-Angela Taylor, *New York Times*

"One of the better publishers of employment almanacs is Adams Media Corporation ... publisher of *The Metropolitan New York JobBank* and similarly named directories of employers in Texas, Boston, Chicago, Northern and Southern California, and Washington DC. A good buy ..."
-*Wall Street Journal's*
National Business Employment Weekly

"For those graduates whose parents are pacing the floor, conspicuously placing circled want ads around the house and typing up resumes, [*The Carolina JobBank*] answers job-search questions."
-*Greensboro News and Record*

"A timely book for Chicago job hunters follows books from the same publisher that were well received in New York and Boston ... [*The Chicago JobBank* is] a fine tool for job hunters ..."
-Clarence Peterson, *Chicago Tribune*

"Because our listing is seen by people across the nation, it generates lots of resumes for us. We encourage unsolicited resumes. We'll always be listed [in *The Chicago JobBank*] as long as I'm in this career."
-Tom Fitzpatrick, Director of Human Resources
Merchandise Mart Properties, Inc.

"Job-hunting is never fun, but this book can ease the ordeal ... [*The Los Angeles JobBank*] will help allay fears, build confidence, and avoid wheel-spinning."
-Robert W. Ross, *Los Angeles Times*

"*The Seattle JobBank* is an essential resource for job hunters."
-Gil Lopez, Staffing Team Manager
Battelle Pacific Northwest Laboratories

"*The Phoenix JobBank* is a first-class publication. The information provided is useful and current."

-Lyndon Denton
Director of Human Resources and Materials Management
Apache Nitrogen Products, Inc.

"Job hunters can't afford to waste time. *The Minneapolis-St. Paul JobBank* contains information that used to require hours of research in the library."

-Carmella Zagone
Minneapolis-based Human Resources Administrator

"*The Florida JobBank* is an invaluable job-search reference tool. It provides the most up-to-date information and contact names available for companies in Florida. I should know -- it worked for me!"

-Rhonda Cody, Human Resources Consultant
Aetna Life and Casualty

"I read through the 'Basics of Job Winning' and 'Resumes' sections [in *The Dallas-Fort Worth JobBank*] and found them to be very informative, with some positive tips for the job searcher. I believe the strategies outlined will bring success to any determined candidate."

-Camilla Norder, Professional Recruiter
Presbyterian Hospital of Dallas

"Through *The Dallas-Fort Worth JobBank,* we've been able to attract high-quality candidates for several positions."

-Rob Bertino, Southern States Sales Manager
CompuServe

"Packed with helpful contacts, *The Houston JobBank* empowers its reader to launch an effective, strategic job search in the Houston metropolitan area."

-Andrew Ceperley, Director
College of Communication Career Services
The University of Texas at Austin

"*The San Francisco Bay Area JobBank* ... is a highly useful guide, with plenty of how-to's ranging from resume tips to interview dress codes and research shortcuts."

-A.S. Ross, *San Francisco Examiner*

"[*The Atlanta JobBank* is] one of the best sources for finding a job in Atlanta!"

-Luann Miller, Human Resources Manager
Prudential Preferred Financial Services

What makes the JobBank series the nation's premier line of employment guides?

With vital employment information on thousands of employers across the nation, the JobBank series is the most comprehensive and authoritative set of career directories available today.

Each book in the series provides information on **dozens of different industries** in a given city or area, with the primary employer listings providing contact information, telephone and fax numbers, e-mail addresses, Websites, a summary of the firm's business, internships, and in many cases descriptions of the firm's typical professional job categories.

All of the reference information in the JobBank series is as up-to-date and accurate as possible. Every year, the entire database is thoroughly researched and verified by mail and by telephone. Adams Media Corporation publishes **more local employment guides more often** than any other publisher of career directories.

The JobBank series offers **28 regional titles**, from Minneapolis to Houston, and from Boston to San Francisco as well as **two industry-specific titles**. All of the information is organized geographically, because most people look for jobs in specific areas of the country.

A condensed, but thorough, review of the entire job search process is presented in the chapter **The Basics of Job Winning**, a feature which has received many compliments from career counselors. In addition, each JobBank directory includes a section on **resumes and cover letters** the *New York Times* has acclaimed as "excellent."

The JobBank series gives job hunters the most comprehensive, timely, and accurate career information, organized and indexed to facilitate your job search. An entire career reference library, JobBank books are designed to help you find optimal employment in any market.

Top career publications from Adams Media Corporation

The JobBank Series:
each JobBank book is $17.95

The Atlanta JobBank, 14th Ed.
The Austin/San Antonio JobBank, 3rd Ed.
The Boston JobBank, 19th Ed.
The Carolina JobBank, 6th Ed.
The Chicago JobBank, 18th Ed.
The Colorado JobBank, 13th Ed.
The Connecticut JobBank, 2nd Ed.
The Dallas-Fort Worth JobBank, 13th Ed.
The Detroit JobBank, 9th Ed.
The Florida JobBank, 15th Ed.
The Houston JobBank, 11th Ed.
The Indiana JobBank, 3rd Ed.
The Las Vegas JobBank, 2nd Ed.
The Los Angeles JobBank, 17th Ed.
The Minneapolis-St. Paul JobBank, 11th Ed.
The Missouri JobBank, 3rd Ed.
The New Jersey JobBank, 1st Ed.
The Metropolitan New York JobBank, 18th Ed.
The Ohio JobBank, 10th Ed.
The Greater Philadelphia JobBank, 14th Ed.
The Phoenix JobBank, 8th Ed.
The Pittsburgh JobBank, 2nd Ed.
The Portland JobBank, 3rd Ed.
The San Francisco Bay Area JobBank, 16th Ed.
The Seattle JobBank, 12th Ed.
The Tennessee JobBank, 5th Ed.
The Virginia JobBank, 3rd Ed.
The Metropolitan Washington DC JobBank, 15th Ed.

The JobBank Guide to Computer & High-Tech Companies, 2nd Ed. ($17.95)
The JobBank Guide to Health Care Companies, 2nd Ed. ($17.95)

The National JobBank, 2003 (Covers the entire U.S.: $450.00 hc)

Other Career Titles:
The Adams Cover Letter Almanac ($12.95)
The Adams Internet Job Search Almanac, 6th Ed. ($12.95)
The Adams Executive Recruiters Almanac, 2nd Ed. ($17.95)
The Adams Job Interview Almanac ($12.95)
The Adams Jobs Almanac, 8th Ed. ($16.95)
The Adams Resume Almanac ($10.95)
Business Etiquette in Brief ($7.95)
Campus Free College Degrees, 8th Ed. ($16.95)
Career Tests ($12.95)
Closing Techniques, 2nd Ed. ($8.95)
Cold Calling Techniques, 4th Ed. ($8.95)
College Grad Job Hunter, 4th Ed. ($14.95)
The Complete Resume & Job Search Book for College Students, 2nd Ed. ($12.95)
Cover Letters That Knock 'em Dead, 5th Ed. ($12.95)
Every Woman's Essential Job Hunting & Resume Book ($11.95)
The Everything Cover Letter Book ($12.95)
The Everything Get-A-Job Book ($12.95)
The Everything Hot Careers Book ($12.95)
The Everything Job Interview Book ($12.95)
The Everything Online Business Book ($12.95)
The Everything Online Job Search Book ($12.95)
The Everything Resume Book ($12.95)
The Everything Selling Book ($12.95)
First Time Resume ($7.95)
How to Start and Operate a Successful Business ($9.95)
Knock 'em Dead, 2003 ($14.95)
Knock 'em Dead Business Presentations ($12.95)
Market Yourself and Your Career, 2nd Ed. ($12.95)
The New Professional Image ($12.95)
The 150 Most Profitable Home Businesses for Women ($9.95)
The Resume Handbook, 3rd Ed. ($7.95)
Resumes That Knock 'em Dead, 5th Ed. ($12.95)
The Road to CEO ($20.00 hc)
The 250 Job Interview Questions You'll Most Likely Be Asked ($9.95)
Your Executive Image ($10.95)

12th Edition
THE Houston
JobBank

Editor:	Erik L. Herman
Assistant Editor:	Sarah Rocha
Researchers:	Maurice Curran
	Megan Danahy
	Emily Mozzone

Adams Media
AVON, MASSACHUSETTS

Published by Adams Media, an F+W Publications Company
57 Littlefield Street, Avon, MA 02322 U.S.A.
www.adamsmedia.com

ISBN: 1-58062-931-8
ISSN: 1098-979X
Manufactured in the United States of America.

The Houston JobBank 2003 (12th Edition) and its cover design are trademarks of F+W Publications, Inc.

Product or brand names used in this book are proprietary property of the applicable firm, subject to trademark protection, and registered with government offices. Any use of these names does not convey endorsement by or other affiliation with the name holder.

Because addresses and telephone numbers of smaller companies change rapidly, we recommend you call each company and verify the information before mailing to the employers listed in this book. Mass mailings are not recommended.

While the publisher has made every reasonable effort to obtain and verify accurate information, occasional errors are possible due to the magnitude of the data. Should you discover an error, or if a company is missing, please write the editors at the above address so that we may update future editions.

"This publication is designed to provide accurate and authoritative information with regard to the subject matter covered. It is sold with the understanding that the publisher is not engaged in rendering legal, accounting, or other professional advice. If legal advice or other expert assistance is required, the services of a competent professional person should be sought."

--From a Declaration of Principles jointly adopted by a Committee of the American Bar
Association and a Committee of Publishers and Associations

This book is available on standing order and at quantity discounts for bulk purchases.
For information, call 800/872-5627 (in Massachusetts, 508/427-7100)
or email at jobbank@adamsonline.com

TABLE OF CONTENTS

- *Automotive Repair Shops*
- *Automotive Stampings*
- *Industrial Vehicles and Moving Equipment*
- *Motor Vehicles and Equipment*
- *Travel Trailers and Campers*

Banking/Savings and Loans/78

Biotechnology, Pharmaceuticals, and Scientific R&D/83
- *Clinical Labs*
- *Lab Equipment Manufacturers*
- *Pharmaceutical Manufacturers and Distributors*

Business Services and Non-Scientific Research/88
- *Adjustment and Collection Services*
- *Cleaning, Maintenance, and Pest Control Services*
- *Credit Reporting Services*
- *Detective, Guard, and Armored Car Services/Security Systems Services*
- *Miscellaneous Equipment Rental and Leasing*
- *Secretarial and Court Reporting Services*

Charities and Social Services/98
- *Job Training and Vocational Rehabilitation Services*

Chemicals/Rubber and Plastics/102
- *Adhesives, Detergents, Inks, Paints, Soaps, Varnishes*
- *Agricultural Chemicals and Fertilizers*
- *Carbon and Graphite Products*
- *Chemical Engineering Firms*
- *Industrial Gases*

Communications: Telecommunications and Broadcasting/110
- *Cable/Pay Television Services*
- *Communications Equipment*
- *Radio and Television Broadcasting Stations*
- *Telephone, Telegraph, and Other Message Communications*

Computer Hardware, Software, and Services/113
- *Computer Components and Hardware Manufacturers*
- *Consultants and Computer Training Companies*
- *Internet and Online Service Providers*
- *Networking and Systems Services*
- *Repair Services/Rental and Leasing*
- *Resellers, Wholesalers, and Distributors*
- *Software Developers/Programming Services*

Educational Services/123
- *Business/Secretarial/Data Processing Schools*
- *Colleges/Universities/Professional Schools*
- *Community Colleges/Technical Schools/Vocational Schools*
- *Elementary and Secondary Schools*
- *Preschool and Child Daycare Services*

Electronic/Industrial Electrical Equipment/131
- *Electronic Machines and Systems*
- *Semiconductor Manufacturers*

Environmental and Waste Management Services/135
- *Environmental Engineering Firms*
- *Sanitary Services*

Fabricated/Primary Metals and Products/140
- *Aluminum and Copper Foundries*
- *Die-Castings*
- *Iron and Steel Foundries/Steel Works, Blast Furnaces, and Rolling Mills*

Financial Services/144
- *Consumer Financing and Credit Agencies*
- *Investment Specialists*

- Mortgage Bankers and Loan Brokers
- Security and Commodity Brokers, Dealers, and Exchanges

Food and Beverages/Agriculture/148
- Crop Services and Farm Supplies
- Dairy Farms
- Food Manufacturers/Processors and Agricultural Producers
- Tobacco Products

Government/160
- Courts
- Executive, Legislative, and General Government
- Public Agencies (Firefighters, Military, Police)
- United States Postal Service

Health Care: Services, Equipment, and Products/163
- Dental Labs and Equipment
- Home Health Care Agencies
- Hospitals and Medical Centers
- Medical Equipment Manufacturers and Wholesalers
- Offices and Clinics of Health Practitioners
- Residential Treatment Centers/Nursing Homes
- Veterinary Services

Hotels and Restaurants/180

Insurance/184

Legal Services/187

Manufacturing: Miscellaneous Consumer/191
- Art Supplies
- Batteries
- Cosmetics and Related Products
- Household Appliances and Audio/Video Equipment
- Jewelry, Silverware, and Plated Ware
- Miscellaneous Household Furniture and Fixtures
- Musical Instruments
- Tools
- Toys and Sporting Goods

Manufacturing: Miscellaneous Industrial/194
- Ball and Roller Bearings
- Commercial Furniture and Fixtures
- Fans, Blowers, and Purification Equipment
- Industrial Machinery and Equipment
- Motors and Generators/Compressors and Engine Parts
- Vending Machines

Mining/Gas/Petroleum/Energy Related/208
- Anthracite, Coal, and Ore Mining
- Mining Machinery and Equipment
- Oil and Gas Field Services
- Petroleum and Natural Gas

Paper and Wood Products/229
- Forest and Wood Products and Services
- Lumber and Wood Wholesale
- Millwork, Plywood, and Structural Members
- Paper and Wood Mills

Printing and Publishing/231
- Book, Newspaper, and Periodical Publishers
- Commercial Photographers
- Commercial Printing Services
- Graphic Designers

Real Estate/235
- Land Subdividers and Developers

SECTION FOUR: INDEX

INTRODUCTION

HOW TO USE THIS BOOK

Right now, you hold in your hands one of the most effective job-hunting tools available anywhere. In *The Houston JobBank*, you will find valuable information to help you launch or continue a rewarding career. But before you open to the book's employer listings and start calling about current job openings, take a few minutes to learn how best to use the resources presented in *The Houston JobBank*.

The Houston JobBank will help you to stand out from other jobseekers. While many people looking for a new job rely solely on newspaper help-wanted ads, this book offers you a much more effective job-search method -- direct contact. The direct contact method has been proven twice as effective as scanning the help-wanted ads. Instead of waiting for employers to come looking for you, you'll be far more effective going to them. While many of your competitors will use trial and error methods in trying to set up interviews, you'll learn not only how to get interviews, but what to expect once you've got them.

In the next few pages, we'll take you through each section of the book so you'll be prepared to get a jump-start on your competition.

Basics of Job Winning

Preparation. Strategy. Time management. These are three of the most important elements of a successful job search. *Basics of Job Winning* helps you address these and all the other elements needed to find the right job.

One of your first priorities should be to define your personal career objectives. What qualities make a job desirable to you? Creativity? High pay? Prestige? Use *Basics of Job Winning* to weigh these questions. Then use the rest of the chapter to design a strategy to find a job that matches your criteria.

In *Basics of Job Winning*, you'll learn which job-hunting techniques work, and which don't. We've reviewed the pros and cons of mass mailings, help-wanted ads, and direct contact. We'll show you how to develop and approach contacts in your field; how to research a prospective employer; and how to use that information to get an interview and the job.

Also included in *Basics of Job Winning*: interview dress code and etiquette, the "do's and don'ts" of interviewing, sample interview questions, and more. We also deal with some of the unique problems faced by those jobseekers who are currently employed, those who have lost a job, and college students conducting their first job search.

Resumes and Cover Letters

The approach you take to writing your resume and cover letter can often mean the difference between getting an interview and never being noticed. In this section, we discuss different formats, as well as what to put on (and what to leave off) your resume. We review the benefits and drawbacks of professional resume writers, and the importance of a follow-up letter. Also included in this section are sample resumes and cover letters which you can use as models.

The Employer Listings

Employers are listed alphabetically by industry. When a company does business under a person's name, like "John Smith & Co.," the company is usually listed by the surname's spelling (in this case "S"). Exceptions occur when a company's name is widely recognized, like "JCPenney" or "Howard Johnson Motor Lodge." In those cases, the company's first name is the key ("J" and "H" respectively).

The Houston JobBank covers a very wide range of industries. Each company profile is assigned to one of the industry chapters listed below.

Accounting and Management Consulting
Advertising, Marketing, and Public Relations
Aerospace
Apparel, Fashion, and Textiles
Architecture, Construction, and Engineering
Arts, Entertainment, Sports, and Recreation
Automotive
Banking/Savings and Loans
Biotechnology, Pharmaceuticals, and
    Scientific R&D
Business Services and Non-Scientific
    Research
Charities and Social Services
Chemicals/Rubber and Plastics
Communications: Telecommunications and
    Broadcasting
Computer Hardware, Software, and Services
Educational Services
Electronic/Industrial Electrical Equipment
Environmental and Waste Management
    Services

Fabricated/Primary Metals and Products
Financial Services
Food and Beverages/Agriculture
Government
Health Care: Services, Equipment, and
    Products
Hotels and Restaurants
Insurance
Legal Services
Manufacturing: Miscellaneous Consumer
Manufacturing: Miscellaneous Industrial
Mining/Gas/Petroleum/Energy Related
Paper and Wood Products
Printing and Publishing
Real Estate
Retail
Stone, Clay, Glass, and Concrete Products
Transportation/Travel
Utilities: Electric/Gas/Water
Miscellaneous Wholesaling

Many of the company listings offer detailed company profiles. In addition to company names, addresses, and phone numbers, these listings also include contact names or hiring departments, and descriptions of each company's products and/or services. Many of these listings also feature a variety of additional information including:

Positions advertised - A list of open positions the company was advertising at the time our research was conducted. Note: Keep in mind that *The Atlanta JobBank* is a directory of major employers in the area, not a directory of openings currently available. Positions listed in this book that were advertised at the time research was conducted may no longer be open. Many of the companies listed will be hiring, others will not. However, since most professional job openings are filled without the placement of help-wanted ads, contacting the employers in this book directly is still a more effective method than browsing the Sunday papers.

Special programs - Does the company offer training programs, internships, or apprenticeships? These programs can be important to first time jobseekers and college students looking for practical work experience. Many employer profiles will include information on these programs.

Parent company - If an employer is a subsidiary of a larger company, the name of that parent company will often be listed here. Use this information to supplement your company research before contacting the employer.

Number of employees - The number of workers a company employs.

Company listings may also include information on other U.S. locations and any stock exchanges the firm may be listed on.

A note on all employer listings that appear in *The Houston JobBank*: This book is intended as a starting point. It is not intended to replace any effort that you, the jobseeker, should devote to your job hunt. Keep in mind that while a great deal of effort has been put into collecting and verifying the company profiles provided in this book, addresses and contact names change regularly. Inevitably, some contact names listed herein have changed even before you read this. We recommend you contact a company before mailing your resume to ensure nothing has changed.

Index
   The Houston JobBank index is listed alphabetically by industry.

THE JOB SEARCH

THE BASICS OF JOB WINNING: A CONDENSED REVIEW

This chapter is divided into four sections. The first section explains the fundamentals that every jobseeker should know, especially first-time jobseekers. The next three sections deal with special situations faced by specific types of jobseekers: those who are currently employed, those who have lost a job, and college students.

THE BASICS:
Things Everyone Needs to Know

Career Planning

The first step to finding your ideal job is to clearly define your objectives. This is better known as career planning (or life planning if you wish to emphasize the importance of combining the two). Career planning has become a field of study in and of itself.

If you are thinking of choosing or switching careers, we particularly emphasize two things. First, choose a career where you will enjoy most of the day-to-day tasks. This sounds obvious, but most of us have at some point found the idea of a glamour industry or prestigious job title attractive without thinking of the key consideration: Would we enjoy performing the *everyday* tasks the position entails?

The second key consideration is that you are not merely choosing a career, but also a lifestyle. Career counselors indicate that one of the most common problems people encounter in jobseeking is that they fail to consider how well-suited they are for a particular position or career. For example, some people, attracted to management consulting by good salaries, early responsibility, and high-level corporate exposure, do not adapt well to the long hours, heavy travel demands, and constant pressure to produce. Be sure to ask yourself how you might adapt to the day-to-day duties and working environment that a specific position entails. Then ask yourself how you might adapt to the demands of that career or industry as a whole.

Choosing Your Strategy

Assuming that you've established your career objectives, the next step of the job search is to develop a strategy. If you don't take the time to develop a plan, you may find yourself going in circles after several weeks of randomly searching for opportunities that always seem just beyond your reach.

The most common jobseeking techniques are:

- following up on help-wanted advertisements (in the newspaper or online)
- using employment services
- relying on personal contacts
- contacting employers directly (the Direct Contact method)

Each of these approaches can lead to better jobs. However, the Direct Contact method boasts twice the success rate of the others. So unless you have specific reasons to employ other strategies, Direct Contact should form the foundation of your job search.

If you choose to use other methods as well, try to expend at least half your energy on Direct Contact. Millions of other jobseekers have already proven that Direct Contact has been twice as effective in obtaining employment, so why not follow in their footsteps?

Setting Your Schedule

Okay, so now that you've targeted a strategy it's time to work out the details of your job search. The most important detail is setting up a schedule. Of course, since job searches aren't something most people do regularly, it may be hard to estimate how long each step will take. Nonetheless, it is important to have a plan so that you can monitor your progress.

When outlining your job search schedule, have a realistic time frame in mind. If you will be job-searching full-time, your search could take at least two months or more. If you can only devote part-time effort, it will probably take at least four months.

You probably know a few people who seem to spend their whole lives searching for a better job in their spare time. Don't be one of them. If you are presently working and don't feel like devoting a lot of energy to jobseeking right now, then wait. Focus on enjoying your present position, performing your best on the job, and storing up energy for when you are really ready to begin your job search.

> **The first step in beginning your job search is to clearly define your objectives.**

Those of you who are currently unemployed should remember that *job-hunting is tough work, both physically and emotionally*. It is also intellectually demanding work that requires you to be at your best. So don't tire yourself out by working on your job campaign around the clock. At the same time, be sure to discipline yourself. The most logical way to manage your time while looking for a job is to keep your regular working hours.

If you are searching full-time and have decided to choose several different strategies, we recommend that you divide up each week, designating some time for each method. By trying several approaches at once, you can evaluate how promising each seems and alter your schedule accordingly. Keep in mind that the *majority of openings are filled without being advertised*. Remember also that positions advertised on the Internet are just as likely to already be filled as those found in the newspaper!

If you are searching part-time and decide to try several different contact methods, we recommend that you try them sequentially. You simply won't have enough time to put a meaningful amount of effort into more than one method at once. Estimate the length of your job search, and then allocate so many weeks or months for each contact method, beginning with Direct Contact. The purpose of setting this schedule is not to rush you to your goal but to help you periodically evaluate your progress.

The Direct Contact Method

Once you have scheduled your time, you are ready to begin your search in earnest. Beginning with the Direct Contact method, the first step is to develop a checklist for categorizing the types of firms for which you'd like to work. You might categorize firms by product line, size, customer type (such as industrial or consumer), growth prospects, or geographical location. Keep in mind, the shorter the list the easier it will be to locate a company that is right for you.

Next you will want to use this *JobBank* book to assemble your list of potential employers. Choose firms where *you* are most likely to be able to find a job. Try matching your skills with those that a specific job demands. Consider where your skills might be in demand, the degree of competition for employment, and the employment outlook at each company.

Separate your prospect list into three groups. The first 25 percent will be your primary target group, the next 25 percent will be your secondary group, and the remaining names will be your reserve group.

After you form your prospect list, begin working on your resume. Refer to the Resumes and Cover Letters section following this chapter for more information.

Once your resume is complete, begin researching your first batch of prospective employers. You will want to determine whether you would be happy working at the firms you are researching and to get a better idea of what their employment needs might be. You also need to obtain enough information to sound highly informed about the company during phone conversations and in mail correspondence. But don't go all out on your research yet! You probably won't be able to arrange interviews with some of these firms, so save your big research effort until you start to arrange interviews. Nevertheless, you should plan to spend several hours researching each firm. Do your research in batches to save time and energy. Start with this book, and find out what you can about each of the firms in your primary target group. For answers to specific questions, contact any pertinent professional associations that may be able to help you learn more about an employer. Read industry publications looking for articles on the firm. (Addresses of associations and names of important publications are listed after each section of employer listings in this book.) Then look up the company on the Internet or try additional resources at your local library. Keep organized, and maintain a folder on each firm.

> The more you know about a company, the more likely you are to catch an interviewer's eye. (You'll also face fewer surprises once you get the job!)

Information to look for includes: company size; president, CEO, or owner's name; when the company was established; what each division does; and benefits that are important to you. An abundance of company information can now be found electronically, through the World Wide Web or commercial online services. Researching companies online is a convenient means of obtaining information quickly and easily. If you have access to the Internet, you can search from your home at any time of day.

You may search a particular company's Website for current information that may be otherwise unavailable in print. In fact, many companies that maintain a site update their information daily. In addition, you may also search articles written about the company online. Today, most of the nation's largest newspapers, magazines, trade publications, and regional business periodicals have online versions of their publications. To find additional resources, use a search engine like Yahoo! or Alta Vista and type in the keyword "companies" or "employers."

If you discover something that really disturbs you about the firm (they are about to close their only local office), or if you discover that your chances of getting a job there are practically nil (they have just instituted a hiring freeze), then cross them off your prospect list. If possible, supplement your research efforts by contacting individuals who know the firm well. Ideally you should make an informal contact with someone at that particular firm, but often a direct competitor or a major customer will be able to supply you with just as much information. At the very least, try to obtain whatever printed information the company has available -- not just annual reports, but product brochures, company profiles, or catalogs. This information is often available on the Internet.

Getting the Interview

Now it is time to make Direct Contact with the goal of arranging interviews. If you have read any books on job-searching, you may have noticed that most of these books tell you to avoid the human resources office like the plague. It is said that the human resources office never hires people; they screen candidates. Unfortunately, this is often the case. If you can identify the appropriate manager with the authority to hire you, you should try to contact that person directly.

The obvious means of initiating Direct Contact are:

- Mail (postal or electronic)
- Phone calls

Mail contact is a good choice if you have not been in the job market for a while. You can take your time to prepare a letter, say exactly what you want, and of course include your resume. Remember that employers receive many resumes every day. Don't be surprised if you do not get a response to your inquiry, *and don't spend weeks waiting for responses that may never come.* If you do send a letter, follow it up (or precede it) with a phone call. This will increase your impact, and because of the initial research you did, will underscore both your familiarity with and your interest in the firm. Bear in mind that your goal is to make your name a familiar one with prospective employers, so that when a position becomes available, your resume will be one of the first the hiring manager seeks out.

DEVELOPING YOUR CONTACTS: NETWORKING

Some career counselors feel that the best route to a better job is through somebody you already know or through somebody to whom you can be introduced. These counselors recommend that you build your contact base beyond your current acquaintances by asking each one to introduce you, or refer you, to additional people in your field of interest.

The theory goes like this: You might start with 15 personal contacts, each of whom introduces you to three additional people, for a total of 45 additional contacts. Then each of these people introduces you to three additional people, which adds 135 additional contacts. Theoretically, you will soon know every person in the industry.

Of course, developing your personal contacts does not work quite as smoothly as the theory suggests because some people will not be able to introduce you to anyone. The further you stray from your initial contact base, the weaker your references may be. So, if you do try developing your own contacts, try to begin with as many people that you know personally as you can. Dig into your personal phone book and your holiday greeting card list and locate old classmates from school. Be particularly sure to approach people who perform your personal business such as your lawyer, accountant, banker, doctor, stockbroker, and insurance agent. These people develop a very broad contact base due to the nature of their professions.

If you send a fax, always follow with a hard copy of your resume and cover letter in the mail. Often, through no fault of your own, a fax will come through illegibly and employers do not often have time to let candidates know.

Another alternative is to make a "cover call." Your cover call should be just like your cover letter: concise. Your first statement should interest the employer in you. Then try to subtly mention your familiarity with the firm. Don't be overbearing; keep your introduction to three sentences or less. Be pleasant, self-confident, and relaxed. This will greatly increase the chances of the person at the other end of the line developing the conversation. But don't press. If you are asked to follow up with "something in the mail," this signals the conversation's natural end. Don't try to prolong the conversation once it has ended, and don't ask what they want to receive in the mail. Always send your resume and a highly personalized follow-up letter, reminding the addressee of the phone conversation. *Always* include a cover letter if you are asked to send a resume, and treat your resume and cover letter as a total package. Gear your letter toward the specific position you are applying for and prove why you would be a "good match" for the position.

> **Always include a cover letter if you are asked to send a resume.**

Unless you are in telephone sales, making smooth and relaxed cover calls will probably not come easily. Practice them on your own, and then with your friends or relatives.

DON'T BOTHER WITH MASS MAILINGS OR BARRAGES OF PHONE CALLS

Direct Contact does not mean burying every firm within a hundred miles with mail and phone calls. Mass mailings rarely work in the job hunt. This also applies to those letters that are personalized -- but dehumanized -- on an automatic typewriter or computer. Don't waste your time or money on such a project; you will fool no one but yourself.

The worst part of sending out mass mailings, or making unplanned phone calls to companies you have not researched, is that you are likely to be remembered as someone with little genuine interest in the firm, who lacks sincerity -- somebody that nobody wants to hire.

If you obtain an interview as a result of a telephone conversation, be sure to send a thank-you note reiterating the points you made during the conversation. You will appear more professional and increase your impact. However, unless specifically requested, don't mail your resume once an interview has been arranged. Take it with you to the interview instead.

You should never show up to seek a professional position without an appointment. Even if you are somehow lucky enough to obtain an interview, you will appear so unprofessional that you will not be seriously considered.

HELP WANTED ADVERTISEMENTS

Only a small fraction of professional job openings are advertised. Yet the majority of jobseekers -- and quite a few people not in the job market -- spend a lot of time studying the help wanted ads. As a result, the competition for advertised openings is often very severe.

A moderate-sized employer told us about their experience advertising in the help wanted section of a major Sunday newspaper:

It was a disaster. We had over 500 responses from this relatively small ad in just one week. We have only two phone lines in this office and one was totally knocked out. We'll never advertise for professional help again.

If you insist on following up on help wanted ads, then research a firm before you reply to an ad. Preliminary research might help to separate you from all of the other professionals responding to that ad, many of whom will have only a passing interest in the opportunity. It will also give you insight about a particular firm, to help you determine if it is potentially a good match. That said, your chances of obtaining a job through the want ads are still much smaller than they are with the Direct Contact method.

Preparing for the Interview

As each interview is arranged, begin your in-depth research. You should arrive at an interview knowing the company upside-down and inside-out. You need to know the company's products, types of customers, subsidiaries, parent company, principal locations, rank in the industry, sales and profit trends, type of ownership, size, current plans, and much more. By this time you have probably narrowed your job search to one industry. Even if you haven't, you should still be familiar with common industry terms, the trends in the firm's industry, the firm's principal competitors and their relative performance, and the direction in which the industry leaders are headed.

Dig into every resource you can! Surf the Internet. Read the company literature, the trade press, the business press, and if the company is public, call your stockbroker (if you have one) and ask for additional information. If possible, speak to someone at the firm before the interview, or if not, speak to someone at a competing firm. The more time you spend, the better. Even if you feel extremely pressed for time, you should set aside several hours for pre-interview research.

> **You should arrive at an interview knowing the company upside-down and inside-out.**

If you have been out of the job market for some time, don't be surprised if you find yourself tense during your first few interviews. It will probably happen every time you re-enter the market, not just when you seek your first job after getting out of school.

Tension is natural during an interview, but knowing you have done a thorough research job should put you more at ease. Make a list of questions that you think might be asked in each interview. Think out your answers carefully and practice them with a friend. Tape record your responses to the problem questions. (*See also in this chapter: Informational Interviews.*) If you feel particularly unsure of your interviewing skills, arrange your first interviews at firms you are not as interested in. (But remember it is common courtesy to seem enthusiastic about the possibility of working for any firm at which you interview.) Practice again on your own after these first few interviews. Go over the difficult questions that you were asked.

Take some time to really think about how you will convey your work history. Present "bad experiences" as "learning experiences." Instead of saying "I hated my position as a salesperson because I had to bother people on the phone," say "I realized that cold-calling was not my strong suit. Though I love working with people, I decided my talents would be best used in a more face-to-face atmosphere." Always find some sort of lesson from previous jobs, as they all have one.

Interview Attire

How important is the proper dress for a job interview? Buying a complete wardrobe, donning new shoes, and having your hair styled every morning are not enough to guarantee you a career position as an investment banker. But on the other hand, if you can't find a clean, conservative suit or won't take the time to wash your hair, then you are just wasting your time by interviewing at all.

Personal grooming is as important as finding appropriate clothes for a job interview. Careful grooming indicates both a sense of thoroughness and self-confidence. This is not the time to make a statement -- take out the extra earrings and avoid any garish hair colors not found in nature. Women should not wear excessive makeup, and both men and women should refrain from wearing any perfume or cologne (it only takes a small spritz to leave an allergic interviewer with a fit of sneezing and a bad impression of your meeting). Men should be freshly shaven, even if the interview is late in the day, and men with long hair should have it pulled back and neat.

Men applying for any professional position should wear a suit, preferably in a conservative color such as navy or charcoal gray. It is easy to get away with wearing the same dark suit to consecutive interviews at the same company; just be sure to wear a different shirt and tie for each interview.

Women should also wear a business suit. Professionalism still dictates a suit with a skirt, rather than slacks, as proper interview garb for women. This is usually true even at companies where pants are acceptable attire for female employees. As much as you may disagree with this guideline, the more prudent time to fight this standard is after you land the job.

The final selection of candidates for a job opening won't be determined by dress, of course. However, inappropriate dress can quickly eliminate a first-round candidate. So while you shouldn't spend a fortune on a new wardrobe, you should be sure that your clothes are adequate. The key is to dress at least as formally or slightly more formally and more conservatively than the position would suggest.

What to Bring

Be complete. Everyone needs a watch, a pen, and a notepad. Finally, a briefcase or a leather-bound folder (containing extra, *unfolded*, copies of your resume) will help complete the look of professionalism.

Sometimes the interviewer will be running behind schedule. Don't be upset, be sympathetic. There is often pressure to interview a lot of candidates and to quickly fill a demanding position. So be sure to come to your interview with good reading material to keep yourself occupied and relaxed.

The Interview

The very beginning of the interview is the most important part because it determines the tone for the rest of it. Those first few moments are especially crucial. Do you smile when you meet? Do you establish enough eye contact, but not too much? Do you walk into the office with a self-assured and confident stride? Do you shake hands firmly? Do you make small talk easily without being garrulous? It is

---

BE PREPARED:
Some Common Interview Questions

Tell me about yourself.

Why did you leave your last job?

What excites you in your current job?

Where would you like to be in five years?

How much overtime are you willing to work?

What would your previous/present employer tell me about you?

Tell me about a difficult situation that you
faced at your previous/present job.

What are your greatest strengths?

What are your weaknesses?

Describe a work situation where you took initiative
and went beyond your normal responsibilities.

Why should we hire you?

---

human nature to judge people by that first impression, so make sure it is a good one. But most of all, try to be yourself.

Often the interviewer will begin, after the small talk, by telling you about the company, the division, the department, or perhaps, the position. Because of your detailed research, the information about the company should be repetitive for you, and the interviewer would probably like nothing better than to avoid this regurgitation of the company biography. So if you can do so tactfully, indicate to the interviewer that you are very familiar with the firm. If he or she seems intent on providing you with background information, despite your hints, then acquiesce.

But be sure to remain attentive. If you can manage to generate a brief discussion of the company or the industry at this point, without being forceful, great. It will help to further build rapport, underscore your interest, and increase your impact.

> **The interviewer's job is to find a reason to turn you down; your job is to not provide that reason.**
>
> ·John L. LaFevre, author,
> *How You Really Get Hired*
>
> Reprinted from the 1989/90 *CPC Annual*, with permission of the National Association of Colleges and Employers (formerly College Placement Council, Inc.), copyright holder.

Soon (if it didn't begin that way) the interviewer will begin the questions, many of which you will have already practiced. This period of the interview usually falls into one of two categories (or somewhere in between): either a structured interview, where the interviewer has a prescribed set of questions to ask; or an unstructured interview, where the interviewer will ask only leading questions to get you to talk about yourself, your experiences, and your goals. Try to sense as quickly as possible in which direction the interviewer wishes to proceed. This will make the interviewer feel more relaxed and in control of the situation.

Remember to keep attuned to the interviewer and make the length of your answers appropriate to the situation. If you are really unsure as to how detailed a response the interviewer is seeking, then ask.

As the interview progresses, the interviewer will probably mention some of the most important responsibilities of the position. If applicable, draw parallels between your experience and the demands of the position as detailed by the interviewer. Describe your past experience in the same manner that you do on your resume: emphasizing results and achievements and not merely describing activities. But don't exaggerate. Be on the level about your abilities.

The first interview is often the toughest, where many candidates are screened out. If you are interviewing for a very competitive position, you will have to make an impression that will last. Focus on a few of your greatest strengths that are relevant to the position. Develop these points carefully, state them again in different words, and then try to summarize them briefly at the end of the interview.

Often the interviewer will pause toward the end and ask if you have any questions. Particularly in a structured interview, this might be the one chance to really show your knowledge of and interest in the firm. Have a list prepared of specific questions that are of real interest to you. Let your questions subtly show your research and your knowledge of the firm's activities. It is wise to have an extensive list of questions, as several of them may be answered during the interview.

Do not turn your opportunity to ask questions into an interrogation. Avoid reading directly from your list of questions, and ask questions that you are fairly certain the interviewer can answer (remember how you feel when you cannot answer a question during an interview).

Even if you are unable to determine the salary range beforehand, do not ask about it during the first interview. You can always ask later. Above all, don't ask about fringe benefits until you have been offered a position. (Then be sure to get all the details.)

Try not to be negative about anything during the interview, particularly any past employer or any previous job. Be cheerful. Everyone likes to work with someone who seems to be happy. Even if you detest your current/former job or manager, do not make disparaging comments. The interviewer may construe this as a sign of a potential attitude problem and not consider you a strong candidate.

Don't let a tough question throw you off base. If you don't know the answer to a question, simply say so -- do not apologize. Just smile. Nobody can answer every question -- particularly some of the questions that are asked in job interviews.

Before your first interview, you may be able to determine how many rounds of interviews there usually are for positions at your level. (Of course it may differ quite a bit even within the different levels of one firm.) Usually you can count on attending at least two or three interviews, although some firms are known to give a minimum of six interviews for all professional positions. While you should be more relaxed as you return for subsequent interviews, the pressure will be on. The more prepared you are, the better.

Depending on what information you are able to obtain, you might want to vary your strategy quite a bit from interview to interview. For instance, if the first interview is a screening interview, then be sure a few of your strengths really stand out. On the other hand, if later interviews are primarily with people who are in a position to veto your hiring, but not to push it forward, then you should primarily focus on building rapport as opposed to reiterating and developing your key strengths.

If it looks as though your skills and background do not match the position the interviewer was hoping to fill, ask him or her if there is another division or subsidiary that perhaps could profit from your talents.

After the Interview

Write a follow-up letter immediately after the interview, while it is still fresh in the interviewer's mind (see the sample follow-up letter format found in the Resumes and Cover Letters chapter). Not only is this a thank-you, but it also gives you the chance to provide the interviewer with any details you may have forgotten (as long as they can be tactfully added in). If you haven't heard back from the interviewer within a week of sending your thank-you letter, call to stress your continued interest in the firm and the position. If you lost any points during the interview for any reason, this letter can help you regain footing. Be polite and make sure to stress your continued interest and competency to fill the position. Just don't forget to proofread it thoroughly. If you are unsure of the spelling of the interviewer's name, call the receptionist and ask.

THE BALANCING ACT:
Looking for a New Job While Currently Employed

For those of you who are still employed, job-searching will be particularly tiring because it must be done in addition to your normal work responsibilities. So don't overwork yourself to the point where you show up to interviews looking exhausted or start to slip behind at your current job. On the other hand, don't be tempted to quit your present job! The long hours are worth it. Searching for a job while you have one puts you in a position of strength.

Making Contact

If you must be at your office during the business day, then you have additional problems to deal with. How can you work interviews into the business day? And if you work in an open office, how can you even call to set up interviews? Obviously, you should keep up the effort and the appearances on your present job. So maximize your use of the lunch hour, early mornings, and late afternoons for calling. If you keep trying, you'll be surprised how often you will be able to reach the executive you are trying to contact during your out-of-office hours. You can catch people as early as 8 a.m. and as late as 6 p.m. on frequent occasions.

Scheduling Interviews

Your inability to interview at any time other than lunch just might work to your advantage. If you can, try to set up as many interviews as possible for your lunch hour. This will go a long way to creating a relaxed atmosphere. But be sure the interviews don't stray too far from the agenda on hand.

Lunchtime interviews are much easier to obtain if you have substantial career experience. People with less experience will often find no alternative to taking time off for interviews. If you have to take time off, you have to take time off. But try to do this as little as possible. Try to take the whole day off in order to avoid being blatantly obvious about your job search, and try to schedule two to three interviews for the same day. (It is very difficult to maintain an optimum level of energy at more than three interviews in one day.) Explain to the interviewer why you might have to juggle your interview schedule; he/she should honor the respect you're showing your current employer by minimizing your days off and will probably appreciate the fact that another prospective employer is interested in you.

> Try calling as early as 8 a.m. and as late as 6 p.m. You'll be surprised how often you will be able to reach the executive you want during these times of the day.

References

What do you tell an interviewer who asks for references from your current employer? Just say that while you are happy to have your former employers contacted, you are trying to keep your job search confidential and would rather that your current employer not be contacted until you have been given a firm offer.

IF YOU'RE FIRED OR LAID OFF:
Picking Yourself Up and Dusting Yourself Off

If you've been fired or laid off, you are not the first and will not be the last to go through this traumatic experience. In today's changing economy, thousands of professionals lose their jobs every year. Even if you were terminated with just cause, do not lose heart. Remember, being fired is not a reflection on you as a person. It is usually a reflection of your company's staffing needs and its perception of your recent job performance and attitude. And if you were not performing up to par or enjoying your work, then you will probably be better off at another company anyway.

> **Be prepared for the question "Why were you fired?" during job interviews.**

A thorough job search could take months, so be sure to negotiate a reasonable severance package, if possible, and determine to what benefits, such as health insurance, you are still legally entitled. Also, register for unemployment compensation immediately. Don't be surprised to find other professionals collecting unemployment compensation -- it is for everyone who has lost their job.

Don't start your job search with a flurry of unplanned activity. Start by choosing a strategy and working out a plan. Now is not the time for major changes in your life. If possible, remain in the same career and in the same geographical location, at least until you have been working again for a while. On the other hand, if the only industry for which you are trained is leaving, or is severely depressed in your area, then you should give prompt consideration to moving or switching careers.

Avoid mentioning you were fired when arranging interviews, but be prepared for the question "Why were you fired?" during an interview. If you were laid off as a result of downsizing, briefly explain, being sure to reinforce that your job loss was not due to performance. If you were in fact fired, be honest, but try to detail the reason as favorably as possible and portray what you have learned from your mistakes. If you are confident one of your past managers will give you a good reference, tell the interviewer to contact that person. Do not to speak negatively of your past employer and try not to sound particularly worried about your status of being temporarily unemployed.

Finally, don't spend too much time reflecting on why you were let go or how you might have avoided it. Think positively, look to the future, and be sure to follow a careful plan during your job search.

THE COLLEGE STUDENT:
Conducting Your First Job Search

While you will be able to apply many of the basics covered earlier in this chapter to your job search, there are some situations unique to the college student's job search.

THE GPA QUESTION

You are interviewing for the job of your dreams. Everything is going well: You've established a good rapport, the interviewer seems impressed with your qualifications, and you're almost positive the job is yours. Then you're asked about your GPA, which is pitifully low. Do you tell the truth and watch your dream job fly out the window?

Never lie about your GPA (they may request your transcript, and no company will hire a liar). You can, however, explain if there is a reason you don't feel your grades reflect your abilities, and mention any other impressive statistics. For example, if you have a high GPA in your major, or in the last few semesters (as opposed to your cumulative college career), you can use that fact to your advantage.

Perhaps the biggest problem college students face is lack of experience. Many schools have internship programs designed to give students exposure to the field of their choice, as well as the opportunity to make valuable contacts. Check out your school's career services department to see what internships are available. If your school does not have a formal internship program, or if there are no available internships that appeal to you, try contacting local businesses and offering your services. Often, businesses will be more than willing to have an extra pair of hands (especially if those hands are unpaid!) for a day or two each week. Or try contacting school alumni to see if you can "shadow" them for a few days, and see what their daily duties are like.

Informational Interviews

Although many jobseekers do not do this, it can be extremely helpful to arrange an informational interview with a college alumnus or someone else who works in your desired industry. You interview them about their job, their company, and their industry with questions you have prepared in advance. This can be done over the phone but is usually done in person. This will provide you with a contact in the industry who may give you more valuable information -- or perhaps even a job opportunity -- in the future. Always follow up with a thank you letter that includes your contact information.

The goal is to try to begin building experience and establishing contacts as early as possible in your college career.

What do you do if, for whatever reason, you weren't able to get experience directly related to your desired career? First, look at your previous jobs and see if there's anything you can highlight. Did you supervise or train other employees? Did you reorganize the accounting system, or boost productivity in some way? Accomplishments like these demonstrate leadership, responsibility, and innovation -- qualities that most companies look for in employees. And don't forget volunteer activities and school clubs, which can also showcase these traits.

On-Campus Recruiting

Companies will often send recruiters to interview on-site at various colleges. This gives students a chance to interview with companies that may not have interviewed them otherwise. This is particularly true if a company schedules "open" interviews, in which the only screening process is who is first in line at the sign-ups. Of course, since many more applicants gain interviews in this format, this also means that many more people are rejected. The on-campus interview is generally a screening interview, to see if it is worth the company's time to invite you in for a second interview. So do everything possible to make yourself stand out from the crowd.

The first step, of course, is to check out any and all information your school's career center has on the company. If the information seems out of date, check out the company on the Internet or call the company's headquarters and ask for any printed information.

Many companies will host an informational meeting for interviewees, often the evening before interviews are scheduled to take place. DO NOT MISS THIS MEETING. The recruiter will almost certainly ask if you attended. Make an effort to stay after the meeting and talk with the company's representatives. Not only does this give you an opportunity to find out more information about both the company and the position, it also makes you stand out in the recruiter's mind. If there's a particular company that you had your heart set on, but you weren't able to get an interview with them, attend the information session anyway. You may be able to persuade the recruiter to squeeze you into the schedule. (Or you may discover that the company really isn't the right fit for you after all.)

Try to check out the interview site beforehand. Some colleges may conduct "mock" interviews that take place in one of the standard interview rooms. Or you may be able to convince a career counselor (or even a custodian) to let you sneak a peek during off-hours. Either way, having an idea of the room's setup will help you to mentally prepare.

Arrive at least 15 minutes early to the interview. The recruiter may be ahead of schedule, and might meet you early. But don't be surprised if previous interviews have run over, resulting in your 30-minute slot being reduced to 20 minutes (or less). Don't complain or appear anxious; just use the time you do have as efficiently as possible to showcase the reasons *you* are the ideal candidate. Staying calm and composed in these situations will work to your advantage.

LAST WORDS

A parting word of advice. Again and again during your job search you will face rejection. You will be rejected when you apply for interviews. You will be rejected after interviews. For every job offer you finally receive, you probably will have been rejected many times. Don't let rejections slow you down. Keep reminding yourself that the sooner you go out, start your job search, and get those rejections flowing in, the closer you will be to obtaining the job you want.

RESUMES AND COVER LETTERS

When filling a position, an employer will often have 100-plus applicants, but time to interview only a handful of the most promising ones. As a result, he or she will reject most applicants after only briefly skimming their resumes.

Unless you have phoned and talked to the employer -- which you should do whenever you can -- you will be chosen or rejected for an interview entirely on the basis of your resume and cover letter. *Your cover letter must catch the employer's attention, and your resume must hold it.* (But remember -- a resume is no substitute for a job search campaign. *You* must seek a job. Your resume is only one tool, albeit a critical one.)

RESUME FORMAT:
Mechanics of a First Impression

The Basics

Employers dislike long resumes, so unless you have an unusually strong background with many years of experience and a diversity of outstanding achievements, keep your resume length to one page. If you must squeeze in more information than would otherwise fit, try using a smaller typeface or changing the margins. Watch also for "widows" at the end of paragraphs. You can often free up some space if you can shorten the information enough to get rid of those single words taking up an entire line. Another tactic that works with some word processing programs is to decrease the font size of your paragraph returns and changing the spacing between lines.

Print your resume on standard 8 1/2" x 11" paper. Since recruiters often get resumes in batches of hundreds, a smaller-sized resume may be lost in the pile. Oversized resumes are likely to get crumpled at the edges, and won't fit easily in their files.

First impressions matter, so make sure the recruiter's first impression of your resume is a good one. Never hand-write your resume (or cover letter)! Print your resume on quality paper that has weight and texture, in a conservative color such as white, ivory, or pale gray. Good resume paper is easy to find at many stores that sell stationery or office products. It is even available at some drug stores. Use *matching* paper and envelopes for both your resume and cover letter. One hiring manager at a major magazine throws out all resumes that arrive on paper that differs in color from the envelope!

Do not buy paper with images of clouds and rainbows in the background or anything that looks like casual stationery that you would send to your favorite aunt. Do not spray perfume or cologne on your resume. Do not include your picture with your resume unless you have a specific and appropriate reason to do so.

Another tip: Do a test print of your resume (and cover letter), to make sure the watermark is on the same side as the text so that you can read it. Also make sure it is right-side up. As trivial as this may sound, some recruiters check for this! One recruiter at a law firm in New Hampshire sheepishly admitted this is the first thing he checks. *"I open each envelope and check the watermarks on the resume and cover letter. Those candidates that have it wrong go into a different pile."*

Getting it on Paper

Modern photocomposition typesetting gives you the clearest, sharpest image, a wide variety of type styles, and effects such as italics, bold-facing, and book-like justified margins. It is also too expensive for many jobseekers. The quality of today's laser printers means that a computer-generated resume can look just as impressive as one that has been professionally typeset.

A computer with a word processing or desktop publishing program is the most common way to generate your resume. This allows you the flexibility to make changes almost instantly and to store different drafts on disk. Word processing and desktop publishing programs also offer many different fonts to choose from, each taking up different amounts of space. (It is generally best to stay between 9-point and 12-point font size.) Many other options are also available, such as bold-facing or italicizing for emphasis and the ability to change and manipulate spacing. It is generally recommended to leave the right-hand margin unjustified as this keeps the spacing between the text even and therefore easier to read. It is not wrong to justify both margins of text, but if possible try it both ways before you decide.

For a resume on paper, the end result will be largely determined by the quality of the printer you use. Laser printers will generally provide the best quality. Do not use a dot matrix printer.

Many companies now use scanning equipment to screen the resumes they receive, and certain paper, fonts, and other features are more compatible with this technology. White paper is preferable, as well as a standard font such as Courier or Helvetica. You should use at least a 10-point font, and avoid bolding, italics, underlining, borders, boxes, or graphics.

Household typewriters and office typewriters with nylon or other cloth ribbons are *not* good enough for typing your resume. If you don't have access to a quality word processing program, hire a professional with the resources to prepare your resume for you. Keep in mind that businesses such as Kinko's (open 24 hours) provide access to computers with quality printers.

Don't make your copies on an office photocopier. Only the human resources office may see the resume you mail. Everyone else may see only a copy of it, and copies of copies quickly become unreadable. Furthermore, sending photocopies of your resume or cover letter is completely unprofessional. Either print out each copy individually, or take your resume to a professional copy shop, which will generally offer professionally-maintained, extra-high-quality photocopiers and charge fairly reasonable prices. You want your resume to represent <u>you</u> with the look of polished quality.

Proof with Care

Whether you typed it or paid to have it produced professionally, mistakes on resumes are not only embarrassing, but will usually remove you from consideration (particularly if something obvious such as your name is misspelled). No matter how much you paid someone else to type, write, or typeset your resume, *you* lose if there is a mistake. So proofread it as carefully as possible. Get a friend to help you. Read your draft aloud as your friend checks the proof copy. Then have your friend read aloud while you check. Next, read it letter by letter to check spelling and punctuation.

If you are having it typed or typeset by a resume service or a printer, and you don't have time to proof it, pay for it and take it home. Proof it there and bring it back later to get it corrected and printed.

If you wrote your resume with a word processing program, use the built-in spell checker to double-check for spelling errors. Keep in mind that a spell checker will not find errors such as "to" for "two" or "wok" for "work." Many spell check programs do not recognize missing or misused punctuation, nor are they set to check the spelling of capitalized words. It's important that you still proofread your resume to check for grammatical mistakes and other problems, even <u>after</u> it has been spellchecked. If you find mistakes, do not make edits in pen or pencil or use white-out to fix them on the final copy!

Electronic Resumes

As companies rely increasingly on emerging technologies to find qualified candidates for job openings, you may opt to create an electronic resume in order to remain competitive in today's job market. Why is this important? Companies today sometimes request that resumes be submitted by e-mail, and many hiring managers regularly check online resume databases for candidates to fill unadvertised job openings. Other companies enlist the services of electronic employment database services, which charge jobseekers a nominal fee to have their resumes posted to the database to be viewed by potential employers. Still other companies use their own automated applicant tracking systems, in which case your resume is fed through a scanner that sends the image to a computer that "reads" your resume, looking for keywords, and files it accordingly in its database.

Whether you're posting your resume online, e-mailing it directly to an employer, sending it to an electronic employment database, or sending it to a company you suspect uses an automated applicant tracking system, you must create some form of electronic resume to take advantage of the technology. Don't panic! An electronic resume is simply a modified version of your conventional resume. An electronic resume is one that is sparsely formatted, but filled with keywords and important facts.

In order to post your resume to the Internet -- either to an online resume database or through direct e-mail to an employer -- you will need to change the way your resume is formatted. Instead of a Word, WordPerfect, or other word processing document, save your resume as a plain text, DOS, or ASCII file. These three terms are basically interchangeable, and describe text at its simplest, most basic level, without the formatting such as boldface or italics that most jobseekers use to make their resumes look more interesting. If you use e-mail, you'll notice that all of your messages are written and received in this format. First, you should remove all formatting from your resume including boldface, italics, underlining, bullets, differing font sizes, and graphics. Then, convert and save your resume as a plain text file. Most word processing programs have a "save as" feature that allows you to save files in different formats. Here, you should choose "text only" or "plain text."

Another option is to create a resume in HTML (hypertext markup language), the text formatting language used to publish information on the World Wide Web. However, the real usefulness of HTML resumes is still being explored. Most of the major online databases do not accept HTML resumes, and the vast majority of companies only accept plain text resumes through their e-mail.

Finally, if you simply wish to send your resume to an electronic employment database or a company that uses an automated applicant tracking system, there is no need to convert your resume to a plain text file. The only change you need to make is to organize the information in your resume by keywords. Employers are likely to do keyword searches for information, such as degree held or knowledge of particular types of software. Therefore, using the right keywords or key phrases in your resume is critical to its ultimate success. Keywords are usually nouns or short phrases that the computer searches for which refer to experience, training, skills, and abilities. For example, let's say an employer searches an employment database for a sales representative with the following criteria:

BS/BA
exceeded quota
cold calls
high energy
willing to travel

Even if you have the right qualifications, neglecting to use these keywords would result in the computer passing over your resume. Although there is no way to know for sure which keywords employers are most likely to search for, you can make educated guesses by checking the help-wanted ads or online job postings for your type of job. You should also arrange keywords in a keyword summary, a paragraph listing your qualifications that immediately follows your name and address (see sample letter in this chapter). In addition, choose a nondecorative font with clear, distinct characters, such as Helvetica or Times. It is more difficult for a scanner to accurately pick up the more unusual fonts. Boldface and all capital letters are best used only for major section headings, such as "Experience" and "Education." It is also best to avoid using italics or underlining, since this can cause the letters to bleed into one another.

For more specific information on creating and sending electronic resumes, see *The Adams Internet Job Search Almanac.*

Types of Resumes

The most common resume formats are the functional resume, the chronological resume, and the combination resume. (Examples can be found at the end of this chapter.) A functional resume focuses on skills and de-emphasizes job titles, employers, etc. A functional resume is best if you have been out of the work force for a long time or are changing careers. It is also good if you want to highlight specific skills and strengths, especially if all of your work experience has been at one company. This format can also be a good choice if you are just out of school or have no experience in your desired field.

Choose a chronological format if you are currently working or were working recently, and if your most recent experiences relate to your desired field. Use reverse chronological order and include dates. To a recruiter your last job and your latest schooling are the most important, so put the last first and list the rest going back in time.

A combination resume is perhaps the most common. This resume simply combines elements of the functional and chronological resume formats. This is used by many jobseekers with a solid track record who find elements of both types useful.

Organization

Your name, phone number, e-mail address (if you have one), and a complete mailing address should be at the top of your resume. Try to make your name stand out by using a slightly larger font size or all capital letters. Be sure to spell out everything. Never abbreviate St. for Street or Rd. for Road. If you are a college student, you should also put your home address and phone number at the top.

Change your message on your answering machine if necessary -- RUSH blaring in the background or your sorority sisters screaming may not come across well to all recruiters. If you think you may be moving within six months then include a second address and phone number of a trusted friend or relative who can reach you no matter where you are.

Remember that employers will keep your resume on file and may contact you months later if a position opens that fits your qualifications. All too often, candidates are unreachable because they have moved and had not previously provided enough contact options on their resume.

Next, list your experience, then your education. If you are a recent graduate, list your education first, unless your experience is more important than your education. (For example, if you have just graduated from a teaching school, have some business experience, and are applying for a job in business, you would list your business experience first.)

Keep everything easy to find. Put the dates of your employment and education on the left of the page. Put the names of the companies you worked for and the schools you attended a few spaces to the right of the dates. Put the city and state, or the city and country, where you studied or worked to the right of the page.

The important thing is simply to break up the text in some logical way that makes your resume visually attractive and easy to scan, so experiment to see which layout works best for your resume. However you set it up, *stay consistent.* Inconsistencies in fonts, spacing, or tenses will make your resume look sloppy. Also, be sure to use tabs to keep your information vertically lined up, rather than the less precise space bar.

RESUME CONTENT:
Say it with Style
Sell Yourself

You are selling your skills and accomplishments in your resume, so it is important to inventory yourself and know yourself. If you have achieved something, say so. Put it in the best possible light, but avoid subjective statements, such as "I am a hard worker" or "I get along well with my coworkers." Just stick to the facts.

While you shouldn't hold back or be modest, don't exaggerate your achievements to the point of misrepresentation. Be honest. Many companies will immediately drop an applicant from consideration (or fire a current employee) upon discovering inaccurate or untrue information on a resume or other application material.

Write down the important (and pertinent) things you have done, but do it in as few words as possible. Your resume will be scanned, not read, and short, concise phrases are much more effective than long-winded sentences. Avoid the use of "I" when emphasizing your accomplishments. Instead, use brief phrases beginning with action verbs.

While some technical terms will be unavoidable, you should try to avoid excessive "technicalese." Keep in mind that the first person to see your resume may be a human resources person who won't necessarily know all the jargon -- and how can they be impressed by something they don't understand?

Keep it Brief

Also, try to hold your paragraphs to six lines or less. If you have more than six lines of information about one job or school, put it in two or more paragraphs. A short resume will be examined more carefully. Remember: Your resume usually has between eight and 45 seconds to catch an employer's eye. So make every second count.

Job Objective

A functional resume may require a job objective to give it focus. One or two sentences describing the job you are seeking can clarify in what capacity your skills will be best put to use. Be sure that your stated objective is in line with the position you're applying for.

Examples:

> An entry-level editorial assistant position in the publishing industry.
> A senior management position with a telecommunications firm.

Don't include a job objective on a chronological resume unless your previous work experiences are <u>completely</u> unrelated to the position for which you're applying. The presence of an overly specific job objective might eliminate you from consideration for other positions that a recruiter feels are a better match for your qualifications. But even if you don't put an objective on paper, having a career goal in mind as you write can help give your resume a solid sense of direction.

USE ACTION VERBS

How you write your resume is just as important as *what* you write. In describing previous work experiences, the strongest resumes use short phrases beginning with action verbs. Below are a few you may want to use. (This list is not all-inclusive.)

achieved	developed	integrated	purchased
administered	devised	interpreted	reduced
advised	directed	interviewed	regulated
arranged	distributed	launched	represented
assisted	established	managed	resolved
attained	evaluated	marketed	restored
budgeted	examined	mediated	restructured
built	executed	monitored	revised
calculated	expanded	negotiated	scheduled
collaborated	expedited	obtained	selected
collected	facilitated	operated	served
compiled	formulated	ordered	sold
completed	founded	organized	solved
computed	generated	participated	streamlined
conducted	headed	performed	studied
consolidated	identified	planned	supervised
constructed	implemented	prepared	supplied
consulted	improved	presented	supported
controlled	increased	processed	tested
coordinated	initiated	produced	trained
created	installed	proposed	updated
determined	instructed	published	wrote

Some jobseekers may choose to include both "Relevant Experience" and "Additional Experience" sections. This can be useful, as it allows the jobseeker to place more emphasis on certain experiences and to de-emphasize others.

Emphasize continued experience in a particular job area or continued interest in a particular industry. De-emphasize irrelevant positions. It is okay to include one opening line providing a general description of each company you've worked at. Delete positions that you held for less than four months (unless you are a very recent college grad or still in school). Stress your <u>results</u> and your achievements, elaborating on how you contributed in your previous jobs. Did you increase sales, reduce costs, improve a product, implement a new program? Were you promoted? Use specific numbers (i.e., quantities, percentages, dollar amounts) whenever possible.

Education

Keep it brief if you have more than two years of career experience. Elaborate more if you have less experience. If you are a recent college graduate, you may choose to include any high school activities that are directly relevant to your career. If you've been out of school for a while you don't need to list your education prior to college.

Mention degrees received and any honors or special awards. Note individual courses or projects you participated in that might be relevant for employers. For example, if you are an English major applying for a position as a business writer, be sure to mention any business or economics courses. Previous experience such as Editor-in-Chief of the school newspaper would be relevant as well.

If you are uploading your resume to an online job hunting site such as CareerCity.com, action verbs are still important, but the key words or key nouns that a computer would search for become more important. For example, if you're seeking an accounting position, key nouns that a computer would search for such as "Lotus 1-2-3" or "CPA" or "payroll" become very important.

Highlight Impressive Skills

Be sure to mention any computer skills you may have. You may wish to include a section entitled "Additional Skills" or "Computer Skills," in which you list any software programs you know. An additional skills section is also an ideal place to mention fluency in a foreign language.

Personal Data

This section is optional, but if you choose to include it, keep it brief. A one-word mention of hobbies such as fishing, chess, baseball, cooking, etc., can give the person who will interview you a good way to open up the conversation.

Team sports experience is looked at favorably. It doesn't hurt to include activities that are somewhat unusual (fencing, Akido, '70s music) or that somehow relate to the position or the company to which you're applying. For instance, it would be worth noting if you are a member of a professional organization in your industry of interest. Never include information about your age, alias, date of birth, health, physical characteristics, marital status, religious affiliation, or political/moral beliefs.

References

The most that is needed is the sentence "References available upon request" at the bottom of your resume. If you choose to leave it out, that's fine. This line is not really necessary. It is understood that references will most likely be asked for and provided by you later on in the interviewing process. Do not actually send references with your resume and cover letter unless specifically requested.

HIRING A RESUME WRITER:
Is it the Right Choice for You?

If you write reasonably well, it is to your advantage to write your own resume. Writing your resume forces you to review your experiences and figure out how to explain your accomplishments in clear, brief phrases. This will help you when you explain your work to interviewers. It is also easier to tailor your resume to each position you're applying for when you have put it together yourself.

If you write your resume, everything will be in your own words; it will sound like you. It will say what you want it to say. If you are a good writer, know yourself well, and have a good idea of which parts of your background employers are looking for, you should be able to write your own resume better than someone else. If you decide to write your resume yourself, have as many people as possible review and proofread it. Welcome objective opinions and other perspectives.

When to Get Help

If you have difficulty writing in "resume style" (which is quite unlike normal written language), if you are unsure which parts of your background to emphasize, or if you think your resume would make your case better if it did not follow one of the standard forms outlined either here or in a book on resumes, then you should consider having it professionally written.

Even some professional resume writers we know have had their resumes written with the help of fellow professionals. They sought the help of someone who could be objective about their background, as well as provide an experienced sounding board to help focus their thoughts.

If You Hire a Pro

The best way to choose a writer is by reputation: the recommendation of a friend, a personnel director, your school placement officer, or someone else knowledgeable in the field.

Important questions:
- "How long have you been writing resumes?"
- "If I'm not satisfied with what you write, will you go over it with me and change it?"
- "Do you charge by the hour or a flat rate?"

There is no sure relation between price and quality, except that you are unlikely to get a good writer for less than $50 for an uncomplicated resume and you shouldn't have to pay more than $300 unless your experience is very extensive or complicated. There will be additional charges for printing. Assume nothing no matter how much you pay. It is your career at stake if there are mistakes on your resume!

Few resume services will give you a firm price over the phone, simply because some resumes are too complicated and take too long to do for a predetermined price. Some services will quote you a price that applies to almost all of their customers. Once you decide to use a specific writer, you should insist on a firm price quote *before* engaging their services. Also, find out how expensive minor changes will be.

COVER LETTERS:
Quick, Clear, and Concise

Always mail a cover letter with your resume. In a cover letter you can show an interest in the company that you can't show in a resume. You can also point out one or two of your skills or accomplishments the company can put to good use.

Make it Personal

The more personal you can get, the better, so long as you keep it professional. If someone known to the person you are writing has recommended that you contact the company, get permission to include his/her name in the letter. If you can get the name of a person to send the letter to, address it directly to that person (after first calling the company to verify the spelling of the person's name, correct title, and mailing address). Be sure to put the person's name and title on both the letter and the envelope. This will ensure that your letter will get through to the proper person, even if a new person now occupies this position. It will not always be possible to get the name of a person. Always strive to get at least a title.

Be sure to mention something about why you have an interest in the company - - *so many candidates apply for jobs with no apparent knowledge of what the company does!* This conveys the message that they just want any job.

Type cover letters in full. Don't try the cheap and easy ways, like using a computer mail merge program or photocopying the body of your letter and typing in the inside address and salutation. You will give the impression that you are mailing to a host of companies and have no particular interest in any one.

Print your cover letter on the same color and same high-quality paper as your resume.

Cover letter basic format

<u>Paragraph 1:</u> State what the position is that you are seeking. It is not always necessary to state how you found out about the position -- often you will apply without knowing that a position is open.

<u>Paragraph 2:</u> Include what you know about the company and why you are interested in working there. Mention any prior contact with the company or someone known to the hiring person if relevant. Briefly state your qualifications and what you can offer. (Do not talk about what you cannot do).

<u>Paragraph 3:</u> Close with your phone number and where/when you can be reached. Make a request for an interview. State when you will follow up by phone (or mail or e-mail if the ad requests no phone calls). Do not wait long -- generally five working days. If you say you're going to follow up, then actually do it! This phone call can get your resume noticed when it might otherwise sit in a stack of 225 other resumes.

Cover letter do's and don'ts

- *Do* keep your cover letter brief and to the point.
- *Do* be sure it is error-free.
- *Do* accentuate what you can offer the company, not what you hope to gain.
- *Do* be sure your phone number and address is on your cover letter just in case it gets separated from your resume (this happens!).
- *Do* check the watermark by holding the paper up to a light -- be sure it is facing forward so it is readable -- on the same side as the text, and right-side up.
- *Do* sign your cover letter (or type your name if you are sending it electronically). Blue or black ink are both fine. Do not use red ink.
- *Don't* just repeat information verbatim from your resume.
- *Don't* overuse the personal pronoun "I."
- *Don't* send a generic cover letter -- show your personal knowledge of and interest in that particular company.

THANK YOU LETTERS:
Another Way to Stand Out

As mentioned earlier, *always* send a thank you letter after an interview (see the sample later in this section). So few candidates do this and it is yet another way for you to stand out. Be sure to mention something specific from the interview and restate your interest in the company and the position.

It is generally acceptable to handwrite your thank you letter on a generic thank you card (but *never* a postcard). Make sure handwritten notes are neat and legible. However, if you are in doubt, typing your letter is always the safe bet. If you met with several people it is fine to send them each an individual thank you letter. Call the company if you need to check on the correct spelling of their names.

Remember to:
- Keep it short.
- Proofread it carefully.
- Send it *promptly*.

FUNCTIONAL RESUME

C.J. RAVENCLAW
129 Pennsylvania Avenue
Washington DC 20500
202/555-6652
e-mail: ravenclaw@dcpress.net

Objective
A position as a graphic designer commensurate with my acquired skills and expertise.

Summary
Extensive experience in plate making, separations, color matching, background definition, printing, mechanicals, color corrections, and personnel supervision. A highly motivated manager and effective communicator. Proven ability to:

- **Create Commercial Graphics**
- **Produce Embossed Drawings**
- **Color Separate**
- **Control Quality**
- **Resolve Printing Problems**
- **Analyze Customer Satisfaction**

Qualifications
Printing:
Knowledgeable in black and white as well as color printing. Excellent judgment in determining acceptability of color reproduction through comparison with original. Proficient at producing four- or five-color corrections on all media, as well as restyling previously reproduced four-color artwork.

Customer Relations:
Routinely work closely with customers to ensure specifications are met. Capable of striking a balance between technical printing capabilities and need for customer satisfaction through entire production process.

Specialties:
Practiced at creating silk screen overlays for a multitude of processes including velo bind, GBC bind, and perfect bind. Creative design and timely preparation of posters, flyers, and personalized stationery.

Personnel Supervision:
Skillful at fostering atmosphere that encourages highly talented artists to balance high-level creativity with maximum production. Consistently beat production deadlines. Instruct new employees, apprentices, and students in both artistry and technical operations.

Experience
Graphic Arts Professor, Ohio State University, Columbus OH (1992-1996).
Manager, Design Graphics, Washington DC (1997-present).

Education
Massachusetts Conservatory of Art, Ph.D. 1990
University of Massachusetts, B.A. 1988

CHRONOLOGICAL RESUME

HARRY SEABORN
557 Shoreline Drive
Seattle, WA 98404
(206) 555-6584
e-mail: hseaborn@centco.com

EXPERIENCE

THE CENTER COMPANY   Seattle, WA
Systems Programmer   1996-present
- Develop and maintain customer accounting and order tracking database using a Visual Basic front end and SQL server.
- Plan and implement migration of company wide transition from mainframe-based dumb terminals to a true client server environment using Windows NT Workstation and Server.
- Oversee general local and wide area network administration including the development of a variety of intranet modules to improve internal company communication and planning across divisions.

INFO TECH, INC.   Seattle, WA
Technical Manager   1994-1996
- Designed and managed the implementation of a network providing the legal community with a direct line to Supreme Court cases across the Internet using SQL Server and a variety of Internet tools.
- Developed a system to make the entire library catalog available on line using PERL scripts and SQL.
- Used Visual Basic and Microsoft Access to create a registration system for university registrar.

EDUCATION

SALEM STATE UNIVERSITY   Salem, OR
    M.S. in Computer Science.   1993
    B.S. in Computer Science.   1991

COMPUTER SKILLS

- Programming Languages: Visual Basic, Java, C++, SQL, PERL
- Software: SQL Server, Internet Information Server, Oracle
- Operating Systems: Windows NT, UNIX, Linux

FUNCTIONAL RESUME

Donna Hermione Moss
703 Wizard's Way
Chicago, IL 60601
(312) 555-8841
e-mail: donna@cowfire.com

OBJECTIVE:
To contribute over five years of experience in promotion, communications, and administration to an entry-level position in advertising.

SUMMARY OF QUALIFICATIONS:
- Performed advertising duties for small business.
- Experience in business writing and communications skills.
- General knowledge of office management.
- Demonstrated ability to work well with others, in both supervisory and support staff roles.
- Type 75 words per minute.

SELECTED ACHIEVEMENTS AND RESULTS:
Promotion:
Composing, editing, and proofreading correspondence and public relations materials for own catering service. Large-scale mailings.

Communication:
Instruction; curriculum and lesson planning; student evaluation; parent-teacher conferences; development of educational materials. Training and supervising clerks.

Computer Skills:
Proficient in MS Word, Lotus 1-2-3, Excel, and Filemaker Pro.

Administration:
Record-keeping and file maintenance. Data processing and computer operations, accounts receivable, accounts payable, inventory control, and customer relations. Scheduling, office management, and telephone reception.

PROFESSIONAL HISTORY:
Teacher; Self-Employed (owner of catering service); Floor Manager; Administrative Assistant; Accounting Clerk.

EDUCATION:
Beloit College, Beloit, WI, BA in Education, 1991

CHRONOLOGICAL RESUME

PERCY ZIEGLER
16 Josiah Court
Marlborough CT 06447
203/555-9641 (h)
203/555-8176, x14 (w)

EDUCATION

Keene State College, Keene NH
Bachelor of Arts in Elementary Education, 1998
- Graduated *magna cum laude*
- English minor
- Kappa Delta Pi member, inducted 1996

EXPERIENCE
September 1998-
Present

Elmer T. Thienes Elementary School, Marlborough CT
Part-time Kindergarten Teacher
- Instruct kindergartners in reading, spelling, language arts, and music.
- Participate in the selection of textbooks and learning aids.
- Organize and supervise class field trips and coordinate in-class presentations.

Summers
1995-1997

Keene YMCA, Youth Division, Keene NH
Child-care Counselor
- Oversaw summer program for low-income youth.
- Budgeted and coordinated special events and field trips, working with Program Director to initiate variations in the program.
- Served as Youth Advocate in cooperation with social worker to address the social needs and problems of participants.

Spring 1997

Wheelock Elementary School, Keene NH
Student Teacher
- Taught third-grade class in all elementary subjects.
- Designed and implemented a two-week unit on Native Americans.
- Assisted in revision of third-grade curriculum.

Fall 1996

Child Development Center, Keene NH
Daycare Worker
- Supervised preschool children on the playground and during art activities.
- Created a "Wishbone Corner," where children could quietly look at books or take a voluntary "time-out."

ADDITIONAL INTERESTS

Martial arts, Pokemon, politics, reading, skiing, writing.

ELECTRONIC RESUME

GRIFFIN DORE
69 Dursley Drive
Cambridge, MA 02138
(617) 555-5555

KEYWORD SUMMARY

Senior financial manager with over ten years experience in Accounting and Systems Management, Budgeting, Forecasting, Cost Containment, Financial Reporting, and International Accounting. MBA in Management. Proficient in Lotus, Excel, Solomon, and Windows.

EXPERIENCE

COLWELL CORPORATION, Wellesley, MA
Director of Accounting and Budgets, 1990 to present
    Direct staff of twenty in General Ledger, Accounts Payable, Accounts Receivable, and International Accounting.
    Facilitate month-end closing process with parent company and auditors.
    Implemented team-oriented cross-training program within accounting group, resulting in timely month-end closings and increased productivity of key accounting staff.
    Developed and implemented a strategy for Sales and Use Tax Compliance in all fifty states.
    Prepare monthly financial statements and analyses.

FRANKLIN AND DELANEY COMPANY, Melrose, MA
Senior Accountant, 1987-1990
    Managed Accounts Payable, General Ledger, transaction processing, and financial reporting. Supervised staff of five.

Staff Accountant, 1985-1987
    Managed Accounts Payable, including vouchering, cash disbursements, and bank reconciliation.
    Wrote and issued policies.
    Maintained supporting schedules used during year-end audits.
    Trained new employees.

EDUCATION

MBA in Management, Northeastern University, Boston, MA, 1989
BS in Accounting, Boston College, Boston, MA, 1985

ASSOCIATIONS

National Association of Accountants

GENERAL MODEL
FOR A COVER LETTER

Your mailing address
Date

Contact's name
Contact's title
Company
Company's mailing address

Dear Mr./Ms. _____:

Immediately explain why your background makes you the best candidate for the position that you are applying for. Describe what prompted you to write (want ad, article you read about the company, networking contact, etc.). Keep the first paragraph short and hard-hitting.

Detail what you could contribute to this company. Show how your qualifications will benefit this firm. Describe your interest in the corporation. Subtly emphasizing your knowledge about this firm and your familiarity with the industry will set you apart from other candidates. Remember to keep this letter short; few recruiters will read a cover letter longer than half a page.

If possible, your closing paragraph should request specific action on the part of the reader. Include your phone number and the hours when you can be reached. Mention that if you do not hear from the reader by a specific date, you will follow up with a phone call. Lastly, thank the reader for their time, consideration, etc.

Sincerely,

(signature)

Your full name (typed)

Enclosure (use this if there are other materials, such as your resume, that are included in the same envelope)

SAMPLE COVER LETTER

16 Josiah Court
Marlborough CT 06447
January 16, 2000

Ms. Leona Malfoy
Assistant Principal
Laningham Elementary School
43 Mayflower Drive
Keene NH 03431

Dear Ms. Malfoy:

Toby Potter recently informed me of a possible opening for a third grade teacher at Laningham Elementary School. With my experience instructing third-graders, both in schools and in summer programs, I feel I would be an ideal candidate for the position. Please accept this letter and the enclosed resume as my application.

Laningham's educational philosophy that every child can learn and succeed interests me, since it mirrors my own. My current position at Elmer T. Thienes Elementary has reinforced this philosophy, heightening my awareness of the different styles and paces of learning and increasing my sensitivity toward special needs children. Furthermore, as a direct result of my student teaching experience at Wheelock Elementary School, I am comfortable, confident, and knowledgeable working with third-graders.

I look forward to discussing the position and my qualifications for it in more detail. I can be reached at 203/555-9641 evenings or 203/555-8176, x14 weekdays. If I do not hear from you before Tuesday of next week, I will call to see if we can schedule a time to meet. Thank you for your time and consideration.

Sincerely,

Percy Ziegler

Percy Ziegler

Enclosure

GENERAL MODEL FOR A
THANK YOU/FOLLOW-UP LETTER

Your mailing address
Date

Contact's name
Contact's title
Company
Company's mailing address

Dear Mr./Ms._____:

Remind the interviewer of the reason (i.e., a specific opening, an informational interview, etc.) you were interviewed, as well as the date. Thank him/her for the interview, and try to personalize your thanks by mentioning some specific aspect of the interview.

Confirm your interest in the organization (and in the opening, if you were interviewing for a particular position). Use specifics to re-emphasize that you have researched the firm in detail and have considered how you would fit into the company and the position. This is a good time to say anything you wish you had said in the initial meeting. Be sure to keep this letter brief; a half page is plenty.

If appropriate, close with a suggestion for further action, such as a desire to have an additional interview, if possible. Mention your phone number and the hours you can be reached. Alternatively, you may prefer to mention that you will follow up with a phone call in several days. Once again, thank the person for meeting with you, and state that you would be happy to provide any additional information about your qualifications.

Sincerely,

(signature)

Your full name (typed)

PRIMARY EMPLOYERS

ACCOUNTING AND MANAGEMENT CONSULTING

You can expect to find the following types of companies in this chapter:
Consulting and Research Firms • Industrial Accounting Firms •
Management Services • Public Accounting Firms •
Tax Preparation Companies

DELOITTE & TOUCHE

333 Clay, Suite 2300, Houston TX 77002. 713/982-2000. **Contact:** Human Resources. **World Wide Web address:** http://www.us.deloitte.com. **Description:** An international firm of certified public accountants providing professional accounting, auditing, tax, and management consulting services to widely diversified clients. The company has a specialized program consisting of national industry groups and functional groups that cross industry lines. Groups are involved in various disciplines including accounting, auditing, taxation management advisory services, small and growing businesses, mergers and acquisitions, and computer applications. **Corporate headquarters location:** Wilton CT. **Number of employees nationwide:** 30,000.

ERNST & YOUNG LLP

100 West Houston Street, Suite 1900, San Antonio TX 78205. 210/228-9696. **Contact:** Human Resources. **World Wide Web address:** http://www.ey.com. **Description:** A certified public accounting firm that also provides management consulting services. Services include data processing, financial modeling, financial feasibility studies, production planning and inventory management, management sciences, health care planning, human resources, cost accounting, and budgeting systems. **Corporate headquarters location:** New York NY. **Other U.S. locations:** Nationwide.

ERNST & YOUNG LLP

700 Lavaca Street, Suite 1400, Austin TX 78701. 512/478-9881. **Contact:** Human Resources. **World Wide Web address:** http://www.ey.com. **Description:** A certified public accounting firm that also provides management consulting services. Services include data processing, financial modeling, financial feasibility studies, production planning and inventory management, management sciences, health care planning, human resources, cost accounting, and budgeting systems. **Corporate headquarters location:** New York NY. **Other U.S. locations:** Nationwide.

KPMG
200 Crescent Court, Suite 300, Dallas TX 75201. 218/840-2000. **Contact:** Human Resources. **World Wide Web address:** http://www.kpmg.com. **Description:** Delivers a wide range of value-added assurance, tax, and consulting services. **Corporate headquarters location:** Montvale NJ. **Parent company:** KPMG International is a leader among professional services firms engaged in capturing, managing, assessing, and delivering information to create knowledge that will help its clients maximize shareholder value. KPMG International has more than 100,000 employees worldwide.

KPMG
700 Louisiana Street, 31st Floor, Bank of America Center, Houston TX 77002. 713/319-2000. **Contact:** Human Resources Department. **World Wide Web address:** http://www.kpmg.com. **Description:** Delivers a wide range of value-added assurance, tax, and consulting services. **Corporate headquarters location:** Montvale NJ. **Parent company:** KPMG International.

PAYCHEX, INC.
4242 Woodcock Drive, Suite 100, San Antonio TX 78228. 512/469-0550. **Contact:** Human Resources. **World Wide Web address:** http://www.paychex.com. **Description:** A payroll accounting firm. **Listed on:** NASDAQ. **Stock exchange symbol:** PAYX.

PRICEWATERHOUSECOOPERS
1201 Louisiana, Suite 2900, Houston TX 77002. 713/356-4000. **Contact:** Human Resources. **World Wide Web address:** http://www.pricewaterhousecoopers.com. **Description:** One of the largest certified public accounting firms in the world. PricewaterhouseCoopers provides public accounting, business advisory, management consulting, and taxation services. **Corporate headquarters location:** New York NY. **Other U.S. locations:** Nationwide.

PRICEWATERHOUSECOOPERS
600 Congress Avenue, Suite 1800, Austin TX 78701. 512/477-1300. **Fax:** 512/477-8681. **Contact:** Human Resources Department. **World Wide Web address:** http://www.pricewaterhousecoopers.com. **Description:** One of the largest certified public accounting firms in the world. PricewaterhouseCoopers provides public accounting, business advisory, management consulting, and taxation services.

Corporate headquarters location: New York NY. **Other U.S. locations:** Nationwide.

ADVERTISING, MARKETING, AND PUBLIC RELATIONS

You can expect to find the following types of companies in this chapter:
Advertising Agencies • Direct Mail Marketers •
Market Research Firms • Public Relations Firms

ADVO INC.

8950 Railwood Drive, Houston TX 77078. 713/636-7200. **Contact:** Human Resources. **World Wide Web address:** http://www.advo. com. **Description:** A direct mail advertising agency. **Positions advertised include:** Client Services Representative; Client Services Account Manager. **Corporate headquarters location:** Windsor CT. **Listed on:** New York Stock Exchange. **Stock exchange symbol:** AD. **Number of employees nationwide:** 4,700.

BRSG (BLACK ROGERS SULLIVAN GOODNIGHT)

1900 St. James Place, Suite 800, Houston TX 77056. 713/781-6666. **Fax:** 713/783-1592. **Contact:** Stacy Jacob, Senior Vice President. **Description:** A marketing communications firm. **Special programs:** Internships. **Office hours:** Monday - Friday, 8:00 a.m. - 5:00 p.m. **Corporate headquarters location:** This location. **Other U.S. locations:** Austin TX. **Operations at this facility include:** Administration; Research and Development.

BATES SOUTHWEST

5847 San Felipe, Suite 400, Houston TX 77057. 713/266-7676. **Contact:** Ann Puleo, Human Resources. **World Wide Web address:** http://www.batessouthwest.com. **Description:** An advertising agency. **Corporate headquarters location:** New York NY. **Other U.S. locations:** Nationwide. **Operations at this facility include:** Administration; Divisional Headquarters. **Number of employees at this location:** 80.

CABLE TIME

401 West Cantu Road, Suite D, Del Rio TX 78840. 830/774-5538. **Contact:** Human Resources. **Description:** Provides advertising services for businesses through major cable networks such as CNN.

DATABASE MARKETING GROUP INC.

2113 Wells Branch Parkway, Suite 4400, Austin TX 78728. 512/990-2000. **Contact:** Human Resources. **World Wide Web address:** http://www.leaddogs.com. **Description:** Provides direct marketing services for high-tech companies including event management and database development.

FOGARTYKLEINMONROE
7155 Old Katy Road, Suite 100, Houston TX 77024. 713/862-5100. **Contact:** Human Resources. **World Wide Web address:** http://www.fkmagency.com. **Description:** A full-service advertising agency.

FREEMAN DECORATING COMPANY
13101 Almeida Road, Houston TX 77045. 713/433-2400. **Contact:** Human Resources. **World Wide Web address:** http://www.totalshow.com. **Description:** Offers set-up and display services for trade shows and conventions.

GSD&M ADVERTISING
828 West Sixth Street, Austin TX 78703. 512/427-4736. **Contact:** Human Resources. **World Wide Web address:** http://www.gsdm.com. **Description:** An advertising agency. **Positions advertised include:** Receptionist; Media Buyer; Producer. **Corporate headquarters location:** This location.

GREENSHEET
P.O. Box 1371, Houston TX 77251. 713/655-3100. **Fax:** 713/371-3541. **Recorded jobline:** 713/371-3542. **Contact:** Recruiter. **World Wide Web address:** http://www.thegreensheet.com. **Description:** *Greensheet* is a free tabloid for business and personal advertising. The company publishes 16 weekly editions, with a readership of over 1 million.

HARTE-HANKS, INC.
P.O. Box 269, San Antonio TX 78291-0269. 210/829-9000. **Contact:** Carolyn Oatman, Director of Human Resources. **World Wide Web address:** http://www.harte-hanks.com. **Description:** Provides direct marketing services for various companies and publishes a weekly shopping guide. **Corporate headquarters location:** This location.

KNOWLEDGEBASE MARKETING
5884 Point West Drive, Houston TX 77036. 713/995-2303. **Fax:** 713/995-2201. **Contact:** Thomas Cope, Recruiter. **Description:** A list brokerage providing a variety of data mining services for direct

marketers, including marketing database development, segmentation analysis, merge/purge, list enhancement, and list rental fulfillment.

ROBERT LAMONS AND ASSOCIATES
1205 Sherwood Forest, Houston TX 77043. 281/558-5555. **Contact:** Human Resources. **World Wide Web address:** http://www.ads2biz.com. **Description:** A business-to-business marketing communications specialist.

MANN & MANN MEDIA SERVICES, INC.
84 NE Loop 410, Suite 126, San Antonio TX 78216. 210/525-8148. **Fax:** 210/525-8246. **Contact:** Wanda Mann, President. **Description:** A media buying firm. Mann & Mann Media Services serves as a negotiator between advertisers and radio and television stations, newspapers, and magazines. Founded in 1986. **NOTE:** Entry-level positions are offered. **Positions advertised include:** Advertising Executive; Marketing Specialist; Media Buyer. **Corporate headquarters location:** This location. **Listed on:** Privately held.

NATIONWIDE ADVERTISING SERVICE INC.
7500 San Felipe, Suite 340, Houston TX 77063. 713/780-0770. **Contact:** Regional Manager. **World Wide Web address:** http://www.hrads.com. **Description:** One of the largest independent, full-service advertising agencies specializing exclusively in human resource communications and promotions. The company offers consultations, campaign planning, ad placement, research, and creative production. **Corporate headquarters location:** Cleveland OH. **Other U.S. locations:** Nationwide. **International locations:** Canada. **Parent company:** McCann-Erickson World Group.

NORWOOD PROMOTIONAL PRODUCTS, INC.
106 East Sixth Street, Suite 300, Austin TX 78701. 512/476-7100. **Contact:** Human Resources. **World Wide Web address:** http://www.norwood.com. **Description:** Through its subsidiaries and divisions, Norwood Promotional Products imprints and distributes over 1,000 promotional items to over 6,500 distributors nationwide. Product lines include badges, business gifts, buttons, headwear, Koozie insulator products, mugs and glassware, paper products, packet specialties, recognition and award items, and writing instruments. The company markets its products under trade names including The Action Line, Barlow, Econ-O-Line, Koozie, RCC, and Salam. **Subsidiaries include:** ArtMold; Barlow; Key; RCC.

PRINT MAILERS
707 West Road, Houston TX 77038. 281/931-8883. **Contact:** Human Resources. **World Wide Web address:** http://www.pminet. com. **Description:** Provides turnkey direct marketing, printing, and mailing services.

SACHNOWITZ & COMPANY
P.O. Box 130939, Houston TX 77219. 713/521-1010. **Contact:** Human Resources. **World Wide Web address:** http:// www.sachnowitz.com. **Description:** An advertising agency specializing in radio, television, and magazine ads.

TL MARKETING INC.
4407 Bee Caves Road, Building 6, 2nd Floor, Suite 622, Austin TX 78746. 512/371-7272. **Contact:** Human Resources. **Description:** A marketing firm representing manufacturers within the electrical industry. **NOTE:** Resumes should be sent to the corporate headquarters at: 14580 Quorum Drive, Suite 100, Dallas TX 75240. **Corporate headquarters location:** Dallas TX.

WEST TELESERVICES
10931 Laureate Drive, Building 3000, San Antonio TX 78249. 210/690-6900. **Contact:** Human Resources. **World Wide Web address:** http://www.west.com. **Description:** A telemarketing company that deals with both outbound (phone sales) and inbound (phone orders) calls. This location handles inbound and outbound calling for *Fortune* 500 companies. **Positions advertised include:** Account Services Supervisor; Performance Assessment Coordinator; Custodial Team Leader; Security Guard; Employee Relations/Training Coordinator; HRMS Analyst; Programmer/Analyst; Senior Secretary; Customer Service Representative. **Listed on:** NASDAQ. **Stock exchange symbol:** WSTC.

AEROSPACE

You can expect to find the following types of companies in this chapter:
Aerospace Products and Services • Aircraft Equipment and Parts

THE BOEING COMPANY
13100 Space Center Boulevard, Houston TX 77059. 281/244-4000.
Contact: Human Resources. **World Wide Web address:** http://
www.boeing.com. **Description:** The Boeing Company is one of the
largest aerospace firms in the United States, one of the nation's top
exporters, and one of the world's leading manufacturers of
commercial jet transports. The company is a major U.S. government
contractor, with capabilities in missile and space, electronic systems,
military aircraft, helicopters, and information systems management.
Operations at this facility include: This location provides
engineering services and other consulting services as a division of
the major aerospace and electronics manufacturer. **Listed on:** New
York Stock Exchange. **Stock Exchange symbol:** BA.

THE BOEING COMPANY
P.O. Box 1824, Kingsville TX 78364-1824. 361/516-8305. **Contact:**
Human Resources. **World Wide Web address:** http://www.boeing.
com. **Description:** The Boeing Company is one of the largest
aerospace firms in the United States, one of the nation's top
exporters, and one of the world's leading manufacturers of
commercial jet transports. The company is a major U.S. government
contractor, with capabilities in missile and space, electronic systems,
military aircraft, helicopters, and information systems management.
Corporate headquarters location: Chicago IL. **Operations at this
facility include:** This location is an aviation training facility for the
U.S. Navy. **Listed on:** New York Stock Exchange. **Stock Exchange
symbol:** BA.

CFAN COMPANY
1000 Technology Way, San Marcos TX 78666. 512/353-2832.
Contact: Human Resources. **World Wide Web address:** http://
www.c-fan.com. **Description:** CFAN Company manufactures
composite fan blades for G.E. aircraft engines.

CONTINENTAL AIRLINES
1600 Smith Street, Houston TX 77002-4330. 713/324-4700. **Fax:**
713/324-5940. **Contact:** Human Resources. **World Wide Web
address:** http://www.continental.com. **Description:** One of the

largest airlines in the United States, offering flights to 126 domestic and 89 international locations daily. Operating through its major hubs in Newark, Houston, and Cleveland, Continental offers extensive service to Latin America and Europe. Founded in 1934. **NOTE:** Entry-level positions and second and third shifts are offered. **Corporate headquarters location:** This location. **Listed on:** New York Stock Exchange. **Stock exchange symbol:** CAL. **Number of employees nationwide:** 42,900.

DELTA AIR LINES, INC.
6763 Hillcrest Avenue, Dallas TX 75261-0348. 800/221-1212. **Contact:** Human Resources. **World Wide Web address:** http://www.delta.com. **Description:** One of the largest airlines in the United States. The company provides scheduled air transportation for passengers, freight, and mail on an extensive route that covers most of the country and extends to 32 foreign nations. The route covers 218 domestic cities in 48 states, the District of Columbia, Puerto Rico, the U.S. Virgin Islands, and 131 cities abroad. Major domestic hubs of Delta include Atlanta, Dallas-Fort Worth, Salt Lake City, and Cincinnati with minor hubs in Los Angeles and Orlando. Delta has over 550 aircraft in its fleet. Founded in 1929. **NOTE:** All hiring is done through Delta Air Lines, Inc., Employment Office, P.O. Box 20530, Hartsfield International Airport, Atlanta GA 30320. 404/715-2600. **Corporate headquarters location:** Atlanta GA. **Listed on:** New York Stock Exchange. **Stock exchange symbol:** DAL.

FAIRCHILD DORNIER CORPORATION
P.O. Box 790490, San Antonio TX 78279-0490. 210/824-9421. **Fax:** 210/824-9476. **Contact:** Human Resources. **World Wide Web address:** http://www.faidor.com. **Description:** Manufactures aircraft and provides a wide range of aviation services. **Corporate headquarters location:** This location.

GB TECH INC.
2200 Space Park Drive, Suite 400, Houston TX 77058. 281/333-3703. **Contact:** Human Resources. **E-mail address:** hr@gbtech.net. **World Wide Web address:** http://www.gbtech.net. **Description:** Performs aerospace and computer engineering services. GB Tech contracts with several organizations including NASA. **Corporate headquarters location:** This location.

GOODRICH AEROSPACE AEROSTRUCTURES GROUP
2005 Technology Way, San Marcos TX 78666. 512/754-3600. **Contact:** Human Resources. **World Wide Web address:** http://www.goodrich.com. **Description:** Designs, integrates, manufactures, sells, and supports aircraft engine nacelle systems and components for large commercial and military aircraft. **Positions advertised include:** Team Leader; Advanced Associate. **Corporate headquarters location:** Charlotte NC. **Parent company:** Goodrich Company provides aircraft systems, components, and services and manufactures a wide range of specialty chemicals. The business units comprising the aerospace division of Goodrich consist of landing systems; sensors and integrated systems; safety systems; and maintenance, repair, and overhaul. Specialty chemical business units include specialty plastics; specialty additives; sealants, coatings, and adhesives; and water systems and services. **Listed on:** New York Stock Exchange. **Stock Exchange Symbol:** GR. **Number of employees nationwide:** 23,000.

DEE HOWARD AIRCRAFT MAINTENANCE, LP
P.O. Box 469004, San Antonio TX 78246-9004. 210/301-8100. **Contact:** Human Resources. **World Wide Web address:** http:/www.deehoward.com. **Description:** Repairs, modifies, and designs aircraft.

LOCKHEED MARTIN SPACE OPERATIONS
2400 NASA Road One, Mail Stop B03, Houston TX 77058. 281/333-5411. **Fax:** 281/333-6100. **Contact:** Human Resources Representative. **World Wide Web address:** http://www.lmco.com. **Description:** Provides a wide range of engineering and scientific support to NASA/Johnson Space Center, which includes operating and maintaining large environment simulation chambers for manned and unmanned engineering tests; designing and managing NASA-sponsored and commercial payloads; supporting all handheld cameras used onboard the space shuttle; designing and building astronaut tools and training aids; and providing development, testing, and implementation of life sciences experiments for space shuttle and space station missions. **NOTE:** Jobseekers are encouraged to submit their resume via the Website: http://www.lockheedmartin.com. **Positions advertised include:** Systems Engineer. **Parent company:** Lockheed Martin Corporation operates in five major areas: Space Systems develops space technology systems such as rocket systems, space shuttle support technology, and other products; Missile Systems produces fleet ballistic missiles for military

applications; Advanced Systems operates as the research and development organization exploring military, commercial, and scientific needs; Information Processing develops comprehensive database systems to process the specific needs of other company divisions; and the Austin Division (Austin TX) is responsible for designing and producing military tactical support systems. **Listed on:** New York Stock Exchange. **Stock exchange symbol:** LM. **Number of employees nationwide:** 125,000.

NEW SYSTEMS
1201 North Industrial Boulevard, Round Rock TX 78681. 512/388-4806. **Contact:** Human Resources. **Description:** Engineers and manufactures kits used for installing navigational equipment in commercial aircraft. **Positions advertised include:** Assembly Engineer; Customer Service Representative; Draftsperson; Electrical/Electronics Engineer.

APPAREL, FASHION, AND TEXTILES

You can expect to find the following types of companies in this chapter:
Broadwoven Fabric Mills • Knitting Mills • Curtains and Draperies •
Footwear • Nonwoven Fabrics • Textile Goods and Finishing •
Yarn and Thread Mills

C C CREATIONS
112 Hollerman Drive, College Station TX 77840. 979/693-9664.
Contact: Human Resources. **World Wide Web address:** http://
www.cccreationsonline.com. **Description:** A custom manufacturer of
screen-printed and embroidered apparel and accessories.

CUSTOM DRAPERY, BLINDS, & CARPET
1312 Live Oak Street, Houston TX 77003. 713/225-9211. **Contact:**
Human Resources. **Description:** Manufactures and installs custom-
designed window treatments and hardware as well as carpeting.

DILLY UNIFORM COMPANY
235 Berry Road, Houston TX 77022. 713/692-7142. **Contact:**
Human Resources. **Description:** Manufactures hospital apparel such
as doctors' and nurses' uniforms.

HOUSTON WIPER & MILL SUPPLY COMPANY
P.O. Box 24962, Houston TX 77229-4962. 713/672-0571. **Toll-free
phone:** 800/633-5968. **Fax:** 713/673-7637. **Contact:** Human
Resources. **World Wide Web address:** http://www.houstonwiper.
com. **Description:** A secondary textile recycler. Founded in 1954.
Office hours: Monday - Friday, 8:00 a.m. - 5:00 p.m. **Corporate
headquarters location:** This location. **Operations at this facility
include:** Manufacturing. **Listed on:** Privately held. **President:** Michael
J. Brown.

KAST FABRICS
P.O. Box 1660, Pasadena TX 77501. 713/473-4848. **Fax:** 713/473-
3130. **Contact:** Human Resources. **World Wide Web address:** http://
www.kastfabrics.com. **Description:** A wholesale distributor of
decorative fabrics for drapes and upholstery. The company also
manufactures bedding such as quilts, bedspreads, and dust ruffles.
Founded in 1952. **Corporate headquarters location:** This location.

TANDY BRANDS ACCESSORIES
500 Airport Road, Yoakum TX 77995. 361/293-2311. **Contact:** Dawne Wendel, Personnel Director. **World Wide Web address:** http://www.tandybrands.com. **Description:** Tandy Brands Accessories manufactures belts, ties, suspenders, and other leather products. **Listed on:** NASDAQ. **Stock exchange symbol:** TBAC.

TEX TAN WESTERN LEATHER COMPANY
808 South U.S. Highway 77A, Yoakum TX 77995. 361/293-2314. **Fax:** 361/293-2369. **Contact:** Charles B. Ratcliff, Personnel Director. **World Wide Web address:** http://www.textan.com. **Description:** Tex Tan Western Leather Company is a manufacturer of various leather products including saddles, riding equipment, belts, and other sundry products. Tex Tan Western Leather Company provides these products to dealers worldwide. **Listed on:** Privately held.

TEXACE CORPORATION
P.O. Box 7429, San Antonio TX 78207-0429. 210/227-7551. **Contact:** Minerva Martinez, Human Resources Director. **World Wide Web address:** http://www.texace.com. **Description:** Texace Corporation manufactures a variety of headwear including golf caps and visors.

WILLIAMSON-DICKIE MANUFACTURING COMPANY
P.O. Box 295, Weslaco TX 78596. 956/968-1567. **Contact:** Human Resources. **World Wide Web address:** http://www.dickies.com. **Description:** Williamson-Dickie Manufacturing Company manufactures apparel for men and boys including casual slacks and work pants. **Corporate headquarters location:** Fort Worth TX. **Operations at this facility include:** This location is primarily engaged in apparel sewing.

WILLIAMSON-DICKIE MANUFACTURING COMPANY
6110 South 42nd Street, McAllen TX 78503. 956/686-6541. **Contact:** Human Resources. **World Wide Web address:** http://www.dickies.com. **Description:** Williamson-Dickie Manufacturing Company manufactures apparel for men and boys including casual slacks and work pants. **Corporate headquarters location:** Fort Worth TX. **Operations at this facility include:** This location manufactures men's work pants.

ARCHITECTURE, CONSTRUCTION, AND ENGINEERING

You can expect to find the following types of companies in this chapter:
Architectural and Engineering Services • Civil and Mechanical Engineering Firms • Construction Products, Manufacturers, and Wholesalers General Contractors/ Specialized Trade Contractors

ABB LUMMUS GLOBAL
3010 Briar Park Drive, Houston TX 77042. 713/821-5000. **Contact:** Personnel Director. **World Wide Web address:** http://www.abb.com. **Description:** An engineering firm serving power plants, chemical plants, and petrochemical and oil refineries, as well as other industries such as aviation and storage. **Listed on:** New York Stock Exchange. **Stock exchange symbol:** ABB.

J.D. ABRAMS INTERNATIONAL INC.
111 Congress Avenue, Suite 2400, Austin TX 78701. 512/322-4000. **Fax:** 512/322-4018. **Contact:** Mr. Dean Bernal, Vice President of Human Resources. **E-mail address:** hr@jdabrams.com. **World Wide Web address:** http://www.jdabrams.com. **Description:** A heavy, civil construction company specializing in public works infrastructure projects. **Positions advertised include:** Estimator; Project Manager; Project Engineer; Field Engineer; Scheduler; Accountant; Human Resources Representative; Clerk. **Corporate headquarters location:** This location.

AMERICAN HOMESTAR CORPORATION
2450 South Shore Boulevard, Suite 300, League City TX 77573. 281/334-9700. **Contact:** Personnel. **World Wide Web address:** http://www.americanhomestar.com. **Description:** Designs, manufactures, and sells houses nationwide. **Corporate headquarters location:** This location. **Other U.S. locations:** OK; LA.

APAC TEXAS, INC.
P.O. Box 20779, Beaumont TX 77720-0779. 409/866-1444. **Contact:** Human Resources. **World Wide Web address:** http://www.apac.com. **Description:** A general contracting company specializing in concrete and asphalt paving work. **Other U.S. locations:** Dallas TX.

ASSOCIATED BUILDING SERVICES COMPANY
1910 Napoleon Street, Houston TX 77003. 713/844-7899. **Contact:** Human Resources. **World Wide Web address:** http://www.abslink. com. **Description:** One of the largest facility maintenance contractors in the nation.

BS&B PROCESS SYSTEMS, INC.
3534 T.C. Juster, Houston TX 77018. 713/939-8686. **Contact:** Operations Manager. **Description:** An engineering firm specializing in the design of oil and gas processing equipment.

BELDON ROOFING COMPANY
P.O. Box 13380, San Antonio TX 78213. 210/341-3100. **Toll-free phone:** 800/688-7663. **Fax:** 210/341-2959. **Contact:** Human Resources. **World Wide Web address:** http://www.beldon.com. **Description:** A construction company that specializes in roofing and sheet metal work for all types of buildings. Founded in 1946. **Positions advertised include:** Accounts Payable Clerk; Single Ply Mechanic; Head Auto Mechanic; Repair Technician; Steel Metal Installer; Roofer. **Office hours:** Monday - Friday, 8:00 a.m. - 5:00 p.m.

THE BERGAILA COMPANIES
11200 Westheimer, Suite 600, Houston TX 77042. 713/780-4227. **Contact:** Human Resources. **World Wide Web address:** http://www.bergaila.com. **Description:** An engineering and drafting service contractor.

BERNARD JOHNSON YOUNG, INC.
9050 North Capital of Texas Highway, Suite 170, Austin TX 78759. 512/231-8900. **Contact:** Human Resources. **World Wide Web address:** http://www.bjy.com. **Description:** An architectural engineering firm. The company also provides technical services, using the Internet to provide a full-time video link to customers. **Special programs:** Internships. **Corporate headquarters location:** This location. **Operations at this facility include:** Administration; Regional Headquarters; Research and Development; Sales. **Listed on:** Privately held.

CARGILL STEEL & WIRE
220 Avenue A, Beaumont TX 77701. 409/835-3712. **Contact:** Human Resources Department. **World Wide Web address:** http://www.cargillsteel.com. **Description:** Manufactures patented concrete-

reinforcing wire mesh for road and building construction customers. **Positions advertised include:** Engineer Manager Trainee; Industrial Sales Trainee. **Corporate headquarters location:** Minneapolis MN. **Parent company:** Cargill Inc., with its subsidiaries and its affiliates, is involved in nearly 50 individual lines of business. The company deals in commodity trading, handling, transporting, processing, and risk management. Cargill is a major trader of grains and oilseeds, as well as a marketer of other agricultural and nonagricultural commodities. As a transporter, the company moves bulk commodities using a network of rail and road systems, inland waterways, and ocean-going routes combining its own fleet and transportation services purchased from outside sources. Agricultural products include a wide variety of feed, seed, fertilizers, and other goods and services for producers worldwide. Cargill is also a leader in producing and marketing seed varieties and hybrids. Cargill Central Research aims to develop new agricultural products to address the needs of customers around the world. The company also provides financial and technical services. Cargill's Financial Markets Division supports Cargill and its subsidiaries with financial products and services, including financial instrument trading, emerging markets instrument trading, value investing, and money management. Cargill's worldwide food processing businesses supply products ranging from basic ingredients used in food production to name brands. The company also operates a number of industrial businesses including the production of steel, industrial-grade starches, ethanol, and salt products. **Listed on:** Privately held. **Number of employees worldwide:** 80,000.

J.C. EVANS CONSTRUCTION COMPANY

P.O. Box 9647, Leander TX 78641. 512/244-1400. **Contact:** Human Resources. **World Wide Web address:** http://www.jcevans.com. **Description:** A general contracting company. **Positions advertised include:** Mechanic. **Corporate headquarters location:** This location.

HERNANDEZ ENGINEERING

16055 Central Boulevard, Suite 725, Houston TX 77062. 281/280-5159. **Contact:** Human Resources. **World Wide Web address:** http://www.hernandez-eng.com. **Description:** Provides technical and engineering services for NASA, the Johnson Space Center, and various high-tech organizations. Founded in 1983. **Positions advertised include:** Editor.

HOUSTON WIRE AND CABLE COMPANY
P.O. Box 23221, Houston TX 77228. 713/609-2100. **Physical address:** 10201 Northloop East, Houston TX 77029. **Contact:** Personnel Director. **World Wide Web address:** http://www.houwire.com. **Description:** Engaged in the distribution of specialty wire and cable. The company also offers cable management and asset management programs.

JALCO, INC.
P.O. Box 27368, Houston TX 77227. 713/728-8480. **Fax:** 713/729-6553. **Contact:** Nilo S. Cruz, Administrative Officer. **E-mail address:** jalcohou@aol.com. **Description:** A heavy-construction company.

KELLOGG, BROWN & ROOT
P.O. Box 3, Houston TX 77001. 713/753-2000. **Contact:** Manager of Employment. **World Wide Web address:** http://www.halliburton.com. **Description:** A full-service design, engineering, procurement, construction, and contract management firm. The company serves the process and energy industries worldwide and is primarily involved in hydrocarbon-processing plants including oil-refining units, petrochemical manufacturing plants, ammonia and fertilizer plants, and gas-processing units. **Positions advertised include:** Account Representative; Field Technology Engineer; Operations Engineer; Product Engineer. **Parent company:** Halliburton Corporation. **Listed on:** New York Stock Exchange. **Stock exchange symbol:** HAL.

LOCKWOOD, ANDREWS & NEWNAM, INC.
1500 City West Boulevard, Houston TX 77042-2343. 713/266-6900. **Fax:** 713/266-7191. **Contact:** Linda Garnett, Human Resources Coordinator. **World Wide Web address:** http://www.lan-inc.com. **Description:** Provides complete architectural, construction management, engineering, planning, and project management. The company also operates within the fields of infrastructure, thermal energy, and transportation. **NOTE:** Part-time jobs are offered. **Positions advertised include:** Architect/Designer; Assistant Engineer; Marketing Assistant; Plants Project Manager; Program Manager; Project Manager. **Special programs:** Internships; Summer Jobs. **Office hours:** Monday - Friday, 7:30 a.m. - 4:30 p.m. **Corporate headquarters location:** This location. **Other U.S. locations:** NE. **Parent company:** Leo A. Daly Company. **Listed on:** Privately held.

LYDA COMPANY
P.O. Box 680907, San Antonio TX 78268. 210/684-1770. **Contact:** Jack Dysart, Senior Vice President. **Description:** One of the largest general commercial contractors in Texas. Past projects included the Alamo Dome.

MAREK BROTHERS
2201 Judiway Street, Houston TX 77018. 713/681-9213. **Contact:** Mike Hamala, Credit Manager. **World Wide Web address:** http://www.marekbros.com. **Description:** A construction contractor. Marek Brothers specializes in drywall and insulation installation for residential buildings.

MARTIN MARIETTA MATERIALS
17910 Interstate Highway 10 West, San Antonio TX 78257. 210/696-8500. **Contact:** Human Resources. **World Wide Web address:** http://www.martinmarietta.com. **Description:** Martin Marietta Materials produces a wide variety of construction aggregates and related materials. **Positions advertised include:** Heavy Equipment Shop Supervisor. **Corporate headquarters location:** Raleigh NC. **Operations at this facility include:** This location is a surface mining company that manufactures products including limestone, base materials, and asphalt. **Listed on:** New York Stock Exchange. **Stock exchange symbol:** MLM.

MUSTANG ENGINEERING
16001 Park 10 Place, Houston TX 77084. 713/215-8000. **Fax:** 713/215-8506. **Contact:** Marty Kunz, Human Resources. **E-mail address:** human.resources@mustangeng.com. **World Wide Web address:** http://www.mustangeng.com. **Description:** An engineering firm that specializes in offshore structures, pipeline systems and services, process plant facilities, environmental services, and process automation and control for the energy industry. Founded in 1987. **NOTE:** Entry-level positions are offered. **Special programs:** Summer Jobs. **Office hours:** Monday - Friday, 7:30 a.m. - 4:30 p.m. **Corporate headquarters location:** This location. **Other U.S. locations:** Monroe LA. **Operations at this facility include:** Administration; Sales. **Listed on:** Privately held. **Number of employees nationwide:** 1,600.

MUSTANG TRACTOR & EQUIPMENT COMPANY
P.O. Box 1373, Houston TX 77252. 713/460-2000. **Fax:** 713/690-2287. **Recorded jobline:** 713/460-7267. **Contact:** Human Resources

Manager. **World Wide Web address:** http://www.mustangcat.com. **Description:** Sells and services Caterpillar heavy equipment and engines. **Special programs:** Apprenticeships. **Corporate headquarters location:** This location. **Operations at this facility include:** Administration; Manufacturing; Sales; Service.

NCI BUILDING SYSTEMS
7301 Fairview TX 77041. 713/466-7788. **Contact:** Human Resources. **World Wide Web address:** http://www.ncilp.com. **Description:** Designs, manufactures, and markets metal building systems and components for commercial, industrial, agricultural, and community service uses.

NACE INTERNATIONAL
1440 South Creek Drive, Houston TX 77084. 281/228-6256. **Fax:** 281/228-6356. **Contact:** Marcie Skinner, Human Resources Manager. **World Wide Web address:** http://www.nace.org. **Description:** NACE (National Association of Corrosion Engineers) International disseminates information about protection/performance in corrosive environments through its two monthly journals, one bimonthly magazine, and a variety of technical reports and journals. **Corporate headquarters location:** This location.

OCEANEERING INTERNATIONAL, INC.
11911 FM 529, Houston TX 77041. 713/329-4500. **Contact:** Human Resources. **World Wide Web address:** http://www.oceaneering.com. **Description:** Offers underwater diving, equipment, and related services to marine and space companies. Founded in 1964. **Listed on:** New York Stock Exchange. **Stock exchange symbol:** OII.

S&B ENGINEERS AND CONSTRUCTORS
7825 Park Place, Houston TX 77087. 713/645-4141. **Contact:** Human Resources. **World Wide Web address:** http://www.sbec.com. **Description:** A construction company. **Positions advertised include:** Project Engineer; Electrical Engineer; Metallurgist/Welding Engineer; Pressure Vessel Engineer; Heat Transfer Engineer; Field Heater Engineer; Civil/Structural Engineer; Project Manager; Senior Estimator; Project Controls Manager.

SCOPE IMPORTS INC.
8020 Blankenship Drive, Houston TX 77055. 713/688-0077. **Contact:** Human Resources. **Description:** An importer of men's apparel, primarily activewear and T-shirts.

WILLIAM A. SMITH CONSTRUCTION COMPANY, INC.
P.O. Box 15217, Houston TX 77220. 713/673-6208. **Contact:** Dan Burg, Controller. **Description:** A railroad construction contractor. **Corporate headquarters location:** This location. **Listed on:** Privately held.

SOUTHERN INVESTORS SERVICE COMPANY
2727 North Loop West, Suite 200, Houston TX 77008. 713/869-7800. **Contact:** Human Resources. **Description:** Offers commercial construction, real estate development, distribution and installation of construction products, and savings and loan services. **Corporate headquarters location:** This location.

SOUTHWEST RESEARCH INSTITUTE
6220 Culebre Road, San Antonio TX 78238. 210/522-2223. **Fax:** 210/522-3990. **Contact:** Human Resources. **E-mail address:** humanresources@swri.org. **World Wide Web address:** http:// www.swri.org. **Description:** An independent, nonprofit, applied engineering and physical science research and development organization. Research is conducted in areas such as automation, intelligent systems, and advanced computer technology; biosciences/bioengineering; nuclear waste regulatory analyses; electronic systems and instrumentation; encapsulation and polymer research; engines, fuels, and lubricants; environmental science; fire technology; fluid and machinery dynamics; engineering and materials sciences; nondestructive evaluation research and development; and space sciences. **Special programs:** Internships. **Corporate headquarters location:** This location. **Listed on:** Privately held.

SPAWGLASS CONSTRUCTION INC.
13603 Westland East Boulevard, Houston TX 77041. 281/970-5300. **Contact:** Human Resources. **E-mail address:** humanresources @spawglass.com. **World Wide Web address:** http://www.spawglass. com. **Description:** A general construction contractor. **Corporate headquarters location:** This location.

SPAWGLASS CONSTRUCTION INC.
9331 Corporate Drive, Selma TX 78154. 210/651-9000. **Contact:** Human Resources. **E-mail address:** humanresources@ spawglass.com. **World Wide Web address:** http://www.spawglass. com. **Description:** A general contracting company specializing in

commercial buildings. **Corporate headquarters location:** Houston TX.

THORPE CORPORATION
P.O. Box 33047, Houston TX 77233. 713/644-1247. **Fax:** 713/644-3011. **Contact:** Human Resources. **World Wide Web address:** http://www.jtthorpe.com. **Description:** An engineering, construction, and refractory company. **NOTE:** Entry-level positions are offered. **Corporate headquarters location:** This location. **Other area locations:** Beaumont TX; Dallas TX. **Other U.S. locations:** Gonzales LA. **Subsidiaries include:** J.T. Thorpe (also at this location); Leacon-Sunbelt, Inc.; Thorpe Products. **Operations at this facility include:** Administration; Manufacturing; Sales; Service. **Listed on:** Privately held.

3D/INTERNATIONAL
1900 West Loop South, Suite 400, Houston TX 77027. 713/871-7000. **Contact:** Personnel. **World Wide Web address:** http://www.3di.com. **Description:** An architectural and interior design firm. The company also provides construction management, engineering, environmental consulting, and program management systems. **Corporate headquarters location:** This location. **Operations at this facility include:** Administration; Sales; Service.

URS CORPORATION
P.O. Box 201088, Austin TX 78720-1088. 512/454-4797. **Contact:** Human Resources. **World Wide Web address:** http://www.urscorp.com. **Description:** An architectural, engineering, and environmental consulting firm that specializes in air transportation, environmental solutions, surface transportation, and industrial environmental and engineering concerns. Founded in 1969. **Positions advertised include:** Accounting Assistant; Chemist; Department Head; Environmental Technician; Graduate Civil Engineer; Mechanical Designer; Project Field Technician; Project Civil Engineer; Rod/Instrument Technician; Senior Chemist. **Corporate headquarters location:** This location. **Listed on:** New York Stock Exchange. **Stock exchange symbol:** URS.

U.S. HOME CORPORATION
P.O. Box 2863, Houston TX 77252-2863. 713/877-2311. **Physical address:** 10707 Clay Road, Houston TX 77041. **Contact:** Human Resources. **World Wide Web address:** http://www.ushome.com. **Description:** Builds and sells single-family houses. **Positions**

advertised include: Internal Auditor. **Parent company:** Lennar. **Listed on:** New York Stock Exchange. **Stock exchange symbol:** LEN. **Number of employees nationwide:** 7,700.

H.B. ZACHRY COMPANY

P.O. Box 240130, San Antonio TX 78224. 210/475-8000. **Fax:** 210/475-8775. **Recorded jobline:** 800/JOB-SUSA. **Contact:** Professional Recruiting. **World Wide Web address:** http://www.zachry.com. **Description:** A construction management company operating through the following seven divisions: Process, Power, Heavy, Maintenance & Service, Commercial, International, and Pipeline. The company primarily builds power plants, highways, and pipelines in the southern United States, as well as in foreign countries. H.B. Zachry Company does not handle residential construction contracts. Founded in 1923. **NOTE:** Entry-level positions are offered. **Positions advertised include:** Accounting Clerk; Messenger; Estimator; Project Superintendent; IT Security Coordinator. **Special programs:** Summer Jobs. **Corporate headquarters location:** This location. **Listed on:** Privately held.

ARTS, ENTERTAINMENT, SPORTS, AND RECREATION

You can expect to find the following types of companies in this chapter:
Botanical and Zoological Gardens • Entertainment Groups • Motion Picture and Video Tape Production and Distribution • Museums and Art Galleries • Physical Fitness Facilities • Professional Sports Clubs • Public Golf Courses • Racing and Track Operations • Sporting and Recreational Camps • Theatrical Producers

AUSTIN NATURE CENTER

301 Nature Center Drive, Austin TX 78746. 512/327-8181. **Contact:** Personnel. **World Wide Web address:** http://www.ci.austin.tx.us/nature-science/generalinfo.htm. **Description:** An indoor/outdoor nature center housing exhibits, live animals, interactive games, and discovery labs. Austin Nature Center is situated on an 80-acre preserve, with more than two miles of hiking trails.

DIVERSE WORKS

1117 East Freeway, Houston TX 77002. 713/223-8346. **Contact:** Hiring Manager. **World Wide Web address:** http://www.diverseworks.org. **Description:** A nonprofit art gallery and theater for the performing and visual arts. Diverse Works is affiliated with the Cultural Arts Council.

GOLFSMITH INTERNATIONAL INC.

11000 North Interstate Highway 35, Austin TX 78753. 512/837-8810. **Fax:** 512/821-4191. **Contact:** Human Resources Manager. **E-mail address:** hr@golfsmith.com. **World Wide Web address:** http://www.golfsmith.com. **Description:** Designs, assembles, and distributes golf equipment. **Positions advertised include:** Receiving Manager; Sales Representative. **Operations at this facility include:** Administration; Manufacturing; Sales; Service.

THE GRAND 1894 OPERA HOUSE

2020 Post Office Street, Galveston TX 77550. 409/763-7173. **Toll-free phone:** 800/821-1894. **Fax:** 409/763-1068. **Contact:** Maureen Patton, Executive Director. **World Wide Web address:** http://www.thegrand.com. **Description:** A 1040-seat opera house offering ballet, symphony, opera, and other musical and theatrical performances.

GREATER TUNA CORPORATION

3660 Stone Ridge Road, Suite C101, Austin TX 78746. 512/328-8862. **Fax:** 512/347-8975. **Contact:** Personnel. **World Wide Web address:** http://www.greatertuna.com. **Description:** Produces a variety of comedic theater performances including *Greater Tuna*, a political satire shown in theaters nationwide. Other shows have included *A Tuna Christmas* and *Red, White and Tuna.*

HOUSTON MUSEUM OF NATURAL SCIENCE

One Herman Circle Drive, Houston TX 77030. 713/639-4600. **Contact:** Human Resources. **World Wide Web address:** http://www.hmns.org. **Description:** Offers numerous educational exhibits in many different areas of natural sciences.

HOUSTON SYMPHONY

615 Louisiana Street, Suite 102, Houston TX 77002. 713/224-4240. **Fax:** 713/222-7024. **Contact:** Human Resources. **E-mail address:** office@houstonsymphony.org. **World Wide Web address:** http://www.houstonsymphony.org. **Description:** A symphony orchestra.

LUTCHER THEATER FOR THE PERFORMING ARTS

P.O. Box 2310, Orange TX 77631. **Toll-free phone:** 800/828-5535. **Contact:** Human Resources. **World Wide Web address:** http://www.lutcher.org. **Description:** A performing arts theater.

THE MUSEUM OF FINE ARTS - HOUSTON

1001 Bissonnet, Houston TX 77005. 713/639-7560. **Fax:** 713/639-7597. **Contact:** Human Resources. **World Wide Web address:** http://www.mfah.org. **Description:** An art museum with exhibits including The Glassell Collection of African Gold, Art of Asia, and Modern and Contemporary Art. **Positions advertised include:** Curatorial Assistant; Master Framer; Mount Maker; Security Officer; Custodian. **Special programs:** Internships. **Corporate headquarters location:** This location. **Number of employees at this location:** 500.

OSHMAN'S SPORTING GOODS INC.

2320 Maxwell Lane, Houston TX 77023. 713/928-3171. **Contact:** Human Resources. **World Wide Web address:** http://www.oshmans.com. **Description:** Offers a broad line of sporting goods and equipment as well as active sports apparel. Most stores operate under the name SuperSports USA. **Corporate headquarters location:** This location.

SEA WORLD OF TEXAS

10500 Sea World Drive, San Antonio TX 78251-3002. 210/523-3600. **Contact:** Human Resources. **World Wide Web address:** http://www.seaworld.com. **Description:** Sea World is home to all types of marine life, and includes such entertainment as shows, exhibits, and a water park.

SIX FLAGS FIESTA TEXAS

17000 Interstate Highway 10 West, San Antonio TX 78257. 210/697-5000. **Contact:** Human Resources. **World Wide Web address:** http://www.sixflags.com. **Description:** A theme park offering attractions, shows, and a water park. **Parent company:** Premier Parks (OK) owns and operates 35 theme parks nationwide.

SIX FLAGS HOUSTON
SIX FLAGS ASTROWORLD, WATERWORLD, & SPLASHTOWN

9001 Kirby Drive, Houston TX 77054. 713/794-3217. **Fax:** 713/799-1030. **Contact:** Human Resources. **World Wide Web address:** http://www.sixflags.com. **Description:** An amusement and theme park. Six Flags AstroWorld offers seven theme lands based on the nations of the world, past and present. Six Flags AstroWorld has 11 roller coasters and also offers Wonderland, filled with rides and activities for younger children. The park also offers entertainment including shows and concerts. Six Flags WaterWorld offers water slides, waterfalls, a fantasy water playground for kids, a game room, specialty shops, a restaurant, and food stands. Six Flags SplashTown is a family-oriented water park. **NOTE:** Jobseekers should apply in person, if possible. Six Flags Houston hires over 3,000 employees each season. Entry-level positions, part-time jobs, and second and third shifts are offered. **Special programs:** Internships; Training; Summer Jobs. **Internship information:** Some paid summer internships are offered and housing is available. For more information, e-mail or write to the Recruitment Coordinator at the above address. **Office hours:** Monday - Friday, 9:00 a.m. - 12:00 p.m., 1:00 p.m. - 6:00 p.m. **Parent company:** Premier Parks (OK) owns and operates 35 theme parks nationwide.

THE STRAND THEATRE

2317 Ships Mechanics Row, Galveston TX 77550. 409/763-4591. **Toll-free phone:** 877/STR-AND9. **Contact:** Personnel. **E-mail address:** strandtheatre@galveston.com. **World Wide Web address:** http://www.galveston.com/strandtheatre. **Description:** A 200-seat theatre that hosts films, comedy shows, concerts, and children's theatre productions. Founded in 1978. **NOTE:** The Strand Theatre welcomes applications for volunteer positions.

ZILKER BOTANICAL GARDEN

2220 Barton Springs Road, Austin TX 78746. 512/477-8672. **Contact:** Human Resources. **World Wide Web address:** http://www.zilkergarden.org. **Description:** Covering 22 acres of land, Zilker Botanical Garden is comprised of a multitude of individual gardens including Xeriscape Garden, Herb and Fragrance Garden, and Rose Garden.

AUTOMOTIVE

You can expect to find the following types of companies in this chapter:
Automotive Repair Shops • Automotive Stampings • Industrial Vehicles and Moving Equipment • Motor Vehicles and Equipment • Travel Trailers and Campers

ANCIRA ENTERPRISES INC.
6111 Bandera Road, San Antonio TX 78238-1643. 210/681-4900. **Contact:** Human Resources. **World Wide Web address:** http://www.ancira.com. **Description:** Sells new and used automobiles including Chevrolet, Subaru, and Volkswagen. This location also has a service, parts, and body shop. **Corporate headquarters location:** This location.

FORETRAVEL, INC.
1221 NW Stallings Drive, Nacogdoches TX 75964. 936/569-7906. **Contact:** Human Resources. **World Wide Web address:** http://www.foretravel.com. **Description:** Manufactures motor homes. **Corporate headquarters location:** This location.

GILLMAN COMPANIES
7611 Bellaire Boulevard, Houston TX 77036. 713/776-7162. **Contact:** Personnel Administration. **World Wide Web address:** http://www.gillmanauto.com. **Description:** An automobile dealership group. Gillman operates dealerships selling Acura, Honda, Hyundai, Lincoln, Mazda, Mercury, Mitsubishi, Nissan, Subaru, and Suzuki automobiles. Founded in 1938. **Positions advertised include:** Assistant Sales Manager; Finance Manager; Service Technician. **Corporate headquarters location:** This location. **Operations at this facility include:** Administration; Sales; Service.

MAC HAIK CHEVROLET INC.
11711 Katy Freeway, Houston TX 77079. 281/497-6600. **Contact:** Personnel Director. **World Wide Web address:** http://www.machaikchevy.com. **Description:** An automobile dealership.

JIFFY LUBE INTERNATIONAL, INC.
P.O. Box 2967, Houston TX 77252-2967. 713/546-4100. **Contact:** Human Resources. **World Wide Web address:** http://www.jiffylube.com. **Description:** Provides automobile maintenance services including oil changes, tire rotations, and wheel balancing.

Corporate headquarters location: This location. **Parent company:** Pennzoil Products.

JACK ROACH FORD

6445 Southwest Freeway, Houston TX 77074. 281/588-5000. **Contact:** Personnel Director. **World Wide Web address:** http://www.jackroach.com. **Description:** A new and used vehicle dealership.

STERLING McCALL TOYOTA

9400 Southwest Freeway, Houston TX 77074. 713/270-3900. **Contact:** Human Resources. **World Wide Web address:** http://www.sterlingmccalltoyota.com. **Description:** Sells and services automobiles.

UNITED SERVICES AUTOMOBILE ASSOCIATION (USAA)

9800 Fredericksburg Road, San Antonio TX 78288. 210/498-2211. **Fax:** 210/498-1489. **Recorded jobline:** 210/498-1289. **Contact:** Strategic Staffing. **World Wide Web address:** http://www.usaa.com. **Description:** An integrated family of companies providing insurance and financial products and services to officers of the U.S. Armed Forces and their families. Products and services include automobile, life, health, property, and rental insurance; a family of mutual funds; credit cards; calling cards; and a federal savings bank (USAA Federal Savings Bank). Members also receive discounts from certain companies. **NOTE:** USAA only accepts resumes and cover letters for jobs listed on the USAA jobline. The company prefers jobseekers to fax their resumes if possible. **Positions advertised include:** Financial/Accounting Technician; Auditor; Financial Planner; Collector. **Special programs:** Internships. **Corporate headquarters location:** This location. **Other U.S. locations:** Sacramento CA; Colorado Springs CO; Tampa FL; Norfolk VA; Reston VA; Seattle WA.

BANKING/SAVINGS AND LOANS

You can expect to find the following types of companies in this chapter:
Banks • Bank Holding Companies and Associations •
Lending Firms/Financial Services Institutions

BANK OF AMERICA
9660 Hillcroft Street, Houston TX 77096. 713/541-7000. **Contact:** Human Resources. **World Wide Web address:** http://www.bankofamerica.com. **Description:** Bank of America is a full-service banking and financial institution. The company operates through four business segments: Global Corporate and Investment Banking, Principal Investing and Asset Management, Commercial Banking, and Consumer Banking. **Corporate headquarters location:** Charlotte NC. **Operations at this facility include:** This location is a bank. **Listed on:** New York Stock Exchange. **Stock exchange symbol:** BAC.

BANK OF AMERICA
2200 NASA Road One, Houston TX 77058. 281/333-8600. **Contact:** Human Resources. **World Wide Web address:** http://www.bankofamerica.com. **Description:** Bank of America is a full-service banking and financial institution. The company operates through four business segments: Global Corporate and Investment Banking, Principal Investing and Asset Management, Commercial Banking, and Consumer Banking. **Positions advertise include:** Banking Center Assistant Manager; Banking Center Manager. **Corporate headquarters location:** Charlotte NC. **Operations at this facility include:** This location is a bank. **Listed on:** New York Stock Exchange. **Stock exchange symbol:** BAC.

BANK ONE SECURITIES
1600 Redbud Boulevard, McKinney TX 75069. 800/695-1111. **Contact:** Human Resources. **World Wide Web address:** http://www.bankone.com. **Description:** Provides financial services in the areas of stocks, bonds, and mutual funds. **Parent company:** Bank One Corporation. **Listed on:** New York Stock Exchange. **Stock exchange symbol:** BAC.

CHASE BANK OF TEXAS
712 Main Street, Houston TX 77002. 713/216-4952. **Contact:** Human Resources. **World Wide Web address:** http://www.chase.com. **Description:** A banking organization, operating

through a network of 40 member banks in Texas. Operations include energy, commercial, real estate, and international banking. **Corporate headquarters location:** This location. **Other U.S. locations:** Denver CO; New York NY. **International locations:** Worldwide.

CITICORP USSC
100 Citibank Drive, San Antonio TX 78245-3214. 210/677-6500. **Contact:** Human Resources. **Description:** A data and customer service center for the nationwide banking company.

FARM CREDIT BANK OF TEXAS
P.O. Box 15919, 6210 Highway 290 East, Austin TX 78723-1023. 512/465-0400. **Contact:** Personnel. **World Wide Web address:** http://www.farmcreditbank.com. **Description:** A bank that provides loans to the agricultural industry. **Positions advertised include:** Senior Accountant; Assistant Loan Closer.

FROST NATIONAL BANK
P.O. Box 179, Galveston TX 77553. 409/763-1151. **Contact:** Human Resources. **World Wide Web address:** http://www.frostbank.com. **Description:** A full-service bank providing a variety of services to both personal and commercial customers. **Corporate headquarters location:** San Antonio TX. **Parent company:** Cullen/Frost Bankers, Inc. has 81 offices across Texas. **Listed on:** New York Stock Exchange. **Stock exchange symbol:** CFR.

FROST NATIONAL BANK
CULLEN/FROST BANKERS, INC.
P.O. Box 1600, San Antonio TX 78296-1400. 210/220-4011. **Recorded jobline:** 210/220-5627. **Contact:** Human Resources. **World Wide Web address:** http://www.frostbank.com. **Description:** A bank that offers online banking, financial management, and loan services. **Corporate headquarters location:** This location. **Parent company:** Cullen/Frost Bankers, Inc. (also at this location) is a multibank holding company with 81 offices across Texas. **Listed on:** New York Stock Exchange. **Stock exchange symbol:** CFR.

HOMETOWN BANK OF GALVESTON
P.O. Box 3909, Galveston TX 77552. 409/763-5252. **Contact:** Human Resources. **World Wide Web address:** http://www.bankofgalveston.com. **Description:** A full-service bank. **Parent company:** Hometown Bank, N.A.

HOMETOWN BANK OF GALVESTON
1801 45th Street, Galveston TX 77550. 409/763-1271. **Contact:** Human Resources. **World Wide Web address:** http://www.bankofgalveston.com. **Description:** A full-service bank. **Corporate headquarters location:** This location. **Parent company:** Hometown Bank, N.A.

INTERNATIONAL BANK OF COMMERCE
P.O. Box 1359, Laredo TX 78042-1359. 956/722-7611. **Physical address:** 1200 San Bernardo Avenue, Laredo TX 78042-1359. **Contact:** Human Resources. **World Wide Web address:** http://www.iboc.com. **Description:** A full-service bank that offers checking and savings accounts, CDs, wire transfers, mortgage loans, ATMs, and Right Checking Accounts.

LAREDO NATIONAL BANK
700 San Bernardo Avenue, Laredo TX 78040. 956/723-1151. **Contact:** Human Resources. **World Wide Web address:** http://www.lnb-online.com. **Description:** A full-service bank that offers checking and savings accounts, CDs, mortgages, and wire transfers.

TEXAS FIRST BANK
6501 Stewart Road, Galveston TX 77552. 409/744-6353. **Contact:** Manager. **World Wide Web address:** http://www.texasfirstbanks com. **Description:** A full-service bank. **Other area locations:** Crystal Beach TX; Dickinson TX; Friendswood TX; Hitchcock TX; Kemah TX; La Marque TX; League City TX; Santa Fe TX; Texas City TX.

TEXAS FIRST BANK
2401 Broadway, Galveston TX 77550. 409/762-7974. **Contact:** Human Resources. **World Wide Web address:** http://www.texasfirstbanks.com. **Description:** The main branch location for the regional full-service bank. **Other area locations:** Crystal Beach TX; Dickinson TX; Friendswood TX; Hitchcock TX; Kemah TX; La Marque TX; League City TX; Santa Fe TX; Texas City TX.

TEXAS FIRST BANK
4165 Pirates Beach, Galveston TX 77554. 409/737-5400. **Contact:** Manager. **World Wide Web address:** http://www.texasfirstbanks.com. **Description:** A full-service bank. **Other area locations:** Crystal Beach TX; Dickinson TX; Friendswood TX; Hitchcock TX; Kemah TX; La Marque TX; League City TX; Santa Fe TX; Texas City TX.

U.S. FEDERAL RESERVE BANK OF HOUSTON
P.O. Box 2578, Houston TX 77252-2578. 713/659-4433. **Contact:** Human Resources. **World Wide Web address:** http://www.dallasfed.org. **Description:** One of 12 regional Federal Reserve banks that, along with the Federal Reserve Board of Governors in Washington DC, and the Federal Open Market Committee, comprise the Federal Reserve System. As the nation's central bank, the Federal Reserve is charged with three major responsibilities: monetary policy, banking supervision and regulation, and processing payments. **Other U.S. locations:** Nationwide.

WELLS FARGO BANK
P.O. Box 1790, Alice TX 78333. 361/668-2400. **Contact:** Human Resources. **World Wide Web address:** http://www.wellsfargo.com. **Description:** A diversified financial institution with over $234 billion in assets. Wells Fargo serves over 17 million customers through 5,300 independent locations worldwide. The company also maintains several stand-alone ATMs and branches within other retail outlets. Services include community banking, credit and debit cards, home equity and mortgage loans, online banking, student loans, and insurance. Wells Fargo also offers a complete line of commercial and institutional financial services. Founded in 1852. **Positions advertised include:** Banker; Teller. **NOTE:** Jobseekers are encouraged to submit resumes via the Website: http://www.wfjobs.com. **Corporate headquarters location:** San Francisco CA. **Other U.S. locations:** Nationwide. **International locations:** Worldwide. **Listed on:** New York Stock Exchange. **Stock exchange symbol:** WFC. **Number of employees worldwide:** 123,000.

WELLS FARGO BANK
P.O. Box 699, Laredo TX 78042. 956/726-8200. **Contact:** Human Resources. **World Wide Web address:** http://www.wellsfargo.com. **Description:** A diversified financial institution with over $234 billion in assets. Wells Fargo serves over 17 million customers through 5,300 independent locations worldwide. The company also maintains several stand-alone ATMs and branches within other retail outlets. Services include community banking, credit and debit cards, home equity and mortgage loans, online banking, student loans, and insurance. Wells Fargo also offers a complete line of commercial and institutional financial services. Founded in 1852. **Positions advertised include:** Banker; Teller. **NOTE:** Jobseekers are encouraged to submit resumes via the Website: http://www.wfjobs.com. **Corporate headquarters location:** San Francisco CA. **Other**

U.S. locations: Nationwide. **International locations:** Worldwide. **Listed on:** New York Stock Exchange. **Stock exchange symbol:** WFC. **Number of employees worldwide:** 123,000.

BIOTECHNOLOGY, PHARMACEUTICALS, AND SCIENTIFIC R&D

You can expect to find the following types of companies in this chapter:
Clinical Labs • Lab Equipment Manufacturers
Pharmaceutical Manufacturers and Distributors

APPLIED BIOSYSTEMS
13215 North Promenade Boulevard, Stafford TX 77477. 281/340-6200. **Contact:** Human Resources. **World Wide Web address:** http://www.appliedbiosystems.com. **Description:** Manufactures products for genetic analysis, molecular agriculture, and human and microbial identification. **Corporate headquarters location:** Foster City CA. **Listed on:** New York Stock Exchange. **Stock exchange symbol:** ABI.

ARONEX PHARMACEUTICALS, INC.
8707 Technology Forest Place, The Woodlands TX 77381-1191. 281/367-1666. **Contact:** Human Resources. **World Wide Web address:** http://www.aronex-pharm.com. **Description:** Develops antiviral and anti-infective pharmaceuticals for the treatment of cancer and other life-threatening diseases. **Parent company:** Antigenics. **Listed on:** NASDAQ. **Stock exchange symbol:** AGEN.

DPT LABORATORIES INC.
307 East Josephine Street, San Antonio TX 78215. 210/223-3281. **Fax:** 210/476-0794. **Contact:** Human Resources. **World Wide Web address:** http://www.dptlabs.com. **Description:** Provides pharmaceutical manufacturing and development services from prototype development to worldwide distribution. **NOTE:** Entry-level positions and second and third shifts are offered. Corporate headquarters location: 318 McCullough Street, San Antonio TX. **Positions advertised include:** Regulatory Affairs Manager; Quality Release Analyst; Quality Control Scientist; Project Manager; Validation Scientist; Bioanalytical Scientist; Principal Research Scientist. **Office hours:** Monday - Friday, 8:00 a.m. - 5:00 p.m.

FISHER SCIENTIFIC COMPANY
9999 Veterans Memorial Drive, Houston TX 77038. 281/878-3500. **Contact:** Human Resources. **World Wide Web address:** http://www.fishersci.com. **Description:** One of the oldest and largest providers of instruments, equipment, and other products to the scientific community. The company offers a selection of more than 150,000 products and services to research centers and industrial

customers worldwide. Fisher serves scientists engaged in biomedical, biotechnology, pharmaceutical, chemical, and other fields of research and development; and scientists in companies, educational and research institutions, and government agencies. The company also supplies clinical laboratories, hospitals, environmental testing centers, remediation companies, quality control laboratories, and other industrial facilities. In addition, Fisher represents its customers as a third-party purchaser of maintenance materials and other basic supplies. **Positions advertised include:** Customer Service Representative; District Sales Manager; Lab Sales Representative; Product Specialist; Safety Sales Representative; Safety Service Technician.

INTERNATIONAL BIOMEDICAL, INC.
8508 Cross Park Drive, Austin TX 78754. 512/873-0033. **Contact:** Human Resources. **World Wide Web address:** http://www.int-bio.com. **Description:** A manufacturer of high-technology medical instruments including infant incubators and radiation gloves. International Biomedical also manufactures electronic equipment used in research, testing, and teaching. **Corporate headquarters location:** Cleburne TX. **Operations at this facility include:** Manufacturing.

LABORATORY CORPORATION OF AMERICA (LABCORP)
4207 James Casey Street, Suite 101, Austin TX 78745. 512/443-0538. **Fax:** 210/735-0512. **Contact:** Personnel. **World Wide Web address:** http://www.labcorp.com. **Description:** One of the nation's leading clinical laboratory companies, providing services primarily to physicians, hospitals, clinics, nursing homes, and other clinical labs nationwide. LabCorp performs tests on blood, urine, and other body fluids and tissue, aiding the diagnosis of disease. **Corporate headquarters location:** Burlington NC. **Other U.S. locations:** Nationwide. **Operations at this facility include:** This location is a blood-drawing facility. **Listed on:** New York Stock Exchange. **Stock exchange symbol:** LH. **Number of employees nationwide:** 19,600.

LABORATORY CORPORATION OF AMERICA (LABCORP)
7207 North Gessner, Houston TX 77040. 713/856-8288. **Contact:** Human Resources. **World Wide Web address:** http://www.labcorp.com. **Description:** One of the nation's leading clinical laboratory companies, providing services primarily to physicians, hospitals, clinics, nursing homes, and other clinical labs nationwide. LabCorp performs tests on blood, urine, and other body fluids and tissue,

aiding the diagnosis of disease. **Positions advertised include:** Laboratory Director. **Corporate headquarters location:** Burlington NC. **Other U.S. locations:** Nationwide. **Listed on:** New York Stock Exchange. **Stock exchange symbol:** LH. **Number of employees nationwide:** 19,600.

LYNNTECH INC.
7610 Eastmark Drive, College Station TX 77840. 979/693-0017. **Contact:** Human Resources. **E-mail address:** hrlynntech@lynntech.com. **World Wide Web address:** http://www.lynntech.com. **Description:** Offers a broad range of research services including environmental and genetic research. Lynntech receives most of its business from government contracts. **Positions advertised include:** Research Scientist; Senior Research Scientist; Research Assistant; Team Leader; Machinist; Shop Supervisor. **Corporate headquarters location:** This location.

NATIONAL INSTITUTIONAL PHARMACY SERVICES, INC. (NIPSI)
2525 Bellfort Street, Suite 130, Houston TX 77054. 713/668-7596. **Contact:** Human Resources. **Description:** Provides a full range of prescription drugs, enteral and perenteral nutritional therapy products, and infusion therapy products. The company offers antibiotic therapy, pain management, and chemotherapy services to over 520 facilities. NIPSI operates a network of 22 pharmacies in nine states.

PPD, INC.
4009 Banister Lane, Austin TX 78704. 512/447-2663. **Contact:** Human Resources. **World Wide Web address:** http://www.ppdi.com. **Description:** Provides research and development services for companies in the biotechnology and pharmaceutical industries. **Positions advertised include:** Global Positioning Logistics Associate; Research Coordination Manager; Project Manager; Research Assistant. **Listed on:** NASDAQ. **Stock exchange symbol:** PPDI.

PHARMERICA
3019 Interstate Drive, San Antonio TX 78219. 210/227-5262. **Contact:** Human Resources. **World Wide Web address:** http://www.pharmerica.com. **Description:** A supplier of pharmaceuticals and related products to long-term care facilities, hospitals, and assisted living communities. PharMerica also provides nurse consultant services, infusion therapy and training, medical records

consulting, and educational programs. **Corporate headquarters location:** Tampa FL.

QUEST DIAGNOSTICS INCORPORATED
8933 Interchange Drive, Houston TX 77054. 713/667-5829. **Contact:** Personnel. **World Wide Web address:** http://www.questdiagnostics.com. **Description:** One of the largest clinical laboratories in North America, providing a broad range of clinical laboratory services to health care clients that include physicians, hospitals, clinics, dialysis centers, pharmaceutical companies, and corporations. The company offers and performs tests on blood, urine, and other bodily fluids and tissues to provide information for health and well-being. **Positions advertised include:** Phlebotomist Group Leader; Billing Coordinator; Customer Service Representative; Medical Technologist; Specimen Technician; Dispatcher; Human Resources Generalist. **Listed on:** New York Stock Exchange. **Stock exchange symbol:** DGX.

TEXAS BIOTECHNOLOGY CORPORATION
7000 Fannin, Floor 20, Houston TX 77030. 713/796-8822. **Fax:** 713/796-8232. **Contact:** Human Resources. **World Wide Web address:** http://www.tbc.com. **Description:** A pharmaceutical research and development firm that specializes in pharmaceuticals for the treatment of acute cardiovascular conditions. **Positions advertised include:** Senior Scientist; Research Assistant; Biostatistician. **Corporate headquarters location:** This location. **Listed on:** NASDAQ. **Stock exchange symbol:** TXBI.

VERTEX PHARMACEUTICALS INCORPORATED
12720 Dairy Ashford, Sugar Land TX 77478. 281/240-1000. **Contact:** Human Resources. **World Wide Web address:** http://www.vpharm.com. **Description:** Develops drugs for viral, autoimmune, inflammatory, and neurodegenerative diseases as well as developing oral active pharmaceuticals for drug-resistant cancer and hemoglobin disorders. **Corporate headquarters location:** Cambridge MA. **Listed on:** NASDAQ. **Stock exchange symbol:** VRTX.

ZONAGEN INC.
2408 Timberloch Place, Suite B-4, The Woodlands TX 77380. 281/367-5892. **Contact:** Human Resources. **World Wide Web address:** http://www.zonagen.com. **Description:** Researches, develops, and markets biopharmaceutical products that deal with a

variety of issues including sexual dysfunction, urology, fertility, and contraception. **Corporate headquarters location:** This location. **Listed on:** NASDAQ. **Stock exchange symbol:** ZONA.

BUSINESS SERVICES AND NON-SCIENTIFIC RESEARCH

You can expect to find the following types of companies in this chapter:
Adjustment and Collection Services • Cleaning, Maintenance, and Pest Control Services • Credit Reporting • Detective, Guard, and Armored Car Services • Miscellaneous Equipment Rental and Leasing • Secretarial and Court Reporting Services

ACCENTURE
2929 Allen Parkway, Suite 2000, Houston TX 77019. 713/837-1500. **Contact:** Human Resources. **World Wide Web address:** http://www.accenture.com. **Description:** A management and technology consulting firm. Accenture offers a wide range of services including business re-engineering, customer service system consulting, data system design and implementation, Internet sales systems research and design, and strategic planning. **Corporate headquarters location:** Hamilton, Bermuda. **Other U.S. locations:** Nationwide. **Listed on:** New York Stock Exchange. **Stock exchange symbol:** ACN.

ACCENTURE
1501 South Mopac Expressway, Suite 300, Austin TX 78746. 512/476-9949. **Contact:** Human Resources. **World Wide Web address:** http://www.accenture.com. **Description:** A management and technology consulting firm. Accenture offers a wide range of services including business re-engineering, customer service system consulting, data system design and implementation, Internet sales systems research and design; and strategic planning. **Corporate headquarters location:** Hamilton, Bermuda. **Other U.S. locations:** Nationwide. **Listed on:** New York Stock Exchange. **Stock exchange symbol:** ACN.

ANALYSTS INTERNATIONAL CORPORATION (AIC)
6207 Bee Cave Road, Suite 220, Austin TX 78746. 512/206-2700. **Fax:** 512/206-2720. **Contact:** Human Resources. **World Wide Web address:** http://www.analysts.com. **Description:** An international computer consulting firm. The company assists clients in developing systems in a variety of industries using diverse programming languages and software. Founded in 1966. **Corporate headquarters location:** Minneapolis MN. **Other U.S. locations:** Nationwide. **International locations:** Canada; England. **Listed on:** NASDAQ. **Stock exchange symbol:** ANLY.

ANALYSTS INTERNATIONAL CORPORATION (AIC)

2550 North Loop West, Suite 200, Houston TX 77008. 713/869-3420. **Fax:** 713/869-8462. **Contact:** Human Resources Department. **World Wide Web address:** http://www.analysts.com/houston. **Description:** An international computer consulting firm. The company assists clients in analyzing, designing, and developing systems using different programming languages and software. Founded in 1966. **Corporate headquarters location:** Minneapolis MN. **Other U.S. locations:** Nationwide. **International locations:** Canada; England. **Listed on:** NASDAQ. **Stock exchange symbol:** ANLY.

AQUENT

1717 West Sixth Street, Suite 340, Austin TX 78703. 512/494-9119. **Contact:** Human Resources. **World Wide Web address:** http://www.aquent.com. **Description:** Engaged in software consulting, training, and staffing.

BAE SYSTEMS

6500 Tracor Lane, Austin TX 78725. 512/926-2800. **Contact:** Recruiting. **World Wide Web address:** http://www.baesystems.com. **Description:** Provides a full spectrum of systems engineering and technical services in the areas of systems development, operation, and maintenance. Technical services include system design, integration, and testing; software development, engineering, and maintenance; and integrated logistics support including safety, reliability, and quality assurance engineering.

THE BENCHMARK COMPANY

907 South Congress Avenue, Suite 7, Austin TX 78704. 512/707-7500. **Fax:** 512/707-7757. **Contact:** Human Resources Department. **World Wide Web address:** http://www.benchmarkresearch.com. **Description:** Gathers data and research about radio listeners. Benchmark is also involved in researching broadcasting companies.

BURNS PINKERTON SECURITY

5825 Callaghan, Suite 107, San Antonio TX 78228. 210/647-9770. **Contact:** Human Resources. **World Wide Web address:** http://www.pinkertons.com. **Description:** A security service that sends out guards to secure various locations and functions. **Parent company:** Securitas.

CIRRUS LOGIC, INC.
P.O. Box 17847, Austin TX 78760. 512/445-7222. **Contact:** Human Resources. **World Wide Web address:** http://www.cirrus.com. **Description:** Designs, markets, and tests computer chips for audio, digital, multimedia, and telecommunication products. Cirrus Logic also supplies high-performance analog circuits. **Positions advertised include:** Mixed Signal Design Engineer; Product Line Manager; Senior Programmer/Analyst; Product Test Engineer.

DRESSER-RAND COMPANY
1200 West Sam Houston Parkway North, Houston TX 77043. 713/467-2221. **Contact:** Human Resources. **World Wide Web address:** http://www.dresser-rand.com. **Description:** Offers high-technology repair services for turbines, compressors, pumps, engines, and blowers. **Corporate headquarters location:** Corning NY.

EMERSON PROCESS MANAGEMENT
8301 Cameron Road, Austin TX 78754-3895. 512/835-2190. **Contact:** Human Resources. **World Wide Web address:** http://www.emersonprocess.com. **Description:** Offers large, medium, and small process management solutions that provide powerful, easy-to-use process control and asset management. **Parent company:** Emerson Electric. **Listed on:** New York Stock Exchange. **Stock exchange symbol:** EMR.

EMERSON PROCESS MANAGEMENT/CSI
15425 North Freeway, Suite 160, Houston TX 77090. 281/873-6000. **Fax:** 281/873-6633. **Contact:** Personnel. **World Wide Web address:** http://www.compsys.com. **Description:** One of the world's largest manufacturers of reliability-based maintenance (RBM) products and allied services. Emerson Process Management/CSI is a technical leader in vibration analysis, with products in three major categories: the periodic survey systems category, the pocket-sized FFT analyzer category, and the advanced machinery analyzer category. The company's tribology products and services include Tribology Mini-Lab, Tribology Total Solution system, and Fluid Analysis Lab. The infrared thermography systems include a focal-plane array camera, which delivers the most accurate temperature measurement in the predictive maintenance field, and IntraPort pen-based analyzer and Infranalysis data/image management system, which provide a systematic route-based approach to IR that saves time and simplifies diagnoses. Emerson Process Management/CSI's

alignment and balancing services include both electromechanical and laser alignment systems. **Corporate headquarters location:** Knoxville TN.

EXPONENT, INC.
10899 Kinghurst Drive, Suite 245, Houston TX 77099. 281/879-6161. **Fax:** 281/879-0687. **Contact:** Personnel. **World Wide Web address:** http://www.exponent.com. **Description:** A technical consulting firm dedicated to the investigation, analysis, and prevention of accidents and failures of an engineering or scientific nature. The company provides a multidisciplinary approach to analyze how failures occur. The company specializes in accident reconstruction, biomechanics, construction/structural engineering, aviation and marine investigations, environmental assessment, materials and product testing, warning and labeling issues, accident statistical data analysis, and risk prevention/mitigation. Founded in 1967. **NOTE:** Send resumes to Exponent Failure Analysis Associates, Human Resources, 149 Commonwealth Drive, Menlo Park CA 94025. **Corporate headquarters location:** Menlo Park CA. **Parent company:** Exponent. **Listed on:** NASDAQ. **Stock exchange symbol:** EXPO.

FUGRO GEOSCIENCES
6105 Rookin, Houston TX 77074. 713/778-5580. **Contact:** Director of Personnel. **World Wide Web address:** http://www.geo.fugro.com. **Description:** An international engineering and geoscience consulting firm serving the offshore, industrial, public works, and commercial industries. The firm offers geosciences, earth sciences, and waste management services. **Positions advertised include:** NDT Level II Technician. **Corporate headquarters location:** This location. **Operations at this facility include:** Administration; Divisional Headquarters.

FUTRON CORPORATION
1120 NASA Road One, Suite 310, Houston TX 77058-3302. 281/333-0190. **Contact:** Human Resources. **E-mail address:** resume@futron.com. **World Wide Web address:** http://www.futron.com. **Description:** Provides management and technical consulting services for aerospace and defense companies. Founded in 1986.

GC SERVICES
6330 Gulfton Street, Houston TX 77081. 713/777-4441. **Contact:** Human Resources. **World Wide Web address:** http://

www.gcserv.com. **Description:** A collection agency. **Positions advertised include:** Assistant Controller.

HVJ ASSOCIATES
6120 South Dairy Ashford Road, Houston TX 77072. 281/933-7388. **Contact:** Human Resources. **World Wide Web address:** http://www.hvj.com. **Description:** A geotechnical, environmental materials testing consultant. Founded in 1985.

HICKAM INDUSTRIES, INC.
11518 Old La Porte Road, La Porte TX 77571. 713/567-2700. **Contact:** Human Resources. **World Wide Web address:** http://www.hickam.com. **Description:** Provides turbine repair services.

HYDROCHEM INDUSTRIAL SERVICES
P.O. Box 478, Baytown TX 77522-0478. 281/834-7767. **Contact:** Human Resources. **World Wide Web address:** http://www.hydrochem.com. **Description:** An industrial cleaning company that provides heavy-duty cleaning services such as high-pressure water blasting and vacuuming for industrial plants. **Corporate headquarters location:** Canal Fulton OH.

I-SECTOR CORPORATION
6401 Southwest Freeway, Houston TX 77074. 713/795-2000. **Fax:** 713/795-2001. **Contact:** Barbara McNeir, Human Resources Director. **E-mail address:** careers@l-sector.com. **World Wide Web address:** http://www.i-sector.com. **Description:** Owns and operates subsidiary companies that are engaged in various aspects of the information and technology industries. **Corporate headquarters location:** This location. **Listed on:** NASDAQ. **Stock exchange symbol:** ISEC. **Number of employees nationwide:** 211.

IKON OFFICE SOLUTIONS
7401 East Ben White Boulevard, Building 2, Austin TX 78741-7418. 512/385-5100. **Contact:** Human Resources. **World Wide Web address:** http://www.ikon.com. **Description:** IKON Office Solutions is one of the largest independent copier distribution networks in North America. **Operations at this facility include:** This location is a sales and service center.

INITIAL SECURITY
3355 Cherry Ridge, Suite 200, San Antonio TX 78230. 210/349-6321. **Toll-free phone:** 800/683-7771. **Contact:** Human Resources.

World Wide Web address: http://www.initialsecurity.com. **Description:** Offers security guard services throughout the greater San Antonio area.

INTERNATIONAL MAINTENANCE CORPORATION
P.O. Box 1029, Beaumont TX 77704. 409/722-8031. **Contact:** Human Resources. **Description:** Provides plant maintenance, including shut-downs and turn-arounds.

ARTHUR D. LITTLE, INC.
1001 McKinney Street, Suite 1700, Houston TX 77002. 713/646-2200. **Contact:** Human Resources. **World Wide Web address:** http://www.arthurdlittle.com. **Description:** Offers services in three areas: management consulting; technology and product development; and environmental, health, and safety consulting. The company's clients include a wide range of firms in manufacturing industries including aerospace, automotive, consumer products, industrial electronics, information and telecommunications, medical products, and pharmaceuticals; process industries including chemicals, energy, food, and metals; and service industries, including financial services, health care, information and communications services, transportation, travel and tourism, and utilities. **Positions advertised include:** Business Analyst; Consultant; Intern.

LOOMIS, FARGO & COMPANY
611 South Presa Street, San Antonio TX 78210. 210/226-0195. **Contact:** Human Resources. **World Wide Web address:** http://www.loomisfargo.com. **Description:** Provides armored transportation, cash vault, and ATM services. **Corporate headquarters location:** Houston TX.

MARSH USA, INC.
1000 Louisiana Street, Suite 4000, Houston TX 77002. 713/654-0400. **Contact:** Human Resources. **World Wide Web address:** http://www.marsh.com. **Description:** Provides advice and services worldwide to clients concerned with the management of assets and risks. Specific services include insurance and risk management services, reinsurance, consulting and financial services, merchandising, and investment management. The company has subsidiaries and affiliates in 57 countries, with correspondents in 20 other countries. **Positions advertised include:** Facilities Manager. **Corporate headquarters location:** New York NY. **Other U.S. locations:** Nationwide. **Parent company:** Marsh & McLennan

Companies (MMC). **Listed on:** New York Stock Exchange. **Stock exchange symbol:** MMC.

MODIS, INC.
1235 North Loop West, Suite 1100, Houston TX 77008. 713/880-0232. **Contact:** Human Resources. **World Wide Web address:** http://www.modisit.com. **Description:** Provides a wide range of computer consulting services. **Corporate headquarters location:** Jacksonville FL. **Parent company:** MPS Group. **Listed on:** New York Stock Exchange. **Stock exchange symbol:** MPS.

PHILIP SERVICES CORPORATION
5151 San Felipe, Suite 1600, Houston TX 77056. 713/623-8777. **Contact:** Human Resources. **World Wide Web address:** http://www.contactpsc.com. **Description:** Provides specialized turn-around maintenance and environmental, electrical, and instrumentation contracting services. Principal markets include petroleum refiners, natural gas processors, petrochemical firms, oil producers, and paper and pulp companies throughout the United States and Europe. Services include turnkey heat exchanger maintenance, tower and vessel maintenance, petroleum and petrochemical storage tank cleaning, and sludge control. In addition, Philip Services Corporation offers turnaround management services, supervising all aspects of periodic maintenance projects. The company also installs electrical and instrumentation systems for offshore production platforms and petrochemical facilities. **Listed on:** NASDAQ. **Stock exchange symbol:** PSCD. **Number of employees worldwide:** 10,000.

PINKERTON SECURITY & INVESTIGATION SERVICES
402 East Hillside, Suite 2, Laredo TX 78041. 956/726-1510. **Contact:** Human Resources. **World Wide Web address:** http://www.pinkertons.com. **Description:** Offers a full range of specialized protective services including premier property and high-rise services, health care and hospital services, special event services, ATM services, and patrol services. The company serves thousands of companies worldwide with investigation, threat assessment, and executive protection services. **Corporate headquarters location:** Westlake Village CA. **Operations at this facility include:** This location is engaged in industrial and private security, investigation, and security consulting. **Parent company:** Securitas.

BECHTEL CORPORATION
P.O. Box 2166, 3000 Post Oak Boulevard, Houston TX 77056. 713/235-2000. **Fax:** 713/960-9031. **Contact:** Human Resources. **World Wide Web address:** http://www.bechtel.com. **Description:** Operates in the following areas: engineering, construction, financing operations, electricity, nuclear fuels, metals, minerals, procurement management, transportation, and pollution control. **Positions advertised include:** Senior Design Engineer; Project Manager.

SAI PEOPLE SOLUTIONS, INC.
2313 Timber Shadows Drive, Suite 200, Kingwood TX 77339. 281/358-1858. **Fax:** 281/358-8952. **Contact:** Human Resources Manager. **World Wide Web address:** http://www.saisoft.com. **Description:** A computer consulting company. Sai People Solutions offers IT staffing expertise and off-site automated software testing services to *Fortune* 500 firms in a wide range of industries including telecommunications, banking, medical, manufacturing, and transportation.

TMP WORLDWIDE RESOURCING
2190 North Loop West, Suite 106, Houston TX 77018. 713/688-4884. **Contact:** Human Resources. **World Wide Web address:** http://www.tmp.com. **Description:** A human resources outsourcing firm. Operations include Monster.com, one of the largest and most successful recruiting Websites; recruitment advertising; executive search and selection; and yellow page advertising. **Positions advertised include:** Client Services Specialist; Marketing Manager; Accounting and Finance Recruiter; Copywriter; Senior Software Engineer; Media Planner; Local Account Executive; Client Service Associate. **Corporate headquarters location:** New York NY.

TABS DIRECT
1002 Texas Parkway, Stafford TX 77477. 281/499-0417. **Fax:** 281/499-7098. **Contact:** Recruiter. **E-mail address:** tabs.hr.resumes@ tabsdirect.com. **World Wide Web address:** http://www.tabsdirect. com. **Description:** A direct mail firm with five subsidiaries engaged in data processing and offset printing. Tabs Direct also has lettershop capabilities. **Positions advertised include:** Pre-Press Specialist; Computer Operator. **Special programs:** Internships. **Corporate headquarters location:** Atlanta GA. **Other U.S. locations:** Los Angeles CA; Chicago IL. **Parent company:** Omnicom. **Operations at this facility include:** Service. **Listed on:** New York Stock Exchange.

Stock exchange symbol: OMC. **Number of employees nationwide:** 400.

TEAMSTAFF
2 Northpoint Drive, Suite 760, Houston TX 77060. 281/405-4300. **Toll-free phone:** 800/600-0374. **Contact:** Human Resources. **World Wide Web address:** http://www.teamstaff.com. **Description:** Offers a full line of services, which include payroll processing, permanent and temporary placement of personnel, in-house hardware and software systems, outsourcing, facility management, employee leasing, and insurance services, including employee benefits. **Listed on:** NASDAQ. **Stock exchange symbol:** TSTF.

TELESCAN, INC.
5959 Corporate Drive, Suite 2000, Houston TX 77036. 281/588-9700. **Fax:** 281/588-9797. **Contact:** Personnel. **World Wide Web address:** http://www.telescan.com. **Description:** Develops customized Internet and online data networks for financial and publishing industries. Telescan also provides proprietary analytics and content to investors. **Corporate headquarters location:** This location. **Other U.S. locations:** Berwyn PA.

TURNER, COLLIE & BRADEN, INC.
P.O. Box 130089, Houston TX 77219. 713/780-4100. **Fax:** 713/784-1546. **Contact:** Human Resources Specialist. **E-mail address:** careers@tcb.aecom.com. **World Wide Web address:** http://www.tcandb.com. **Description:** A consulting firm providing technical services including engineering and design for the transportation, public works, environmental, and land development industries and does engineering economics and feasibility studies. Founded in 1946. **NOTE:** Entry-level positions and part-time jobs are offered. **Special programs:** Internships; Co-ops; Summer Jobs. **Office hours:** Monday - Friday, 7:30 a.m. - 4:30 p.m. **Corporate headquarters location:** This location. **Other area locations:** Austin TX; Dallas TX; San Antonio TX. **Other U.S. locations:** Denver CO. **Parent company:** AECOM. **Operations at this facility include:** Administration; Divisional Headquarters; Sales. **Listed on:** Privately held.

VIGNETTE CORPORATION
1601 South MoPac Expressway, Building 3, Austin TX 78746-5776. 512/741-4300. **Contact:** Human Resources. **World Wide Web address:** http://www.vignette.com. **Description:** Supplies e-business

applications to online business clients. **Corporate headquarters location:** This location. **Listed on:** NASDAQ. **Stock exchange symbol:** VIGN.

XEROX CORPORATION
6836 Austin Center Boulevard, Suite 300, Austin TX 78731. 512/343-5600. **Contact:** Human Resources Center. **World Wide Web address:** http://www.xerox.com. **Description:** Xerox is a leader in the global document market providing document solutions that enhance business productivity. Xerox develops, manufactures, markets, sells, and services a full range of document processing products and solutions. **Corporate headquarters location:** Stamford CT. **Operations at this facility include:** This location is a regional sales and service office. **Listed on:** New York Stock Exchange. **Stock exchange symbol:** XRX.

XEROX OMNIFAX
P.O. Box 80709, Austin TX 78708. 512/719-5566. **Fax:** 512/490-6308. **Contact:** Personnel Manager. **World Wide Web address:** http://www.omnifax.com. **Description:** Manufacture communications systems, telewriters, and facsimile recording devices. **Parent company:** Xerox Corporation. **Listed on:** New York Stock Exchange. **Stock exchange symbol:** XRX.

CHARITIES AND SOCIAL SERVICES

You can expect to find the following types of organizations in this chapter:

Social and Human Service Agencies • Job Training and Vocational Rehabilitation Services • Nonprofit Organizations

AIDS SERVICES OF AUSTIN
P.O. Box 4874, Austin TX 78765. 512/458-2437. **Fax:** 512/452-3299. **Contact:** Personnel. **World Wide Web address:** http://www.asaustin.org. **Description:** This organization has 600 volunteers that work together to assist the community and individuals who are HIV-positive. AIDS Services of Austin is involved in philanthropy, wellness educational programs, safe sex seminars, counseling, and financial aid for HIV-positive individuals.

AMERICAN RED CROSS
3642 East Houston Street, San Antonio TX 78219. 210/224-5151. **Contact:** Human Resources. **World Wide Web address:** http://www.redcross.org. **Description:** A humanitarian organization that aids disaster victims, gathers blood for crisis distribution, trains individuals to respond to emergencies, educates individuals on various diseases, and raises funds for other charitable establishments.

AMERICAN RED CROSS
908 West Pine Avenue, Orange TX 77630. 409/883-2322. **Contact:** Human Resources Department. **World Wide Web address:** http://www.redcross.org. **Description:** A humanitarian organization that aids disaster victims, gathers blood for crisis distribution, trains individuals to respond to emergencies, educates individuals on various diseases, and raises funds for other charitable establishments.

BAYTOWN YMCA
201 Wye Drive, Baytown TX 77521. 281/427-1797. **Contact:** Human Resources. **Wide Web address:** http://www.ymcahouston.org. **Description:** One of the nation's largest and most comprehensive service organizations. The YMCA provides health and fitness services, social and personal development, sports and recreation, education and career development, and camps and conferences to children, youths, adults, the elderly, families, the disabled, refugees and foreign nationals, YMCA residents, and community residents, through a broad range of programs. **Corporate headquarters location:** Chicago IL.

COMMUNITIES IN SCHOOL
2150 West 18th Street, Suite 100, Houston TX 77008. 713/654-1515. **Contact:** Human Resources Department. **World Wide Web address:** http://www.cishouston.org. **Description:** A social service agency offering school programs to prevent dropouts.

GOODWILL INDUSTRIES
P.O. Box 3963, Beaumont TX 77701. 409/838-9911. **Contact:** Director. **World Wide Web address:** http://www.goodwill.org. **Description:** A nonprofit provider of employment training for the disabled and the poor, operating 1,800 thrift stores nationwide. **Other U.S. locations:** Nationwide.

HOUSTON AREA URBAN LEAGUE
1301 Texas Avenue, Houston TX 77002. 713/393-8700. **Contact:** James Lacy, Manager of Operations. **World Wide Web address:** http://www.haul.org. **Description:** A social service agency that also provides employment services.

LADY BIRD JOHNSON WILDFLOWER CENTER
4801 La Crosse Avenue, Austin TX 78739. 512/292-4200. **Contact:** Human Resources. **World Wide Web address:** http://www.wildflower.org. **Description:** A nonprofit organization that serves to educate people on the value and beauty of native plants. Lady Bird Johnson Wildflower Center also houses Wild Ideas: The Store, a retail store offering books, art, and clothing dedicated to generating an interest in plant life; and The Wildflower Cafe, a coffee shop and eatery. **Special programs:** Internships. **Corporate headquarters location:** This location.

LIFE RESOURCE
SPINDLE TOP MENTAL HEALTH & MENTAL RETARDATION
2750 South Eighth Street, Beaumont TX 77701. 409/839-1000. **Contact:** Director. **Description:** A crisis resolution and counseling center providing addiction recovery programs. **Other U.S. locations:** Port Arthur TX; Orange TX.

LIGHTHOUSE OF HOUSTON
P.O. Box 130345, Houston TX 77219-0435. 713/527-9561. **Contact:** Human Resources. **World Wide Web address:** http://www.thelighthouseofhouston.org. **Description:** A nonprofit organization for the blind offering adult day care, recreational activities, and social services.

MARTIN LUTHER HOMES OF TEXAS INC.
332 South Loop 123 Business, Suite 400, Seguin TX 78155. 830/372-3075. **Contact:** Jerome Boeck, Recruiter. **World Wide Web address:** http://www.mlhs.com. **Description:** An agency that provides housing and support services for individuals with mental retardation.

NEIGHBORHOOD CENTERS INC.
P.O. Box 271389, Houston TX 77277-1389. 713/667-9400. **Contact:** Director. **World Wide Web address:** http://www.neighborhood-centers.org. **Description:** A human services organization offering a variety of programs to assist low-income families. Some of the programs offered include Healthy Start, which provides prenatal services and Early Head Start, which promotes the emotional and physical growth of children. Founded in 1907. **Parent company:** United Way.

THE RONALD McDONALD HOUSE OF GALVESTON
P.O. Box 1045, Galveston TX 77553. 409/762-0609. **Fax:** 409/762-5338. **Contact:** Executive Director. **E-mail address:** ronmcd@galveston.com. **World Wide Web address:** http://www.galveston.com/ronald. **Description:** A nonprofit organization providing support services for families of children afflicted with serious illnesses.

SERVICE CORPORATION INTERNATIONAL (SCI)
1929 Allen Parkway, Houston TX 77219. 713/522-5141. **Contact:** Human Resources. **World Wide Web address:** http://www.sci-corp.com. **Description:** Engaged in the operation of cemeteries and also provides cremation services and grief counseling. **Positions advertised include:** Staff Auditor; Outside Sales Representative; Family Service Counselor; Voice Services Specialist. **Listed on:** New York Stock Exchange. **Stock exchange symbol:** SRV. **Number of employees nationwide:** 24,000.

UNITED WAY OF THE TEXAS GULF COAST
P.O. Box 924507, Houston TX 77292-4507. 713/685-2300. **Contact:** Human Resources. **World Wide Web address:** http://www.uwtgc.org. **Description:** The United Way provides necessary job and life skills training in order to help people become independent, responsible citizens, capable of making a contribution to society; empowers communities and individuals to care for themselves; provides opportunities to maintain physical and mental

well-being; supports all children with a safe, nurturing environment through positive role models, developmental experiences, social stimulation, and interaction; ensures the opportunity for individuals to maintain an independent life; provides resources that give people a safe and secure living environment and provides for basic needs; and provides social and emotional support to family members so that they can function in society at their optimal potential.

CHEMICALS/RUBBER AND PLASTICS

You can expect to find the following types of companies in this chapter:
Adhesives, Detergents, Inks, Paints, Soaps, Varnishes • Agricultural Chemicals and Fertilizers • Carbon and Graphite Products • Chemical Engineering Firms• Industrial Gases

ALBEMARLE CORPORATION

P.O. Box 2500, Pasadena TX 77501-2500. 713/740-1000. **Contact:** Human Resources. **World Wide Web address:** http://www.albemarle.com. **Description:** Albemarle Corporation is a global supplier of specialty and performance chemicals that enhance consumer products. The company serves markets for petroleum and agricultural chemicals, detergents, polymers, electronics, and pharmaceuticals and is one of the world's leading producers of alpha olefins, bromine chemicals, and ibuprofen. **Operations at this facility include:** This location manufactures specialty chemicals for plastics manufacturing.

ATOFINA CHEMICAL

2231 Haden Road, Houston TX 77015. 713/455-1211. **Contact:** Resources Manager. **World Wide Web address:** http://www.atofinachemicals.com. **Description:** A chemical manufacturer with products that include polymers, fluorochemicals, carbons, and specialty chemicals.

ATOFINA PETROCHEMICALS, INC.

P.O. Box 849, Port Arthur TX 77641-0849. 409/962-4421. **Contact:** Human Resources. **World Wide Web address:** http://www.petrochemicals.atofina.com. **Description:** Explores for crude oil and natural gas; markets natural gas; refines, supplies, transports, and markets petroleum products; manufactures and markets specialty chemicals, primarily petrochemicals and plastics including polypropylene, polystyrene, styrene monomer, high-density polyethylene, and aromatics; licenses certain chemical processes; and manufactures and markets paints and coatings.

BASF CORPORATION

602 Copper Road, Freeport TX 77541. 979/238-6100. **Contact:** Human Resources. **World Wide Web address:** http://www.basf.com. **Description:** An international manufacturer and distributor of chemical products, doing business in five operating groups: Agricultural Chemicals; Chemicals; Colors and Auxiliaries; Pigments

and Organic Specialties; and Polymers. **Corporate headquarters location:** Mount Olive NJ.

BP CHEMICAL COMPANY
P.O. Box 1489, Baytown TX 77522. 281/421-2972. **Contact:** Human Resources. **World Wide Web address:** http:// www.bpamoco.com. **Description:** Manufactures polypropylene products used in fibers and packaging. **Corporate headquarters location:** Joliet IL. **Listed on:** New York Stock Exchange. **Stock exchange symbol:** BP.

BAKER PETROLITE
P.O. Box 5050, Sugar Land TX 77487. 281/276-5400. **Physical address:** 12645 West Airport Boulevard, Sugar Land TX 77478. **Fax:** 281/275-7392. **Contact:** Human Resources. **World Wide Web address:** http://www.bakerhughes.com. **Description:** Engaged in the manufacture and sale of chemicals. **Positions advertised include:** Technical Manager; Systems Analyst; Senior Development Scientist; Compliance Accountant; Financial Analyst; HSE Specialist; Department Administrator. **Corporate headquarters location:** This location. **Other U.S. locations:** Anchorage AK; Bakersfield CA; Los Angeles CA; Tulsa OK. **International locations:** Caracas, Venezuela; Liverpool, England. **Parent company:** Baker Hughes Inc. **Listed on:** New York Stock Exchange. **Stock exchange symbol:** BHI.

BASELL POLYOLEFINS
12001 Bay Area Boulevard, Pasadena TX 77507. 281/474-4481. **Contact:** Human Resources. **World Wide Web address:** http:// www.basell.com. **Description:** Produces polypropylene resins and advanced materials supplied to manufacturers in the plastics, synthetic fibers, automobiles, and household products industries. **Operations at this facility include:** Administration; Manufacturing.

CELANESE CORPORATION
P.O. Box 509, Bay City TX 77404. 979/241-4000. **Contact:** Human Resources. **World Wide Web address:** http://www.celanese.com. **Description:** Manufactures industrial inorganic chemicals. **Parent company:** Celanese AG is an industrial chemical company operating in five business segments: Acetyl Products; Chemical Intermediates; Celanese Acetate Textiles; Ticona Technical Polymers; and Nurtovina Performance Products.

CELANESE CORPORATION
Highway 77 South, P.O. Box 428, Bishop TX 78343. 361/584-6000. **Contact:** Human Resources. **World Wide Web address:** http:// www.celanese.com. **Description:** A manufacturing plant producing chemicals and plastics. **Parent company:** Celanese AG is an industrial chemical company operating in five business segments: Acetyl Products; Chemical Intermediates; Celanese Acetate Textiles; Ticona Technical Polymers; and Nutrovina Performance Products.

CONTINENTAL CARBON COMPANY
333 Cypress Run, Suite 100, Houston TX 77094. 281/647-3700. **Contact:** Human Resources. **World Wide Web address:** http:// www.continentalcarbon.com. **Description:** Manufactures carbon black for the tire and rubber industries. **Corporate headquarters location:** This location.

CONTINENTAL PLASTIC CONTAINERS, INC.
6831 Silsbee Road, Houston TX 77033. 713/643-2638. **Contact:** Christine Daigle, Human Resources Administrator. **Description:** Manufactures and distributes plastic packaging products such as bottles for the chemical and food industries.

DX SERVICE COMPANY
P.O. Box 130410, Houston TX 77219. 713/863-1947. **Contact:** Human Resources. **World Wide Web address:** http:// www.dixiechemical.com. **Description:** A holding company with subsidiaries that manufacture and distribute chemicals.

DOW CHEMICAL COMPANY
P.O. Box 685, La Porte TX 77572-0685. 713/246-0369. **Contact:** Human Resources Department. **World Wide Web address:** http:// www.dow.com. **Description:** Manufactures petrochemicals.

DOW CHEMICAL COMPANY
400 West Sam Houston Parkway South, Houston TX 77042. 713/978-2971. **Contact:** Human Resources Department. **World Wide Web address:** http://www.dow.com. **Description:** Provides drafting, construction, and other services for Dow U.S.A.

ENGINEERED CARBONS, INC.
9300 Needlepoint Road, Baytown TX 77521. 281/421-2500. **Contact:** Human Resources. **Description:** Produces carbon black for highly sophisticated applications such as conductive and

nonconductive electrical cables, superthin rubber membranes, plastic applications, printing ink, and other specialty products.

FLINT HILLS RESOURCES LP
P.O. Box 2608, Corpus Christi TX 78403-2608. 361/241-4811. **Contact:** Human Resources. **World Wide Web address:** http://www.fhr.com. **Description:** A manufacturer of chemicals. **Positions advertised include:** Instrument Technician. **Corporate headquarters location:** Wichita KS. **Parent company:** Koch Industries.

GSE LINING TECHNOLOGY, INC.
19103 Gundle Road, Houston TX 77073-3598. 281/230-5832. **Toll-free phone:** 800/435-2008. **Fax:** 281/230-8607. **Contact:** Human Resources. **World Wide Web address:** http://www.gseworld.com. **Description:** Manufactures and installs plastic environmental liners for ponds and landfills. **Special programs:** Internships. **Corporate headquarters location:** This location. **Listed on:** New York Stock Exchange. **Stock exchange symbol:** GSE. **President/CEO:** Samir Badawi.

GOODYEAR CHEMICAL
P.O. Box 26003, Beaumont TX 77720-6003. 409/794-5230. **Contact:** Employment. **World Wide Web address:** http://www.goodyear.com. **Description:** Goodyear Tire & Rubber Company manufactures and sells thousands of products including metal, rubber, and plastic products for the transportation industry, and various industrial and consumer markets; synthetic rubber; and numerous high-technology products for aerospace, defense, and nuclear energy applications. The company's principal business is the development, manufacture, distribution, and sale of tires of every type. **Corporate headquarters location:** Akron OH. **Operations at this facility include:** This location manufactures synthetic rubber and hydrocarbon resins. **Parent company:** Goodyear Tire & Rubber Company. **Listed on:** New York Stock Exchange. **Stock exchange symbol:** GT.

LUBRIZOL CORPORATION
P.O. Box 158, Deer Park TX 77536-0158. 281/479-2851. **Contact:** Human Resources. **World Wide Web address:** http://www.lubrizol.com. **Description:** A diversified specialty chemical company engaged in chemical, mechanical, and genetic research to develop products for transportation, industry, and agriculture. **Listed on:** New York Stock Exchange. **Stock exchange symbol:** LZ.

LYONDELL CHEMICAL COMPANY
10801 Choate Road, Pasadena TX 77507. 281/474-4191. **Contact:** Human Resources. **World Wide Web address:** http://www.lyondell. com. **Description:** Specializes in the production of propylene derivatives, olefins, and refining chemicals. **Corporate headquarters location:** Houston TX. **Other area locations:** Channelview TX; Dallas TX. **Operations at this facility include:** This location is one of the world's leading producers of propylene oxide, propylene glycol, and styrene monomer. **Subsidiaries include:** Equistar Chemicals, LP; Lyondell Methanol Company, LP; Lyondell-Citgo Refining Company, Ltd. **Listed on:** New York Stock Exchange. **Stock exchange symbol:** LYO.

LYONDELL CHEMICAL COMPANY
EQUISTAR CHEMICALS, LP
P.O. Box 3646, Houston TX 77252. 713/652-7200. **Contact:** Human Resources. **World Wide Web address:** http://www.lyondell.com. **Description:** Specializes in the production of propylene derivatives, olefins, and refining chemicals. Equistar Chemicals, LP (also at this location) produces ethylene, propylene, and polyethelene as well as color compounds, resins, and fine powders. **Corporate headquarters location:** This location. **Operations at this facility include:** This location is one of the world's leading producers of propylene oxide, propylene glycol, and styrene monomer. **Subsidiaries include:** Lyondell Methanol Company, LP; Lyondell-Citgo Refining Company, Ltd. **Listed on:** New York Stock Exchange. **Stock exchange symbol:** LYO.

MAINTENANCE ENGINEERING CORPORATION
P.O. Box 1729, Houston TX 77251. 713/222-2351. **Contact:** Brian Banks, Controller. **World Wide Web address:** http://www.meco. com. **Description:** Manufactures and distributes water conditioning chemicals and related products.

MERISOL
11821 East Freeway, Houston TX 77029. 713/428-5400. **Contact:** Human Resources. **World Wide Web address:** http://www.merisol. com. **Description:** Manufactures water conditioning chemicals used in cooling towers and boiler treatments.

NL INDUSTRIES, INC.
16825 Northchase, Suite 1200, Houston TX 77060. 281/423-3300. **Contact:** Human Resources. **World Wide Web address:** http://

www.nl-ind.com. **Description:** Manufactures and markets titanium dioxide pigments and other specialty chemicals used in a wide variety of products including paints, plastics, inks, and paper. **Corporate headquarters location:** This location. **International locations:** Worldwide. **Subsidiaries include:** Kronos, Inc.; Rheox, Inc. **Listed on:** New York Stock Exchange. **Stock exchange symbol:** NL.

NOVA CHEMICAL CORPORATION
12222 Port Road, Pasadena TX 77507. 281/474-1000. **Contact:** Human Resources. **World Wide Web address:** http://www.novachem.com. **Description:** Manufactures plastics materials including films, thermoplastic resins, and other synthetic resins; polyethylene; and polypropylene. The company's products are used to make a wide variety of products ranging from dashboards to diapers and medical supplies.

OCCIDENTAL CHEMICAL CORPORATION
P.O. Box 500, Deer Park TX 77536. 281/476-2000. **Contact:** Employment Office. **World Wide Web address:** http://www.oxychem.com. **Description:** Occidental Chemical Corporation manufactures commodity and specialty chemicals. The company has approximately 25 manufacturing facilities nationwide. **Corporate headquarters location:** Dallas TX. **Other U.S. locations:** Nationwide. **Operations at this facility include:** This location produces plastic materials and synthetic resins. **Parent company:** Occidental Petroleum Corporation. **Listed on:** New York Stock Exchange. **Stock exchange symbol:** OXY. **Number of employees nationwide:** 8,200.

OCCIDENTAL CHEMICAL CORPORATION
P.O. Box 849, Pasadena TX 77501. 281/884-4009. **Contact:** Human Resources. **World Wide Web address:** http://www.oxychem.com. **Description:** Manufactures commodity and specialty chemicals. The company has approximately 25 manufacturing facilities nationwide. **Corporate headquarters location:** Dallas TX. **Other U.S. locations:** Nationwide. **Parent company:** Occidental Petroleum Corporation. **Listed on:** New York Stock Exchange. **Stock exchange symbol:** OXY. **Number of employees nationwide:** 8,200.

ONDECO NALCO ENERGY SERVICES L.P.
P.O. Box 87, Sugar Land TX 77487-0087. 281/263-7000. **Contact:** Bill Aimone, Manager of Employment. **World Wide Web address:** http://www.nalco.com. **Description:** Engaged in the manufacture

and sale of highly specialized service chemicals used in water treatment, pollution control, energy conservation, oil production, oil refining, steelmaking, papermaking, mining, and other industrial processes. **Positions advertised include:** Industry Analyst; Applications Engineer; Technical Sales Representative. **Corporate headquarters location:** Naperville IL.

ROHM & HAAS COMPANY
1900 Tidal Road, Deer Park TX 77536. 281/228-8100. **Contact:** Human Resources. **World Wide Web address:** http:// www.rohmhaas.com. **Description:** Rohm & Haas Company is a specialty chemicals company operating in four industry segments: Polymers, Resins, and Monomers; Plastics; Industrial Chemicals; and Agricultural Chemicals. Rohm & Haas Company is also engaged in nonchemical industries such as forestry products, carpet production, and biomedical testing. **Corporate headquarters location:** Philadelphia PA. **Operations at this facility include:** This location manufactures a variety of chemicals including ammonia and cyanide. **Listed on:** New York Stock Exchange. **Stock exchange symbol:** ROH.

SILGAN PLASTICS CORPORATION
6814 Kirbyville, Houston TX 77033. 713/644-5201. **Contact:** Human Resources. **World Wide Web address:** http:// www.silganplastics.com. **Description:** Produces a wide range of plastic closures, bottles, dispensers, and packaging. **Corporate headquarters location:** Triadelphia WV. **Operations at this facility include:** This location manufactures plastic sanitary containers.

STERLING CHEMICALS, INC.
P.O. Box 1311, Texas City TX 77592-1311. 409/945-4431. **Physical address:** 201 Bay Street, Texas City TX 77590. **Contact:** Human Resources. **World Wide Web address:** http://www. sterlingchemicals.com. **Description:** Engaged in the production of sodium chlorate, lactic acid, acetic acid, plasticizers, and sodium cyanide. **Corporate headquarters location:** Houston TX. **Operations at this facility include:** Manufactures petrochemicals.

STERLING CHEMICALS, INC.
1200 Smith Street, Suite 1900, Houston TX 77002. 713/650-3700. **Contact:** Human Resources. **World Wide Web address:** http:// www.sterlingchemicals.com. **Description:** A chemical manufacturer engaged in the production of sodium chlorate, lactic acid, acetic

acid, plasticizers, and sodium cyanide. **NOTE:** Send resumes to: Sterling Chemicals, Inc., Human Resources, P.O. Box 1311, Texas City TX 77592-1311. **Corporate headquarters location:** This location.

SUNOCO CHEMICALS CORPORATION

P.O. Box 600, Pasadena TX 77501. 281/884-4400. **Fax:** 281/884-4402. **Contact:** Dan Gilbert, Manager of Human Resources Department. **World Wide Web address:** http:// www.sunocochemicals.com. **Description:** Sunoco Chemicals Corporation is a diversified chemicals manufacturer, marketing a broad range of products that are converted into consumer items. Markets served include automotive, construction, marine, and recreational. The company's product lines include phenol, bisphenol-A, polypropylene, acrylic sheet, coal chemicals, dibasic acids, cumene, plasticizers, and unsaturated polyester resins. **NOTE:** Second and third shifts are offered. **Special programs:** Internships; Training; Co-ops; Summer Jobs. **Corporate headquarters location:** Philadelphia PA. **Other U.S. locations:** OH; PA; WV. **Operations at this facility include:** This location manufactures 2-ethylhexanol and phthalic anhydride.

TEXAS PETROCHEMICALS CORPORATION

8600 Park Place Boulevard, Houston TX 77017. 713/477-9211. **Contact:** Human Resources. **Description:** Manufactures petroleum-based compounds and chemicals including ether and butane. **World Wide Web address:** http://www.txpetrochem.com. **Corporate headquarters location:** This location.

COMMUNICATIONS: TELECOMMUNICATIONS AND BROADCASTING

You can expect to find the following types of companies in this chapter:
*Cable/Pay Television Services • Communications Equipment•
Radio and Television Broadcasting Systems • Telephone, Telegraph, and
other Message Communications*

ARCH WIRELESS
5177 Richmond Avenue, Suite 140, Houston TX 77056. 713/881-2000. **Contact:** Human Resources. **World Wide Web address:** http://www.arch.com. **Description:** A leading provider of wireless messaging and information services across the United States and Canada. **Positions advertised include:** Wireless Sales Executive. **Corporate headquarters location:** Westborough MA.

CHANNEL 2 KPRC-TV
P.O. Box 2222, Houston TX 77252. 713/222-2222. **Physical address:** 8181 SW Freeway, Houston TX 77074. **Contact:** Human Resources. **World Wide Web address:** http://www.kprc.com. **Description:** A television broadcasting company and NBC affiliate.

CLEAR CHANNEL COMMUNICATIONS
P.O. Box 659512, San Antonio TX 78265-9512. 210/822-2828. **Fax:** 210/822-2299. **Contact:** Personnel. **World Wide Web address:** http://www.clearchannel.com. **Description:** A nationwide television and radio broadcasting company. Clear Channel Communications operates approximately 1,225 radio and 37 television stations in the United States. **Positions advertised include:** Radio Account Executive; Traffic Director. **Corporate headquarters location:** This location. **Listed on:** New York Stock Exchange. **Stock exchange symbol:** CCU.

HARRIS CORPORATION
5727 Farinon Drive, San Antonio TX 78249. 210/561-7300. **Contact:** Human Resources. **World Wide Web address:** http://www.harris.com. **Description:** Harris Corporation is a communications equipment company that provides broadcast, network, government, and wireless support products and systems. Founded in 1895. **Corporate headquarters location:** Melbourne FL. **Operations at this facility include:** This location develops and manufactures wireless microwave radios. **Listed on:** New York Stock

Exchange. **Stock exchange symbol:** HRS. **Number of employees nationwide:** 10,500.

QVC SAN ANTONIO INC.
9855 West Stover Hills Boulevard, San Antonio TX 78251. 210/522-4300. **Contact:** Human Resources. **World Wide Web address:** http://www.qvc.com. **Description:** A nationwide home shopping television network.

SBC COMMUNICATIONS INC.
SOUTHWESTERN BELL
175 East Houston Street, San Antonio TX 78205. 210/821-4105. **Recorded jobline:** 210/820-6832. **Contact:** Human Resources. **World Wide Web address:** http://www.sbc.com. **Description:** Provides telecommunications products and services throughout the United States and internationally. **Corporate headquarters location:** This location. **Subsidiaries include:** Ameritech, CellularOne, Nevada Bell, Pacific Bell, SBC Telecom, SNET, and Southwestern Bell (also at this location) provides local telephone and cellular services. **Listed on:** New York Stock Exchange. **Stock exchange symbol:** SBC. **Number of employees worldwide:** 200,000.

TIME WARNER CABLE
8400 West Tidwell Road, Houston TX 77040. 713/462-9000. **Contact:** Human Resources. **World Wide Web address:** http://www.twchouston.com. **Description:** Provides residential cable television services.

VTEL CORPORATION
9208 Waterford Centre Boulevard, Austin TX 78758. 512/821-7000. **Contact:** Human Resources. **World Wide Web address:** http://www.vtel.com. **Description:** A leading provider of interactive videoconferencing systems in the distance learning and health care markets. VTEL products are distributed primarily through resellers and co-marketers. **Corporate headquarters location:** This location.

VERIZON COMMUNICATIONS
6210 Rothway Street, Houston TX 77040. 713/867-6600. **Contact:** Human Resources. **World Wide Web address:** http://www.verizon.com. **Description:** A full-service communications services provider. Verizon offers residential local and long distance telephone services and Internet access; wireless service plans, cellular phones, and data services; a full-line of business services including Internet access,

data services, and telecommunications equipment and services; and government network solutions including Internet access, data services, telecommunications equipment and services, and enhanced communications services. **NOTE:** Resumes must be submitted via the Website: http://www.verizon.com/careers. **Corporate headquarters location:** New York NY. **Listed on:** New York Stock Exchange. **Stock exchange symbol:** VZ.

WORLDCOM
One Fluor Daniel Drive, Building C, Sugar Land TX 77478. 281/276-4000. **Contact:** Human Resources. **World Wide Web address:** http://www.wcom.com. **Description:** One of the world's largest suppliers of local, long-distance, and international telecommunications services, and a global Internet service provider. **Corporate headquarters location:** Clinton MS. **International locations:** Worldwide. **Listed on:** NASDAQ. **Stock exchange symbol:** WCOM.

COMPUTER HARDWARE, SOFTWARE, AND SERVICES

You can expect to find the following types of companies in this chapter:
Computer Components and Hardware Manufacturers • Consultants and Computer Training Companies • Internet and Online Service Providers • Networking and Systems Services • Repair Services/Rental and Leasing • Resellers, Wholesalers, and Distributors • Software Developers/Programming Services • Web Technologies

APPLE COMPUTER, INC.
2420 Ridgepoint Drive, Austin TX 78754. 674/919-2000. **Contact:** Employment. **World Wide Web address:** http://www.apple.com. **Description:** Apple Computer manufactures personal computers and computer-related products for home, business, scientific, industrial, professional, and educational use. **Corporate headquarters location:** Cupertino CA. **Operations at this facility include:** This location offers sales and technical support to companies and educational institutions. **Listed on:** NASDAQ. **Stock exchange symbol:** AAPL.

ASPEN TECHNOLOGY, INC.
1293 Eldridge Parkway, Houston TX 77077. 281/584-1000. **Contact:** Human Resources. **World Wide Web address:** http://www.aspentech.com. **Description:** Aspen Technology, Inc. supplies computer-aided chemical engineering software to the chemical, petroleum, pharmaceutical, metal, mineral, food product, consumer product, and utility industries. **Positions advertised include:** Engineering Business Consultant; Proposal Specialist. **Corporate headquarters location:** Cambridge MA. **International locations:** Belgium; England; Hong Kong; Japan. **Operations at this facility include:** This location develops software. **Listed on:** NASDAQ. **Stock exchange symbol:** AZPN. **Number of employees worldwide:** 1,850.

BMC SOFTWARE, INC.
2101 City West Boulevard, Houston TX 77042-2827. 713/918-8800. **Contact:** Human Resources. **World Wide Web address:** http://www.bmc.com. **Description:** Develops, markets, and supports standard systems software products to enhance and increase the performance of large-scale (mainframe) computer database management systems and data communications software systems. Founded in 1980. **Positions advertised include:** Senior Product Developer; Financial Analyst; Inside Sales Associate; Internal Audit Manager; Database Marketing Manager; Pricing Analyst;

Programmer/Analyst; Sales Representative. **Listed on:** New York Stock Exchange. **Stock exchange symbol:** BMC. **Annual sales/revenues:** More than $1.5 billion.

CSC CONTINUUM INC.
400 West Cesar Chavez Street, Austin TX 78701. 512/345-5700. **Contact:** Donna Monroe, Director of Human Resources. **World Wide Web address:** http://www.csc.com. **Description:** Develops software and provides related services for the financial services industry. **Positions advertised include:** GL Accountant. **Parent company:** Computer Sciences Corporation (El Segundo CA). **Listed on:** New York Stock Exchange. **Stock exchange symbol:** CNU. **Number of employees worldwide:** 68,000.

COMPAQ COMPUTER CORPORATION
P.O. Box 692000, MC-50016, Houston TX 77269-2000. 281/370-0670. **Contact:** Human Resources. **World Wide Web address:** http://www.hp.com. **Description:** Designs, manufactures, sells, and services computers, peripheral equipment, and related software and supplies. Applications and programs include scientific research, computation, communications, education, data analysis, industrial control, time sharing, commercial data processing, graphic arts, word processing, health care, instrumentation, engineering, and simulation. **NOTE:** Compaq is now part of Hewlett Packard. See the Website for more information. **Other U.S. locations:** Nationwide.

COMPUTIZE
1008 Wirt Road, Suite 150, Houston TX 77055. 713/957-0057. **Fax:** 713/613-4866. **Contact:** Human Resources. **World Wide Web address:** http://www.computize.com. **Description:** A computer reseller. Computize also offers e-commerce development, networking, and IS project support through its technical division, DomiNet. Founded in 1983. **Positions advertised include:** Sales Representative. **Annual sales/revenues:** More than $100 million.

CYPRESS SEMICONDUCTOR TEXAS INCORPORATED
17 Cypress Boulevard, Round Rock TX 78664. 512/244-7789. **Contact:** Human Resources. **World Wide Web address:** http://www.cypress.com. **Description:** Manufactures semiconductors.

DELL COMPUTER CORPORATION
One Dell Way, Round Rock TX 78682. 512/338-4400. **Contact:** Human Resources. **World Wide Web address:** http://www.dell.com.

Description: Designs, develops, manufactures, markets, services, and supports personal computer systems and related equipment including servers, workstations, notebooks, and desktop systems. The company also offers over 4,000 software packages and peripherals. **Corporate headquarters location:** This location. **International locations:** Ireland; United Kingdom. **Listed on:** NASDAQ. **Stock exchange symbol:** DELL. **Number of employees worldwide:** 34,600.

ECOM ELITE COMPUTER CONSULTANTS
10333 NW Freeway, Suite 414, Houston TX 77092. 713/686-9740. **Contact:** Human Resources. **World Wide Web address:** http://www.ecom-inc.com. **Description:** A computer consulting firm.

EPSIIA CORPORATION
1101 South Capital of Texas Highway, Building K, Suite 200, Austin TX 78746. 512/329-0081. **Contact:** Human Resources. **World Wide Web address:** http://www.epsiia.com. **Description:** Develops retrieval and conversion software. **Positions advertised include:** Sales Account Executive. **Corporate headquarters location:** This location. **Parent company:** Fiserv Resources.

GRC INTERNATIONAL, INC.
6100 Bandera Road, Suite 505, San Antonio TX 78238. 210/520-7878. **Fax:** 210/520-7881. **Contact:** Human Resources Department. **World Wide Web address:** http://www.grci.com. **Description:** GRC International creates large-scale, decision-support systems and software engineering environments; applies operations research and mathematical modeling to business and management systems; and implements advanced database technology. GRC International also provides studies and analysis capabilities for policy development and planning; modeling and simulation of hardware and software used in real-time testing of sensor, weapon, and battlefield management command, control, and communication systems; and testing and evaluation. GRC International's services are offered primarily to government and commercial customers. **Corporate headquarters location:** Vienna VA. **Other U.S. locations:** Nationwide. **Operations at this facility include:** This location is involved in technical research. **Parent company:** AT&T Corporation. **Listed on:** New York Stock Exchange. **Stock exchange symbol:** T.

GALACTIC TECHNOLOGIES, INC.
400 North Loop 1604 East, Suite 210, San Antonio TX 78232. 210/496-7250. **Fax:** 210/490-6790. **Contact:** Cynthia J. Chatelain, Director of Programs. **World Wide Web address:** http:// www.galactictech.com. **Description:** Provides computer hardware and software engineering, PC support, and networking services. Galactic Technologies also operates as a value-added reseller. **Positions advertised include:** Software Engineer; PC Technician. **Office hours:** Monday - Friday, 7:30 a.m. - 5:00 p.m. **Corporate headquarters location:** This location.

GLOBAL SHOP SOLUTIONS
975 Evergreen Circle, The Woodlands TX 77380-3637. 281/681-1959. **Fax:** 281/681-2663. **Contact:** Dick Alexander, President. **World Wide Web address:** http://www.globalshopsolutions.com. **Description:** Designs and sells manufacturing software systems. Founded in 1976.

HONEYWELL
8440 Westglen Drive, Houston TX 77063. 713/780-6500. **Contact:** Personnel Director. **World Wide Web address:** http:// www.honeywell.com. **Description:** Engaged in the research, development, manufacture, and sale of advanced technology products and services for the satellite technology field. Overall, Honeywell is engaged in the research, development, manufacture, and sale of advanced technology products and services in the fields of chemicals, electronics, automation, and controls. The company's major businesses are home and building automation and control, performance polymers and chemicals, industrial automation and control, space and aviation systems, and defense and marine systems. **Positions advertised include:** Industrial Sales Consultant. **Listed on:** New York Stock Exchange. **Stock exchange symbol:** HON.

IBM CORPORATION
11400 Burnett Road, Austin TX 78758. 512/823-0000. **Toll-free phone:** 800/796-7876. **Recorded jobline:** 800/964-4473. **Contact:** Human Resources. **World Wide Web address:** http://www.ibm.com. **Description:** IBM Corporation is a developer, manufacturer, and marketer of advanced information processing products including computers and microelectronic technology, software, networking systems, and information technology-related services. **NOTE:** Jobseekers should send a resume to IBM Staffing Services, 1DP/051,

3808 Six Forks Road, Raleigh NC 27609. **Corporate headquarters location:** Armonk NY. **International locations:** Worldwide. **Operations at this facility include:** This location is a sales office. **Subsidiaries include:** IBM Credit Corporation; IBM Instruments, Inc.; IBM World Trade Corporation. **Listed on:** New York Stock Exchange. **Stock exchange symbol:** IBM.

INSITUFORM TECHNOLOGIES, INC.
16619 Aldine Westfield Road, Houston TX 77032. 281/821-7070. **Contact:** Human Resources. **E-mail address:** careers@ insituform.com. **World Wide Web address:** http://www.insituform. com. **Description:** Insituform Technologies, Inc. uses various trenchless technologies for rehabilitation, new construction, and improvements of pipeline systems including sewers; gas lines; industrial waste lines; water lines; and oil field, mining, and industrial process pipelines. **Parent company:** Insituform Technologies, Inc. provides a wide variety of technologies including Insituform, PALTEM, Tite Liner, and tunneling. **Operations at this facility include:** This location conducts pipeline rehabilitation. **Listed on:** NASDAQ. **Stock exchange symbol:** INSUA.

LIANT SOFTWARE CORPORATION
8911 Burnet Road, Building C-21, Austin TX 78757. 512/371-7028. **Fax:** 512/371-7609. **Contact:** Human Resources. **World Wide Web address:** http://www.liant.com. **Description:** Develops software including Relativity, an SQL relational access through ODBC to COBOL managed data for client/server Windows applications, and Open PL/I, which offers transitions of PL/I mainframe and minicomputer applications from legacy systems to open, client/server environments. **Corporate headquarters location:** Framingham MA. **Operations at this facility include:** This location is engaged in software packaging and distribution.

LIANT SOFTWARE CORPORATION
RYAN McFARLAND
8911 North Capital of Texas Highway, Suite 4300, Austin TX 78759. 512/343-1010. **Toll-free phone:** 800/762-6265. **Contact:** Human Resources. **World Wide Web address:** http://www.liant.com. **Description:** Develops software including Relativity, an SQL relational access through ODBC to COBOL managed data for client/server Windows applications, and Open PL/I, which offers transitions of PL/I mainframe and minicomputer applications from legacy systems to open, client/server environments. Ryan McFarland

(also at this location) manufactures COBOL software development tools and technologies for applications in client/server environments. **Corporate headquarters location:** Framingham MA.

MESQUITE SOFTWARE, INC.
8500 North MoPac, Suite 825, Austin TX 78759. 512/338-9153. **Contact:** Human Resources. **World Wide Web address:** http://www.mesquite.com. **Description:** Develops software and provides support services for the system simulation market. The company's product line includes CSIM18-The Simulation Engine. **Corporate headquarters location:** This location.

METROWERKS INC.
9801 Metric Boulevard, Suite 100, Austin TX 78758. **Toll-free phone:** 800/377-5416. **Fax:** 512/997-5505. **Contact:** Cheryl Harper, Human Resources Coordinator. **World Wide Web address:** http://www.metrowerks.com. **Description:** Develops and markets software development and programming tools for Windows and Macintosh applications. Founded in 1985. **NOTE:** Entry-level positions are offered. **Other U.S. locations:** Cupertino CA; Woburn MA. **International locations:** Worldwide.

MIILLE APPLIED RESEARCH COMPANY
P.O. Box 87634, Houston TX 77287-7634. 713/472-6272. **Physical address:** 1730 South Richey, Pasadena TX 77502. **Fax:** 713/472-0318. **Contact:** Human Resources. **World Wide Web address:** http://www.miille.com. **Description:** Manufactures and distributes modems and protocol converters for computers.

NEWTEK INC.
5131 Beckwith Boulevard, San Antonio TX 78249. 210/370-8000. **Contact:** Human Resources. **World Wide Web address:** http://www.newtek.com. **Description:** Designs and develops software used for animation and graphics.

PER-SE TECHNOLOGIES, INC.
7701 North Lamar, Suite 124, Austin TX 78752. 512/459-3061. **Contact:** Human Resources. **World Wide Web address:** http://www.per-se.com. **Description:** A leading provider of comprehensive business management services, financial and clinical software, and Internet solutions to physicians and other healthcare professionals. **Corporate headquarters location:** Atlanta GA. **Listed on:** NASDAQ. **Stock exchange symbol:** PSTI.

PERVASIVE SOFTWARE INC.

12365 Riata Trace Parkway, Building Two, Austin TX 78727. 512/231-6000. **Fax:** 512/231-6010. **Contact:** Recruiter. **E-mail address:** greatjobs@pervasive.com. **World Wide Web address:** http://www.pervasive.com. **Description:** Develops embedded database software. **Corporate headquarters location:** This location. **International locations:** Belgium; Canada; England; France; Germany; Hong Kong; Ireland; Japan. **Listed on:** NASDAQ. **Stock exchange symbol:** PVSW.

RADISYS

5959 Corporate Drive, Houston TX 77036. 713/541-8200. **Toll-free phone:** 800/627-8700. **Contact:** Personnel. **World Wide Web address:** http://www.radisys.com. **Description:** A provider of internetwork servers for the Novell marketplace. Radisys has an OEM agreement with Novell and manufactures industry standard servers, CPUs, chassis, mobile systems, and monitors. Founded in 1976. **Listed on:** NASDAQ. **Stock exchange symbol:** RSYS.

SAMSUNG AUSTIN SEMICONDUCTOR

12100 Samsung Boulevard, Austin TX 78754. 512/672-1000. **Contact:** Human Resources. **World Wide Web address:** http://www.sas.samsung.com. **Description:** Manufactures semiconductors.

SEMATECH

2706 Montopolis Drive, Austin TX 78741. 512/356-3588. **Contact:** Human Resources. **E-mail address:** staffing@sematech.com. **World Wide Web address:** http://www.sematech.org. **Description:** SEMATECH is a consortium of U.S. semiconductor manufacturers, working with government and academia, to sponsor and conduct research in semiconductor manufacturing technology for the United States. Results are transferred to consortium members including the Department of Defense for both military and commercial applications. **Operations at this facility include:** This location develops advanced semiconductor manufacturing methods, materials, and equipment.

SONY SEMICONDUCTOR COMPANY OF AMERICA

One Sony Place, San Antonio TX 78245. 210/681-9000. **Fax:** 210/647-6492. **Recorded jobline:** 210/647-6255. **Contact:** Senior Recruiter. **E-mail address:** resumes@ssa-sa.sel.sony.com. **World Wide Web address:** http://www.sel.sony.com. **Description:** Manufactures semiconductor devices with CMOS, BiCMOS, gallium arsenide, and Bipolar technology. **Listed on:** New York Stock Exchange. **Stock exchange symbol:** SNE.

TECHWORKS, INC.
4030 West Braker Lane, Suite 350, Austin TX 78759. 512/794-8533. **Contact:** Human Resources Department. **World Wide Web address:** http://www.techworks.com. **Description:** Manufactures and sells computer memory.

TEXAS INSTRUMENTS, INC. (TI)
P.O. Box 1443, Houston TX 77251-1443. 281/274-2000. **Contact:** Human Resources. **World Wide Web address:** http://www.ti.com. **Description:** Texas Instruments (TI) is one of the world's largest suppliers of semiconductor products. TI's defense electronics business is a leading supplier of avionics, infrared, and weapons guidance systems to the U.S. Department of Defense and U.S. allies. The company is also a technology leader in high-performance notebook computers and model-based software development tools. TI sensors monitor and regulate pressure and temperature in products ranging from automobiles to air conditioning systems. **Corporate headquarters location:** Dallas TX. **Operations at this facility include:** This location manufactures semiconductors. **Listed on:** New York Stock Exchange. **Stock exchange symbol:** TXN. **Number of employees worldwide:** 34,000.

TEXAS INSTRUMENTS, INC. (TI)
P.O. Box 655474, MS 328, Dallas TX 75265. **Contact:** Human Resources. **World Wide Web address:** http://www.ti.com. **Description:** One of the world's largest technology companies, with sales and manufacturing operations in more than 25 countries. Texas Instruments (TI) is one of the world's largest suppliers of semiconductor products. TI's defense electronics business is a leading supplier of avionics, infrared, and weapons guidance systems to the U.S. Department of Defense and U.S. allies. The company is also a technology leader in high-performance notebook computers and model-based software development tools. TI sensors monitor and regulate pressure and temperature in products ranging from automobiles to air conditioning systems. **Corporate headquarters location:** This location. **Listed on:** New York Stock Exchange. **Stock exchange symbol:** TXN. **Number of employees worldwide:** 34,000.

TRILOGY DEVELOPMENT GROUP

5001 Plaza on the Lake, Austin TX 78746. 512/874-3100. **Contact:** Joseph Oiemandt, CEO. **World Wide Web address:** http://www.trilogy.com. **Description:** A developer of configuration software for a variety of industries including automotive, utilities, insurance, shipping, and computers. **Positions advertised include:** Software Developer; Technical Consultant; Application Developer; Configuration Expert; Software Development Manager; Business Development Associate.

UNISYS CORPORATION

13105 NW Freeway, Suite 825, Houston TX 77040. 713/744-2666. **Contact:** Human Resources. **World Wide Web address:** http://www.unisys.com. **Description:** Unisys Corporation provides information services, technology, and software. The company's Enabling Software Team creates a variety of software projects that facilitate the building of user applications and the management of distributed systems. The company's Platforms Group is responsible for UNIX Operating Systems running across multiple processor server platforms including all peripheral and communication drivers. The Unisys Commercial Parallel Processing Team develops microkernel-based operating systems, I/O device drivers, ATM hardware, diagnostics, and system architectures. The System Management Group is in charge of the overall management of development programs for UNIX desktop and entry-server products. **Positions advertised include:** IT Manager; Business Relationship Manager; Reception/Help Desk Supervisor. **Office hours:** Monday - Friday, 8:00 a.m. - 5:00 p.m. **Corporate headquarters location:** Blue Bell PA. **Other U.S. locations:** Nationwide. **Operations at this facility include:** This location manufactures and sells computers.

UNIVERSAL COMPUTER SYSTEMS, INC. (UCS)
DEALER COMPUTER SYSTEMS, INC. (DCS)

6700 Hollister, Houston TX 77040. 713/718-1800. **Toll-free phone:** 800/883-3031. **Contact:** Human Resources Department. **World Wide Web address:** http://www.universalcomputersys.com. **Description:** Supplies computer software and hardware systems specifically designed for the business of automobile dealerships. **NOTE:** Entry-level positions, part-time jobs, and second and third shifts are offered. **Positions advertised include:** Marketing Assistant; Data Entry Clerk; File Clerk; Recruiting Assistant; Maintenance Assistant; Pressman Trainee; Bilingual Software Education Trainee; Technical Writer; Windows Developer. **Special programs:**

Internships; Co-ops. **Corporate headquarters location:** This location. **Other U.S. locations:** Southfield MI; College Station TX. **International locations:** Worldwide. **Listed on:** Privately held. **Number of employees nationwide:** 2,600.

WELCOM SOFTWARE TECHNOLOGY
15990 North Barkers Landing, Suite 350, Houston TX 77079. 281/558-0514. **Fax:** 281/584-7828. **Contact:** Human Resources. **E-mail address:** personnel@welcom.com. **World Wide Web address:** http://www.welcom.com. **Description:** Designs, develops, and markets project- and cost-management software. Founded in 1984. **NOTE:** Entry-level positions are offered. **Positions advertised include:** Earned Value and Project Management Consultant; Software Quality Test Engineer; Technical Consultant. **Special programs:** Internships; Training; Summer Jobs. **Office hours:** Monday - Friday, 8:00 a.m. - 5:00 p.m. **Corporate headquarters location:** This location.

EDUCATIONAL SERVICES

You can expect to find the following types of facilities in this chapter:
Business/Secretarial/Data Processing Schools •
Colleges/Universities/Professional Schools • Community Colleges/Technical
Schools/Vocational Schools • Elementary and Secondary Schools •
Preschool and Child Daycare Services

AUSTIN COMMUNITY COLLEGE
5930 Middle Fiskville Road, Austin TX 78752. 512/223-7000. **Contact:** Human Resources. **World Wide Web address:** http://www.austin.cc.tx.us. **Description:** A two-year community college.

DALLAS COUNTY COMMUNITY COLLEGE DISTRICT
1402 Corinth Street, Dallas TX 75215. **Contact:** Human Resources. **World Wide Web address:** http://www.dcccd.edu. **Description:** A community college district. **Positions advertised include:** Director of Human Resources; Accounting Professor; Music Instructor; Administrative Assistant; Admissions Specialist; Tutor Coordinator. **Corporate headquarters location:** This location. **Operations at this facility include:** Administration; Research and Development.

GALVESTON COLLEGE
4015 Avenue Q, Galveston TX 77550-7496. 409/763-6551. **Fax:** 409/762-0973. **Contact:** Human Resources. **E-mail address:** hrmail@gc.edu. **World Wide Web address:** http://www.gc.edu. **Description:** A community college with an enrollment of 2,500. **Positions advertised include:** Director of Accounting Services.

GIDDINGS STATE SCHOOL
P.O. Box 600, Giddings TX 78942. 979/542-3686x214. **Fax:** 979/542-0177. **Contact:** Human Resources. **World Wide Web address:** http://www.tyc.state.tx.us. **Description:** A government-run school and home for juvenile offenders. **NOTE:** Jobseekers must obtain an application from the state employment agency and submit it along with a resume. **Parent company:** Texas Youth Commission.

HUMBLE INDEPENDENT SCHOOL DISTRICT
P.O. Box 2000, Humble TX 77346. 281/540-5000. **Contact:** Human Resources. **World Wide Web address:** http://www.humble.k12.tx.us. **Description:** Offices for the Humble school district, which comprises fifteen elementary schools, six middle schools, and five high schools.

Positions advertised include: Bilingual Education Teacher; Certified Librarian; Pathologist; Summer School Assistant Principal.

LAMAR UNIVERSITY
P.O. Box 11127, Beaumont TX 77710. 409/880-8375. **Contact:** Human Resources. **World Wide Web address:** http://www.lamar. edu. **Description:** A university offering associate's, bachelor's, master's, and doctoral degrees. Both two- and four-year programs are available. Approximately 7,300 undergraduate and 700 graduate students attend Lamar University. **Corporate headquarters location:** This location.

LAREDO COMMUNITY COLLEGE
West End Washington Street, Laredo TX 78040. 956/722-0521. **Contact:** Human Resources. **World Wide Web address:** http:// www.laredo.cc.tx.us. **Description:** Offers a variety of associate's degrees in programs including business, computers, electronics, and nursing. Approximately 6,900 students attend the college. Founded in 1947. **Positions advertised include:** Catalog Librarian; History Instructor; Reading Instructor; Grant Developer.

RICE UNIVERSITY
Mail Stop 56, P.O. Box 1892, Houston TX 77252-1892. 713/348-4074. **Fax:** 713/348-5496. **Recorded jobline:** 713/348-6080. **Contact:** Employment Coordinator. **World Wide Web address:** http://employment.rice.edu. **Description:** An independent, co-educational, private university for undergraduate and graduate studies, research, and professional training in selected disciplines. Rice University has an undergraduate student enrollment of approximately 2,700; a graduate and professional student enrollment of approximately 1,400. **Positions advertised include:** Accounting assistant; Executive Assistant; Summer School/Education Certification Program Coordinator; Network Architect; Research Technician; Chemistry Department Administrator. **Office hours:** Monday - Friday, 8:00 a.m. - 5:00 p.m.

ST. EDWARD'S UNIVERSITY
Campus Mailbox 1042, 3001 South Congress Avenue, Austin TX 78748. 512/448-8587. **Fax:** 512/464-8813. **Recorded jobline:** 512/448-8541. **Contact:** Human Resources. **World Wide Web address:** http://www.stedwards.edu/humr/jobs.htm. **Description:** A private university affiliated with the Catholic Church. St. Edward's University offers a liberal arts program to undergraduate and

graduate students interested in business or human services. **Positions advertised include:** Assistant Marketing Professor; Systems Librarian; Vice President of Enrollment Management; Senior Secretary; Assistant Women's Basketball Coach; Resident Aide; Fitness and Recreation Specialist; Teacher's Aide; Teacher. **Corporate headquarters location:** This location. **Operations at this facility include:** Administration. **Listed on:** Privately held.

ST. MARY'S UNIVERSITY
One Camino Santa Maria, San Antonio TX 78228-8565. 210/436-3725. **Fax:** 210/431-2223. **Contact:** Director of Human Resources. **World Wide Web address:** http://www.stmarytx.edu. **Description:** A liberal arts university affiliated with the Catholic Church. St. Mary's University has three undergraduate programs and two graduate programs including a law school. The school is one of the oldest and largest Catholic universities in the Southwest. Founded in 1852. **Special programs:** Internships. **Corporate headquarters location:** This location. **Operations at this facility include:** Administration; Research and Development; Service. **Listed on:** Privately held.

SAM HOUSTON STATE UNIVERSITY
P.O. Box 2356, Huntsville TX 77341. 936/294-1111. **Contact:** Human Resources. **World Wide Web address:** http://www.shsu.edu. **Description:** A four-year state university offering programs through its four colleges: Arts & Sciences, Business Administration, Criminal Justice, and Educational and Applied Sciences.

SAN JACINTO COLLEGE DISTRICT
4624 Fairmont Parkway, Suite 106, Pasadena TX 77504. 281/998-6115. **Contact:** Personnel Director. **World Wide Web address:** http://www.sjcd.cc.tx.us. **Description:** This location houses the administrative offices for the community college. Campuses are located in Pasadena and Houston.

SOUTH TEXAS COLLEGE OF LAW
1303 San Jacinto Street, Houston TX 77002-7000. 713/646-1812. **Fax:** 713/646-1833. **Contact:** Margaret Kautz, Director of Human Resources. **World Wide Web address:** http://www.stcl.edu. **Description:** A private law school with an enrollment of approximately 1,250 students. Founded in 1923. **Positions advertised include:** Vice President of Information Technology. **Corporate headquarters location:** This location. **Operations at this facility include:** Administration. **Listed on:** Privately held.

STEPHEN F. AUSTIN STATE UNIVERSITY
P.O. Box 13039, Nacogdoches TX 75962. 936/468-2304. **Contact:** Human Resources. **World Wide Web address:** http://www.sfasu.edu. **Description:** A four-year college offering bachelor's and master's degrees.

SYLVAN LEARNING CENTER
4356 Dowlen Road, Beaumont TX 77706. 409/899-9798. **Recorded jobline:** 877/SYL-VAN6. **Contact:** Personnel. **World Wide Web address:** http://www.sylvan.net. **Description:** Provides educational instruction and tutoring through reading and math programs, study skills courses, SAT/ACT prep classes, and homework support. **Positions advertised include:** Adult Learning Instructor. **Other U.S. locations:** Nationwide. **Parent company:** Sylvan Learning Systems provides educational services and programs to families, schools, and industries.

TEXAS A&M UNIVERSITY
809 East University Drive, Suite 101A, College Station TX 77843-1475. 979/845-5154. **Contact:** Office of Human Resources. **World Wide Web address:** http://www.hr.tamu.edu. **Description:** A university that offers a wide range of bachelor's, master's, doctoral and professional programs. Texas A&M also provides continuing education programs that serve the needs of area businesses and professionals. **Positions advertised include:** Accountant; Administrative Assistant; Analytical Chemist; Assistant Research Scientist; Business Coordinator; Custodial Worker; Mechanical Equipment Foreman. **Corporate headquarters location:** This location.

TEXAS A&M UNIVERSITY
6300 Ocean Drive, USC Services, Room 121, Corpus Christi TX 78411. 361/825-2630. **Fax:** 361/825-5871. **Contact:** Debra Cortinas, Director of Human Resources. **World Wide Web address:** http://www.tamucc.edu. **Description:** A university that offers a wide range of undergraduate degree programs, master's degree programs, and doctoral and professional programs. The university also provides continuing education programs that serve the needs of area businesses and professionals. **Positions advertised include:** Cadet Training Officer; Custodial Worker; Early Childhood Lead Teacher; Engineering Technician. **Corporate headquarters location:** College Station TX. **Operations at this facility include:** Administration;

Education; Research and Development. **Number of employees at this location:** 600.

TEXAS A&M UNIVERSITY

Campus Box 105, Kingsville TX 78363. 361/593-2111. **Contact:** Human Resources. **World Wide Web address:** http://www.tamu.edu. **Description:** A university that offers a wide range of undergraduate degree programs, master's degree programs, and doctoral and professional programs. **Positions advertised include:** Accountant; Administrative Assistant; Analytical Chemist; Assistant Research Scientist; Business Coordinator; Custodial Worker; Mechanical Equipment Foreman. **Corporate headquarters location:** College Station TX.

TEXAS CHIROPRACTIC COLLEGE

5912 Spencer Highway, Pasadena TX 77505. 281/998-6003. **Toll-free phone:** 800/468-6839. **Fax:** 281/991-5237. **Contact:** Director of Human Resources. **World Wide Web address:** http://www.txchiro.edu. **Description:** Offers Doctor of Chiropractic and Bachelor of Science in Human Biology degrees.

TEXAS HIGHER EDUCATION COORDINATING BOARD

P.O. Box 12788, Austin TX 78711-2788. 512/427-6100. **Recorded jobline:** 512/427-6574. **Contact:** Betty Sharp, Personnel Director. **World Wide Web address:** http://www.thecb.state.tx.us. **Description:** A governmental board that regulates educational issues in Texas.

TEXAS SOUTHERN UNIVERSITY

3100 Cleburne Avenue, Houston TX 77004. 713/313-7011. **Contact:** Personnel Director. **World Wide Web address:** http://www.tsu.edu. **Description:** A four-year university offering both undergraduate and graduate degree programs.

TRINITY UNIVERSITY

715 Stadium Drive, San Antonio TX 78212. 210/999-7011. **Contact:** Human Resources. **E-mail address:** hr@trinity.edu. **World Wide Web address:** http://www.trinity.edu. **Description:** A four-year college with majors including education, biology, communications, business administration, and engineering. The current enrollment is approximately 2,400. Founded in 1869.

UNIVERSITY OF HOUSTON/DOWNTOWN
One Main Street, Suite 9105 South, Houston TX 77002. 713/221-8427. **Contact:** Human Resources. **World Wide Web address:** http://www.dt.uh.edu. **Description:** One of four campuses within the University of Houston system.

UNIVERSITY OF HOUSTON/UNIVERSITY PARK
4800 Calhoun, Houston TX 77204. 713/743-5770. **Contact:** Human Resources. **World Wide Web address:** http://www.uh.edu. **Description:** The main campus of the University of Houston. **Special programs:** Internships. **Operations at this facility include:** Accounting/Auditing; Research and Development; Service.

UNIVERSITY OF ST. THOMAS
3800 Montrose Boulevard, Houston TX 77006. 713/522-7911. **Fax:** 713/525-3896. **Contact:** Personnel. **World Wide Web address:** http://www.stthom.edu. **Description:** A liberal arts university affiliated with the Catholic Church. The university has an enrollment of 2,700 students. **NOTE:** Entry-level positions and part-time jobs are offered. **Positions advertised include:** Dean of Scholarship and Financial Aide; Registrar; Administrative Assistant; Assistant English Professor. **Corporate headquarters location:** This location.

UNIVERSITY OF TEXAS AT AUSTIN
University of Texas at Austin, Austin TX 78712. 512/471-1795. **Contact:** Human Resources. **World Wide Web address:** http://www.utexas.edu. **Description:** One location of the state university. **Positions advertised include:** Postdoctoral Fellow; Associate Director for Development; Associate Director of Recreational Sports; Engineering Services Manager; Program Manager. **Operations at this facility include:** Administration; Research and Development; Service.

UNIVERSITY OF TEXAS AT BROWNSVILLE
80 Fort Brown Street, Brownsville TX 78520. 956/544-8200. **Fax:** 956/982-0175. **Contact:** Human Resources. **World Wide Web address:** http://www.utb.edu. **Description:** University of Texas at Brownsville and Texas Southmost College are partner institutions offering the following programs of study: College of Liberal Arts, College of Science, Mathematics & Technology, School of Business, School of Education, and School of Health Sciences. Founded in 1973. **Positions advertised include:** Accounting Clerk; Accounting Group Supervisor; Central Store Clerk; Chess Coach; Child Care

Specialist; Counselor; Dean of Graduate Studies; Groundskeeper; Security Guard; Learning Instructional Specialist; Maintenance Worker; Police Cadet.

UNIVERSITY OF TEXAS MEDICAL BRANCH
4700 Broadway, Galveston TX 77551. 409/747-7960. **Fax:** 409/772-0728. **Contact:** Employment Office. **World Wide Web address:** http://www.hr.utmb.edu. **Description:** Educates health professionals and offers extensive medical services through a network of hospitals and health clinics. Founded in 1891. **Positions advertised include:** Assistant Instructor; Audiologist; Psychological Associate; Assistant Nurse Manager; Animal Attendant; Administrative Secretary.

UNIVERSITY OF TEXAS-PAN AMERICAN
1201 West University Drive, Edinburg TX 78539. 956/381-2511. **Fax:** 956/381-2340. **Recorded jobline:** 956/381-2551. **Contact:** Human Resources. **World Wide Web address:** http://www.panam.edu. **Description:** One location of the state university. **Positions advertised include:** Orientation Coordinator; Business/Economic Research Assistant; Coordinator of Student Development; Library Clerk; Duplicating Equipment Operator; Staff Nurse; Student Development Specialist. **Office hours:** Monday - Friday, 8:00 a.m. - 5:00 p.m. **Corporate headquarters location:** Austin TX. **Operations at this facility include:** Administration; Service.

UNIVERSITY OF THE INCARNATE WORD
4301 Broadway Street, Box 320, San Antonio TX 78209. 210/829-6019. **Contact:** Human Resources. **World Wide Web address:** http://www.uiw.edu. **Description:** A Catholic, co-educational, four-year university offering liberal arts and professional studies. The university offers such majors as fine arts, nursing, preprofessional studies, business, and education. The enrollment for the college is approximately 3,000 undergraduate and graduate students. Founded in 1881.

WINDHAM SCHOOL DISTRICT
P.O. Box 40, Huntsville TX 77342-0040. 936/291-5321. **Fax:** 936/291-4622. **Contact:** Minnie Madison, Personnel Officer for Applications. **E-mail address:** personnel@wsdtx.org. **World Wide Web address:** http://www.windhamschooldistrict.org. **Description:** Responsible for correctional education for the Texas Department of Criminal Justice. **NOTE:** Windham School District is governed by the Texas Education Agency and hires only certified teachers and

administrators, some positions requiring a degree, and clerical positions. **Operations at this facility include:** Administration; Regional Headquarters.

ELECTRONIC/INDUSTRIAL ELECTRICAL EQUIPMENT

You can expect to find the following types of companies in this chapter:
Electronic Machines and Systems • Semiconductor Manufacturers

ADVANCED MICRO DEVICES, INC. (AMD)
5204 East Ben White Boulevard, Mail Stop 556, Austin TX 78741. 512/385-8542. **Contact:** Employment. **World Wide Web address:** http://www.amd.com. **Description:** Designs, develops, manufactures, and markets complex, monolithic integrated circuits for use by electronic equipment and systems manufacturers, primarily in instrument applications and products for computation and communication. **Positions advertised include:** Software Engineer; Group Controller; Sales Representative; Senior Design Engineer; Senior Architect; Senior Programmer/Analyst. **Corporate headquarters location:** Sunnyvale CA. **International locations:** Worldwide. **Operations at this facility include:** This location manufactures semiconductors. **Listed on:** New York Stock Exchange. **Stock exchange symbol:** ASD. **Number of employees nationwide:** 14,000.

AVNET ELECTRONICS MARKETING
7433 Harwin Drive, Houston TX 77036. 800/408-8353. **Contact:** Human Resources. **World Wide Web address:** http://www.em.avnet.com. **Description:** Distributes electronic parts and equipment including connectors, printers, and semiconductors.

AVNET, INC.
1321 Rutherford Lane, Suite 200, Austin TX 78753. 512/835-1152. **Contact:** Human Resources. **World Wide Web address:** http://www.avnet.com. **Description:** Avnet is the world's largest distributor of semiconductors, interconnect, passive, and electromechanical components, computer products, and embedded systems from leading manufacturers. **Corporate headquarters location:** Phoenix AZ. **Other U.S. locations:** Nationwide. **Listed on:** New York Stock Exchange. **Stock exchange symbol:** AVT.

BENCHMARK ELECTRONICS, INC.
3000 Technology Drive, Angleton TX 77515. 979/849-6550. **Contact:** Human Resources. **World Wide Web address:** http://www.bench.com. **Description:** Assembles printed circuit boards for original equipment manufacturers. **Corporate headquarters location:**

This location. **Listed on:** New York Stock Exchange. **Stock exchange symbol:** BHE.

COOPER INDUSTRIES INC.
P.O. Box 4446, Houston TX 77210. 713/209-8400. **Contact:** Brad Davison, Manager of Training. **World Wide Web address:** http://www.cooperindustries.com. **Description:** Cooper Industries is a *Fortune* 500 company engaged in tools and hardware manufacturing and electrical and electronic products manufacturing. **Positions advertised include:** Senior Legal Secretary. **Corporate headquarters location:** This location. **Listed on:** New York Stock Exchange. **Stock exchange symbol:** CBE. **Number of employees nationwide:** 30,500.

ELECTROTEX INC.
P.O. Box 981149, Houston TX 77098-8149. 713/526-3456. **Physical address:** 2300 Richmond Avenue, Houston TX 77098. **Contact:** Human Resources. **World Wide Web address:** http://www.electrotex.com. **Description:** Distributes electrical components used in televisions, VCRs, and computers.

HISCO, INC.
8330 Cross Park Drive, Austin TX 78754. 512/834-9773. **Fax:** 512/834-8583. **Contact:** Jackie Moras, Office Manager. **E-mail address:** hr@hisonic.com. **World Wide Web address:** http://www.hiscoinc.com. **Description:** A distributor for the electronics industry. Hisco's clients include IBM, Motorola, and Compaq. Founded in 1970. **Corporate headquarters location:** Houston TX. **Other U.S. locations:** Nationwide. **Listed on:** Privately held.

IEC EDINBURG TEXAS
1920 Industrial Park Drive, Edinburg TX 78539. 956/380-8700. **Fax:** 956/318-1028. **Contact:** Human Resources Manager. **World Wide Web address:** http://www.iec-electronics.com. **Description:** A contract electrical manufacturing firm that manufactures printed circuit board (PCB) assemblies for computers, telecommunications, medical, and industrial equipment companies. **NOTE:** Second and third shifts are offered. **Special programs:** Training. **Corporate headquarters location:** Newark NY. **Parent company:** IEC Electronics Corp. **Listed on:** NASDAQ. **Stock exchange symbol:** IECE.

INTEGRATED ELECTRICAL SERVICES INC.
1800 West Loop South, Suite 500, Houston TX 77027-9408. 713/860-1500. **Toll-free phone:** 800/696-1044. **Fax:** 713/860-1599. **Contact:** Margie Harris, Vice President of Human Resources. **World Wide Web address:** http://www.ielectric.com. **Description:** An electrical contractor providing construction and maintenance services to a variety of business segments. The company's services include design and installation work for new and renovation projects, preventative maintenance, and emergency repair work. **Company slogan:** The power of partnership. **Corporate headquarters location:** This location. **Other U.S. locations:** Nationwide. **Listed on:** New York Stock Exchange. **Stock exchange symbol:** IEE. **Number of employees nationwide:** 15,000.

KASPER WIRE WORKS INC.
P.O. Box 667, Shiner TX 77984-0667. 361/594-3327. **Contact:** Human Resources. **World Wide Web address:** http://www.kwire. com. **Description:** A manufacturer of newspaper vending machines.

LSI SPECIALTY ELECTRICAL PRODUCTS
1231 Shadowdale, Houston TX 77043. 713/464-1393. **Fax:** 713/464-7731. **Contact:** Human Resources. **World Wide Web address:** http://www.lsispecialty.com. **Description:** Distributes electrical products used in hazardous areas and harsh environments. **Corporate headquarters location:** This location. **Other U.S. locations:** Lafayette LA; Oklahoma City OK. **Operations at this facility include:** Administration; Sales.

MOTOROLA, INC.
6501 William Cannon Drive West, Austin TX 78735. 512/895-2000. **Contact:** Human Resources. **World Wide Web address:** http://www.mot.com. **Description:** Motorola manufactures communications equipment and electronic products including car radios, cellular phones, semiconductors, computer systems, cellular infrastructure equipment, pagers, cordless phones, and LAN systems. **Corporate headquarters location:** Schaumburg IL. **Other U.S. locations:** Nationwide. **International locations:** Worldwide. **Operations at this facility include:** This location is engaged in cellular communications. **Listed on:** New York Stock Exchange. **Stock exchange symbol:** MOT. **Number of employees worldwide:** 111,000.

NATIONAL ELECTRIC COIL

3330 East 14th Street, Brownsville TX 78521. 956/541-1759. **Fax:** 956/982-7525. **Contact:** Edward K. Rice, Human Resources Manager. **World Wide Web address:** http://www.national-electric-coil.com. **Description:** Manufactures and installs high-voltage generator windings. **Corporate headquarters location:** Nashville TN. **Operations at this facility include:** Administration; Manufacturing; Sales; Service. **Number of employees nationwide:** 850.

RELIABILITY INC.

P.O. Box 218370, Houston TX 77218. 281/492-0550. **Fax:** 281/492-0615. **Contact:** Human Resources. **World Wide Web address:** http://www.relinc.com. **Description:** Engaged in the testing of electronic components. **Office hours:** Monday - Thursday, 7:00 a.m. - 5:00 p.m.; Friday, 7:00 a.m. - 11:00 a.m. **Corporate headquarters location:** This location. **Operations at this facility include:** Manufacturing; Research and Development; Sales; Service. **Listed on:** NASDAQ. **Stock exchange symbol:** REAL.

SILICON HILLS DESIGN, INC.

9101 Burnet Road, Suite 107, Austin TX 78758. 512/836-1088. **Contact:** Harold Tantaze, President. **World Wide Web address:** http://www.siliconhills.com. **Description:** Designs printed circuit boards for computers as well as for the space and satellite markets.

SUNTRON CORPORATION

1111 Gillingham Lane, Sugar Land TX 77478. 281/243-5000. **Fax:** 281/243-5107. **Contact:** Human Resources. **World Wide Web address:** http://www.suntroncorp.com. **Description:** A global provider of vertically integrated electronics manufacturing services supplying high mix solutions for aerospace, industrial controls and instrumentation, medical, semiconductor, networking and telecommunications industries. **Corporate headquarters location:** Phoenix AZ. **Listed on:** NASDAQ. **Stock exchange symbol:** SUNT.

WEATHERFORD INTERNATIONAL, INC.

P.O. Box 27608, Houston TX 77227. 713/693-4000. **Physical address:** 515 Post Oak Boulevard, Suite 200, Houston TX 77027. **Contact:** Human Resources. **World Wide Web address:** http://www.weatherford.com. **Description:** Manufactures and services oil field equipment.

ENVIRONMENTAL AND WASTE MANAGEMENT SERVICES

You can expect to find the following types of companies in this chapter:
Environmental Engineering Firms • Sanitary Services

ALLIED WASTE INDUSTRIES
8101 Little York, Houston TX 77016. 713/635-6666. **Contact:** Human Resources. **World Wide Web address:** http://www.alliedwaste.com. **Description:** Engaged primarily in the collection and disposal of solid waste for commercial, industrial, and residential customers. Services provided include landfill services, waste-to-energy programs, hazardous waste removal, and liquid waste removal. The company has worldwide operations at more than 500 facilities. **Corporate headquarters location:** Scottsdale AZ. **Other U.S. locations:** Nationwide. **Listed on:** New York Stock Exchange. **Stock exchange symbol:** AW.

ALLIED WASTE INDUSTRIES
757 North Eldridge, Houston TX 77079. 281/870-8100. **Contact:** Human Resources. **World Wide Web address:** http://www.alliedwaste.com. **Description:** Engaged in the collection and disposal of solid waste for commercial, industrial, and residential customers. Services provided include landfill services, waste-to-energy programs, hazardous waste removal, and liquid waste removal. **Corporate headquarters location:** Scottsdale AZ. **Other U.S. locations:** Nationwide. **Listed on:** New York Stock Exchange. **Stock exchange symbol:** AW.

ALLIED WASTE INDUSTRIES
11315 West Little York, Building Two, Houston TX 77041. 713/937-9955. **Contact:** Human Resources. **World Wide Web address:** http://www.alliedwaste.com. **Description:** Engaged in the collection and disposal of solid waste for commercial, industrial, and residential customers. Services provided include landfill services, waste-to-energy programs, hazardous waste removal, and liquid waste removal. **Corporate headquarters location:** Scottsdale AZ. **Other U.S. locations:** Nationwide. **Listed on:** New York Stock Exchange. **Stock exchange symbol:** AW.

ASHBROOK CORPORATION
11600 East Hardy Road, Houston TX 77093. 281/449-0322. **Contact:** Human Resources. **World Wide Web address:** http://

www.ashbrookcorp.com. **Description:** Manufactures wastewater treatment equipment and dewatering devices for sanitation plants.

ENSR INC.
3000 Richmond Avenue, Suite 400, Houston TX 77098. 713/520-9900. **Contact:** Human Resources. **World Wide Web address:** http://www.ensr.com. **Description:** Offers comprehensive environmental services including consulting, engineering, and remediation. **Positions advertised include:** Client Service Center Manager; Staff Geologist.

NATIONAL MARINE FISHERIES SERVICE
4700 Avenue U, Galveston TX 77551. 409/766-3500. **Contact:** Human Resources. **World Wide Web address:** http://galveston.ssp.nmfs.gov/galv. **Description:** A laboratory that researches the management processes of commercial and recreational shellfish and works to protect coastal habitats. **NOTE:** Applicants are asked to forward resumes, college transcripts, and a list of references. **Special programs:** Internships.

ONYX ENVIRONMENTAL
1800 South Highway 146, Baytown TX 77520. 281/427-4099. **Contact:** Human Resources. **World Wide Web address:** http://www.onyxes.com. **Description:** A provider of comprehensive waste management services, as well as engineering and construction, industrial, and related services, with operations in 19 countries. **Other U.S. locations:** Nationwide.

SEVERN TRENT LABORATORIES, INC.
14046 Summit Drive, Suite 111, Austin TX 78728. 512/244-0855. **Fax:** 512/244-0160. **Contact:** Human Resources. **World Wide Web address:** http://www.stl-inc.com. **Description:** Provides a complete range of environmental testing services to private industry, engineering consultants, and government agencies in support of federal and state environmental regulations. The company also possesses analytical capabilities in the fields of air toxins, field analytical services, radiochemistry/mixed waste, and advanced technology.

TANKNOLOGY-NDE INTERNATIONAL, INC.
8900 Shoal Creek Boulevard, Building 200, Austin TX 78757. 512/451-6334. **Contact:** Human Resources Department. **E-mail address:** thebestjobsare@tankology.com. **World Wide Web address:**

http://www.tanknde.com. **Description:** Through its subsidiaries, Tanknology-NDE provides environmental compliance, information, and management services to owners and operators of underground storage tanks. The company has three principal lines of business: domestic underground storage tank testing; domestic tank management; and international underground storage tank testing. The company's primary service is tank tightness testing, tank integrity testing, or precision testing. This service involves testing underground storage tanks and associated piping to determine if they are leaking. **Positions advertised include:** Associate Technician; Technician; Corrosion Technician.

TEAM INDUSTRIAL SERVICES, INC.

P.O. Box 123, Alvin TX 77512. 281/331-6154. **Contact:** Human Resources. **World Wide Web address:** http://www.teamindustrialservices.com. **Description:** Provides a wide variety of environmental services for industrial corporations including consulting, engineering, monitoring, and leak repair. Founded in 1973. **Positions advertised include:** Driver; Machinist; Welder. **Corporate headquarters location:** This location. **Other U.S. locations:** Nationwide. **International locations:** Worldwide. **Listed on:** American Stock Exchange. **Stock exchange symbol:** TMI. **Number of employees worldwide:** 800.

UNITED WASTE SERVICE CENTER

1300A Bay Area Boulevard, Houston TX 77058. 281/282-6000. **Contact:** Human Resources. **Description:** United Waste Service Center provides integrated solid waste management services to commercial, industrial, and residential customers. These services include nonhazardous landfill operations, waste collection services, waste reuse and reduction programs (such as composting and recycling), and related environmental services. Fourteen nonhazardous landfill locations are currently in operation, as well as 11 waste collection companies serving over 215,000 customers and operating 16 waste transfer stations. United Waste Service Center also owns and operates several facilities with waste reuse and reduction programs including four composting facilities. **Corporate headquarters location:** This location. **Other U.S. locations:** KY; MA; MI; MS; PA.

VERITAS D.G.C.

10300 Town Park Drive, Houston TX 77072. 832/351-8300. **Contact:** Human Resources. **World Wide Web address:** http://

www.veritasdgc.com. **Description:** Engaged in land and marine seismic surveying, as well as the processing of collected work.

WAID AND ASSOCIATES
14205 Burnet Road, Suite 600, Austin TX 78728. 512/255-9999. **Fax:** 512/255-8780. **Contact:** Human Resources. **E-mail address:** waid@waid.com. **World Wide Web address:** http://www.waid.com. **Description:** An engineering and environmental services firm. The company specializes in air quality services for industrial clients, particularly involving emissions control; permitting and compliance. Waid and Associates also provides services in waste and wastewater management, environmental management, and environmental information systems. Founded in 1978. **NOTE:** Entry-level positions are offered. **Office hours:** Monday - Friday, 8:00 a.m. - 5:00 p.m. **Corporate headquarters location:** This location. **Parent company:** Waid Corporation. **Listed on:** Privately held.

WASTE MANAGEMENT, INC.
2175 West Cardinal Drive, Beaumont TX 77705. 409/842-0045. **Contact:** Human Resources. **World Wide Web address:** http://www.wm.com. **Description:** Engaged in residential and commercial refuse collection. **Corporate headquarters location:** Houston TX. **Other U.S. locations:** Nationwide. **Listed on:** New York Stock Exchange. **Stock exchange symbol:** WMI.

WASTE MANAGEMENT, INC.
P.O. Box 475, McGregor TX 76657. 800/234-7478. **Contact:** Human Resources. **World Wide Web address:** http://www.wm.com. **Description:** Engaged in residential and commercial refuse collection. **Corporate headquarters location:** Houston TX. **Other U.S. locations:** Nationwide. **Listed on:** New York Stock Exchange. **Stock exchange symbol:** WMI.

WASTE MANAGEMENT, INC.
1001 Fannin Street, Suite 4000, Houston TX 77002. 713/512-6200. **Contact:** Human Resources. **World Wide Web address:** http://www.wm.com. **Description:** An international provider of comprehensive waste management services as well as engineering, construction, industrial, and related service. **Positions advertised include:** Administrative Assistant; Senior Executive Assistant; Customer Service Representative; Financial Analyst; Human Resources Coordinator. **Corporate headquarters location:** This

location. **Other U.S. locations:** Nationwide. **Listed on:** New York Stock Exchange. **Stock exchange symbol:** WMI.

WASTE MANAGEMENT, INC.
P.O. Box 201450, San Antonio TX 78220. 210/224-4651. **Physical address:** 4730 SE Loop 410, San Antonio TX 78222. **Contact:** Human Resources. **World Wide Web address:** http://www.wm.com. **Description:** Engaged in residential and commercial refuse collection. **Positions advertised include:** Commercial Driver; Customer Service Representative; Heavy Equipment Operator; Vehicle Maintenance Technician; Welder. **Corporate headquarters location:** Houston TX. **Other U.S. locations:** Nationwide. **Listed on:** New York Stock Exchange. **Stock exchange symbol:** WMI.

WASTE MANAGEMENT, INC.
1901 Afton, Houston TX 77055. 713/686-6666. **Fax:** 713/957-6921. **Contact:** Human Resources. **World Wide Web address:** http:// www.wm.com. **Description:** Engaged in residential and commercial refuse collection. **Corporate headquarters location:** Houston TX. **Positions advertised include:** Commercial Driver; Customer Service Representative; Heavy Equipment Operator; Vehicle Maintenance Technician; Welder. **Office hours:** Monday - Friday, 8:00 a.m. - 5:00 p.m. **Other U.S. locations:** Nationwide. **Listed on:** New York Stock Exchange. **Stock exchange symbol:** WMI.

FABRICATED/PRIMARY METALS AND PRODUCTS

You can expect to find the following types of companies in this chapter:
Aluminum and Copper Foundries • Die-Castings • Iron and Steel Foundries • Steel Works, Blast Furnaces, and Rolling Mills

ALAMO IRON WORKS, INC.
P.O. Box 231, San Antonio TX 78219. 210/223-6161. **Physical address:** 943 Coliseum Road, San Antonio TX 78291. **Fax:** 210/704-8409. **Contact:** Vice President of Human Resources. **Recorded jobline:** 210/704-8491. **World Wide Web address:** http://www.aiwnet.com. **Description:** Distributes industrial supplies and operates a foundry and a steel service center. **Positions advertised include:** Welder; Mechanic; Sales Trainee; Counter Sales Representative; Material Handler. **Corporate headquarters location:** This location. **Operations at this facility include:** Administration; Manufacturing; Sales. **Listed on:** Privately held.

ALCOA (ALUMINUM COMPANY OF AMERICA)
P.O. Box 101, Point Comfort TX 77978. 361/987-2631. **Contact:** Helen Ross, Employment Supervisor. **World Wide Web address:** http://www.alcoa.com. **Description:** Engaged in all aspects of the aluminum industry including mining, refining, smelting, fabricating, and recycling. ALCOA also manufactures ceramic packaging for the semiconductor industry, alumina chemicals, plastic bottle closures, vinyl siding, packaging machinery, and electrical distribution systems for automobiles. **Special programs:** Internships. **Corporate headquarters location:** Pittsburgh PA. **International locations:** Worldwide. **Operations at this facility include:** Manufacturing. **Listed on:** New York Stock Exchange. **Stock exchange symbol:** AA. **Annual sales/revenues:** More than $22 billion. **Number of employees worldwide:** 129,000.

AMFELS, INC.
P.O. Box 3107, Brownsville TX 78523. 956/831-8220. **Physical address:** 20000 South Highway 48, Brownsville TX 75821. **Contact:** Norma Bennett, Human Resources. **World Wide Web address:** http://www.amfels.com. **Description:** A shipyard that fabricates steel.

DOT METAL PRODUCTS
18757 Bracken Drive, San Antonio TX 78266. 210/651-6331. **Contact:** Office Manager. **World Wide Web address:** http://

www.gibraltar1.com. **Description:** Manufactures a variety of metal products including metal edging. **Parent company:** Gibraltar. **Listed on:** NASDAQ. **Stock exchange symbol:** ROCK.

FRIEDMAN INDUSTRIES, INC.

4001 Homestead Road, Houston TX 77028. 713/672-9433. **Contact:** Human Resources Manager. **World Wide Web address:** http://www.friedmanindustries.com. **Description:** Engaged in the steel processing and distribution business. The company has two product classifications: hot-rolled steel sheet and plate, and tubular products. At its facilities in Lone Star TX, Houston TX, and Hickman AK, the company processes semifinished, hot-rolled steel coils into flat, finished sheet and plate, and sells these products on a wholesale, rapid-delivery basis in competition with steel mills, importers, and steel service centers. The company also processes customer-owned coils on a fee basis. Products and services are sold principally to steel distributors and to customers fabricating steel products such as storage tanks, steel buildings, farm machinery and equipment, construction equipment, transportation equipment, conveyors, and other similar products. The company, through its Texas Tubular Products operation (Lone Star TX), also markets and processes pipe.

LUFKIN INDUSTRIES, INC.

P.O. Box 849, Lufkin TX 75902. 936/634-2211. **Contact:** Viron Barbay. **E-mail address:** vbarbay@Lufkin.com. **World Wide Web address:** http://www.lufkin.com. **Description:** Designs and fabricates gears for power transmission products; iron castings; oil field pumps; and platforms and dump trailers for the over-the-road transportation industry. **Positions advertised include:** Accountant; CNC Machine Operator; Electrician; Electronics Technician; Maintenance Mechanic; Manufacturing Engineer; Welder. **Corporate headquarters location:** This location. **Listed on:** NASDAQ. **Stock exchange symbol:** LUFK.

MMI PRODUCTS, INC.

515 West Greens Road, Suite 710, Houston TX 77067. 281/876-0080. **Contact:** Human Resources. **World Wide Web address:** http://www.merchantsmetals.com. **Description:** A manufacturer and distributor of wire and fabricated steel.

MAXXAM INC.
KAISER ALUMINUM CORPORATION
5847 San Felipe, Suite 2600, Houston TX 77057. 713/975-7600. **Contact:** Human Resources. **World Wide Web address:** http://www.kaiseral.com. **Description:** A diversified holding company. Kaiser Aluminum Corporation (also at this location, 713/267-3777) manufactures aluminum and related products for the transportation, can-making, and aerospace markets. **Corporate headquarters location:** This location. **Subsidiaries include:** Pacific Lumber Company produces lumber and owns or operates 187,000 acres of forestland in California; Maxxam Property Company develops resorts, single- and multiple-family homes, and has large land holdings.

METALS USA , INC.
2900 Patio Drive, Houston TX 77017. 713/946-9000. **Toll-free phone:** 800/231-4009. **Contact:** Human Resources. **World Wide Web address:** http://www.metalsusa.com. **Description:** Manufactures aluminum. Founded in 1954. **Corporate headquarters location:** This location.

PARKVIEW METAL PRODUCTS INC.
400 Barnes Drive, San Marcos TX 78666. 512/754-0200. **Contact:** Human Resources. **World Wide Web address:** http://www.parkviewmetal.com. **Description:** A manufacturer of metal stamping and metal parts for computers, radios, and VCRs.

QUANEX CORPORATION
1900 West Loop South, Suite 1500, Houston TX 77027. 713/961-4600. **Contact:** Human Resources. **World Wide Web address:** http://www.quanex.com. **Description:** Engaged in the manufacture of carbon-alloy steel pipes, bars, and tubing. Quanex also manufactures aluminum products for the home improvement, commercial construction, and lawn and garden industries. **Listed on:** New York Stock Exchange. **Stock exchange symbol:** NX.

SAFETY STEEL SERVICE INC.
P.O. Box 2298, Victoria TX 77902. 361/575-4561. **Contact:** Human Resources. **Description:** Provides a variety of services for the steel industry including manufacturing rebar and structural pipes.

TEX-TUBE COMPANY
1503 North Post Oak, Houston TX 77055. 713/686-4351. **Fax:** 713/685-3222. **Contact:** Human Resources. **World Wide Web address:** http://www.tex-tube.com. **Description:** Manufactures steel pipe and tubular products. **Positions advertised include:** Janitor; Mill Helper; Toolwright; Crane Operator; Machinist; Inside Sales Representative; Outside Sales Representative. **Other U.S. locations:** MD; ME; OH. **Operations at this facility include:** Manufacturing; Sales. **Listed on:** Privately held.

TRINITY INDUSTRIES, INC.
P.O. Box 1579, Houston TX 77251-1579. 713/861-8181. **Contact:** Human Resources. **World Wide Web address:** http://www.trin.net. **Description:** Manufactures fabricated steel structures. **Positions advertised include:** Sales Management Trainee. **Listed on:** New York Stock Exchange. **Stock exchange symbol:** TRN.

VULCRAFT
P.O. Box 186, Grapeland TX 75844-0186. 936/687-4665. **Contact:** Human Resources. **World Wide Web address:** http://www.vulcraft. com. **Description:** Manufactures steel joists and steel decking. **Parent company:** Nucor Corporation is a steel and steel products manufacturer with mills in North and South Carolina, Nebraska, Texas, Utah, and Arizona. Products include hot-rolled and cold-finished steel shapes, girders, and beams.

FINANCIAL SERVICES

You can expect to find the following types of companies in this chapter:
Consumer Finance and Credit Agencies • Investment Specialists •
Mortgage Bankers and Loan Brokers •
Security and Commodity Brokers, Dealers, and Exchanges

AIM MANAGEMENT GROUP INC.
11 Greenway Plaza, Suite 100, Houston TX 77046. 713/626-1919.
Contact: Human Resources. **World Wide Web address:** http://
www.aiminvestments.com. **Description:** Manages mutual funds.
Listed on: Privately held.

AMERICAN EXPRESS FINANCIAL ADVISORS
9442 Capital of Texas Highway North, Plaza One Suite 800, Austin
TX 78759. 512/346-5400. **Fax:** 512/338-1705. **Contact:** Recruiting
Coordinator. **World Wide Web address:** http://www.
americanexpress.com/advisors. **Description:** Offers financial
planning, annuities, mutual funds, insurance, investment certificates,
and institutional investment advisory trust, tax preparation, and retail
securities brokerage services. **Positions advertised include:** Financial
Consultant. **Other U.S. locations:** Nationwide. **Parent company:**
American Express Company (New York NY).

AMERICAN PHYSICIANS SERVICE GROUP, INC. (APS)
1301 Capital of Texas Highway, Suite C-300, Austin TX 78746.
512/328-0888. **Fax:** 512/314-4398. **Contact:** Bill Hayes, Chief
Financial Officer. **World Wide Web address:** http://www.amph.com.
Description: A management and financial services firm with
subsidiaries and affiliates that provide medical malpractice insurance
services for doctors, brokerage and investment services to institutions
and individuals, lithotripsy services in 34 states, refractive vision
surgery, and dedicated care facilities for Alzheimer's patients.
Corporate headquarters location: This location. **Subsidiaries
include:** APS Asset Management, Inc.; APS Consulting, Inc.; APS
Facilities Management, Inc.; APS Financial Corporation; APS
Insurance Services, Inc.; APS Investment Services, Inc.; APS Realty,
Inc.; APSC, Inc.; APSFM, Inc.; American Physicians Insurance
Agency, Inc; Syntera Technologies, Inc. **Listed on:** NASDAQ. **Stock
exchange symbol:** AMPH.

CLARKE AMERICAN CHECKS, INC.

10931 Laureate Drive, San Antonio TX 78249. 210/697-8888. **Recorded jobline:** 210/690-6500. **Contact:** Human Resources. **World Wide Web address:** http://www.clarkeamerican.com. **Description:** A leading printer of checks and share drafts for the financial industry. Founded in 1874. **Special programs:** Internships. **Corporate headquarters location:** This location. **Other U.S. locations:** Nationwide. **Parent company:** Novar plc. **Operations at this facility include:** Regional Headquarters. **Listed on:** Privately held. **Number of employees nationwide:** 3,500.

FISERV, INC.

595 Orleans Street, Beaumont TX 77701. 409/839-0600. **Contact:** Human Resources. **World Wide Web address:** http://www.fiserv. com. **Description:** An independent provider of data processing outsourcing capabilities and related products and services for financial institutions. FiServ's system applications are designed to increase the operating efficiency, customer service, and marketing capability of banks, credit unions, mortgage banks, savings institutions, and other financial intermediaries. **Corporate headquarters location:** Brookfield WI. **Other U.S. locations:** Nationwide. **Listed on:** NASDAQ. **Stock exchange symbol:** FISV.

JEFFERIES & COMPANY, INC.

909 Fannin Street, Suite 3100, Houston TX 77010. 713/658-1100. **Contact:** Human Resources. **World Wide Web address:** http://www.jefco.com. **Description:** Engaged in equity, convertible debt and taxable fixed income securities brokerage and trading, and corporate finance. Jefferies & Company is one of the leading national firms engaged in the distribution and trading of blocks of equity securities primarily in the third market. Founded in 1962. **Parent company:** Jefferies Group, Inc. is a holding company which, through its primary subsidiaries Jefferies & Company; Investment Technology Group; Inc., Jefferies International Limited; and Jefferies Pacific Limited, is engaged in securities brokerage and trading, corporate finance, and other financial services.

MFC FINANCE COMPANY

P.O. Box 87688, Houston TX 77287. **Toll-free phone:** 800/547-5632. **Contact:** Human Resources. **Description:** MFC Finance Company provides financing for car loans and sometimes engages in financing personal loans for established customers.

PRINCIPAL FINANCIAL GROUP
7330 San Pedro Street, Suite 700, San Antonio TX 78216. 210/349-5454. **Contact:** Human Resources. **World Wide Web address:** http://www.principal.com. **Description:** Provides financial services including annuities, home mortgages, mutual funds, and retirement plans. The Principal Financial Group also offers dental, disability, health, life, and vision insurance policies. **Corporate headquarters location:** Des Moines IA.

RAYMOND JAMES & ASSOCIATES
6034 West Courtyard Drive, Suite 305, Austin TX 78730. 512/418-1700. **Contact:** Human Resources. **World Wide Web address:** http://www.raymondjames.com. **Description:** An investment brokerage firm offering financial planning, investment banking, asset management, and trust services. Founded in 1962.

SOUTHWEST SECURITIES GROUP, INC.
1103D Williams Drive, Georgetown TX 78628. 512/869-1586. **Contact:** Human Resources. **World Wide Web address:** http://www.swst.com. **Description:** A broker/dealer clearing firm that operates a securities brokerage business. Southwest Securities, Inc. is a member of the New York Stock Exchange, the American Stock Exchange, major regional exchanges, and the National Association of Securities Dealers. The company provides a full range of investment banking services to corporations, municipalities, and other political subdivisions. The firm also trades over-the-counter stock and bonds. **Parent company:** Southwest Securities Group, Inc. (Dallas TX). **Listed on:** New York Stock Exchange. **Stock exchange symbol:** SWS. **Number of employees worldwide:** 1,100.

SOUTHWEST SECURITIES GROUP, INC.
4040 Broadway, Suite 301, San Antonio TX 78209. 210/826-3655. **Contact:** Human Resources. **World Wide Web address:** http://www.swst.com. **Description:** A broker/dealer clearing firm that operates a securities brokerage business. Southwest Securities, Inc. is a member of the National Association of Securities Dealers. The company provides a full range of investment banking services to corporations, municipalities, and other political subdivisions. The firm also trades over-the-counter stock and bonds. **Parent company:** Southwest Securities Group, Inc. (Dallas TX). **Listed on:** New York Stock Exchange. **Stock exchange symbol:** SWS. **Number of employees worldwide:** 1,100.

TELECHECK SOUTHWEST
5251 Westheimer, Suite 1000, Houston TX 77056-5404. 713/331-7700. **Contact:** Personnel. **World Wide Web address:** http://www.telecheck.com. **Description:** A check verification company.

WORLD FINANCIAL GROUP
2600 Via Fortuna, Suite 220, Austin TX 78746. 512/328-4220. **Contact:** Human Resources. **World Wide Web address:** http://www.wfg-online.com. **Description:** Offers a wide variety of financial services including mutual funds, debt consolidation, securities, mortgages, health insurance, and life insurance. **Parent company:** AEGON.

FOOD AND BEVERAGES/ AGRICULTURE

You can expect to find the following types of companies in this chapter:
Crop Services and Farm Supplies • Dairy Farms • Food Manufacturers/Processors and Agricultural Producers • Tobacco Products

AGRILINK FOODS
P.O. Box 367, Uvalde TX 78802. 830/278-4525. **Contact:** Office Manager. **World Wide Web address:** http://www.agrilinkfoods.com. **Description:** Packages frozen vegetables.

ALAMO GROUP, INC.
P.O. Box 549, Seguin TX 78156. 830/379-1480. **Fax:** 830/372-9616. **Contact:** Gabrielle Garcia, Personnel Manager. **World Wide Web address:** http://www.alamo-group.com. **Description:** A manufacturer of agricultural and industrial machinery. **Corporate headquarters location:** This location. **Listed on:** New York Stock Exchange. **Stock exchange symbol:** ALG.

AMERICAN RICE, INC. (ARI)
10700 North Freeway, Suite 800, Houston TX 77037. 281/272-8800. **Contact:** Human Resources. **World Wide Web address:** http://www.amrice.com. **Description:** An international agribusiness company active in all phases of rice milling, processing, and marketing. ARI markets parboiled rice, white rice, instant rice, brown rice, and rice mixes, primarily under proprietary, trademarked brand names throughout the world. ARI operates rice-processing facilities in the United States, Jamaica, and Haiti. Founded in 1987. **Corporate headquarters location:** This location.

ANHEUSER-BUSCH, INC.
1800 West Loop South, Suite 1100, Houston TX 77027. 713/622-2400. **Contact:** Human Resources. **World Wide Web address:** http://www.budweiser.com. **Description:** A brewer with a high-tech brewing process and high-speed packaging lines. Brand names include Budweiser, Michelob, and Busch beers. **Corporate headquarters location:** St. Louis MO. **Parent company:** Anheuser-Busch Companies is a diverse company involved in the entertainment, brewing, baking, and manufacturing industries. Anheuser-Busch Companies is one of the largest domestic brewers, operating 13 breweries throughout the United States and distributing

through over 900 independent wholesalers. Beer brands include Budweiser, Michelob, Busch, King Cobra, and O'Doul's nonalcoholic beverages. Related businesses include can manufacturing, paper printing, and barley malting. Anheuser-Busch Companies is also one of the largest operators of theme parks in the United States, with locations in Florida, Virginia, Texas, Ohio, and California. Through subsidiary Campbell Taggart Inc., Anheuser-Busch is one of the largest commercial baking companies in the United States, producing foods under the Colonial brand name, among others. Anheuser-Busch Companies also has various real estate interests.

ANHEUSER-BUSCH, INC.
775 Gellhorn Drive, Houston TX 77029. 713/675-2311. **Contact:** Human Resources. **World Wide Web address:** http://www.budweiser.com. **Description:** A brewer with a high-tech brewing process and high-speed packaging lines. Brand names include Budweiser, Michelob, and Busch beers. **Corporate headquarters location:** St. Louis MO. **Parent company:** Anheuser-Busch Companies is a diverse company involved in the entertainment, brewing, baking, and manufacturing industries. Anheuser-Busch Companies is one of the largest domestic brewers, operating 13 breweries throughout the United States and distributing through over 900 independent wholesalers. Beer brands include Budweiser, Michelob, Busch, King Cobra, and O'Doul's nonalcoholic beverages. Related businesses include can manufacturing, paper printing, and barley malting. Anheuser-Busch Companies is also one of the largest operators of theme parks in the United States, with locations in Florida, Virginia, Texas, Ohio, and California. Through subsidiary Campbell Taggart Inc., Anheuser-Busch is one of the largest commercial baking companies in the United States, producing foods under the Colonial brand name, among others. Anheuser-Busch Companies also has various real estate interests.

BROOKSHIRE BROTHERS INC.
P.O. Box 1688, Lufkin TX 75902. 936/634-8155. **Contact:** Human Resources. **World Wide Web address:** http://www.brookshirebrothers.com. **Description:** Operates a retail grocery chain. **Corporate headquarters location:** This location.

CHUNG'S GOURMET FOOD
3907 Dennis Street, Houston TX 77004. 713/741-2118. **Contact:** Human Resources. **Description:** Manufactures food products including egg rolls and other Chinese entrees.

COCA-COLA BOTTLING COMPANY
2400 West Expressway 83, McAllen TX 78501. 956/632-3700. **Contact:** Ms. Chris Munoz, Employee Relations Manager. **World Wide Web address:** http://www.coca-cola.com. **Description:** This location is packages Coca-Cola, Barq's, and Dr. Pepper. **Corporate headquarters location:** Atlanta GA. **Other U.S. locations:** Nationwide. **Parent company:** Coca-Cola Company is one of the world's largest marketers, distributors, and producers of bottle and can products. Coca-Cola Enterprises, part of the Coca-Cola Company, is in the liquid nonalcoholic refreshment business, which includes traditional carbonated soft drinks, still and sparkling waters, juices, isotonics, and teas. The company operates in 38 states, the District of Columbia, the U.S. Virgin Islands, the Islands of Tortola and Grand Cayman, and the Netherlands. Including recent acquisitions, Coca-Cola Enterprises franchise territories encompass a population of over 154 million people, representing 54 percent of the population of the United States. Coca-Cola Enterprises operates 268 facilities, approximately 24,000 vehicles, and over 860,000 vending machines, beverage dispensers, and coolers used to market, distribute, and produce the company's products. **Listed on:** New York Stock Exchange. **Stock exchange symbol:** KO. **Number of employees worldwide:** 38,000.

COCA-COLA BOTTLING COMPANY
3012 Industrial Terrace, Austin TX 78758. 512/836-7272. **Contact:** Human Resources. **World Wide Web address:** http://www.coca-cola.com. **Description:** A distribution plant that bottles and ships Coca-Cola products to the surrounding area. **Corporate headquarters location:** Atlanta GA. **Other U.S. locations:** Nationwide. **Parent company:** Coca-Cola Company is one of the world's largest marketers, distributors, and producers of bottle and can products. Coca-Cola Enterprises, part of the Coca-Cola Company, is in the liquid nonalcoholic refreshment business, which includes traditional carbonated soft drinks, still and sparkling waters, juices, isotonics, and teas. The company operates in 38 states, the District of Columbia, the U.S. Virgin Islands, the Islands of Tortola and Grand Cayman, and the Netherlands. Including recent acquisitions, Coca-Cola Enterprises franchise territories encompass a

population of over 154 million people, representing 54 percent of the population of the United States. Coca-Cola Enterprises operates 268 facilities, approximately 24,000 vehicles, and over 860,000 vending machines, beverage dispensers, and coolers used to market, distribute, and produce the company's products. **Listed on:** New York Stock Exchange. **Stock exchange symbol:** KO. **Number of employees worldwide:** 38,000.

DAVIS FOOD CITY INC.
P.O. Box 8748, Houston TX 77249-8748. 713/695-2826. **Contact:** Human Resources. **World Wide Web address:** http://www.davisfoodcity.com. **Description:** Operates a grocery store chain. **Corporate headquarters location:** This location.

DEL MONTE FOODS
2205 Old Uvalde Highway, Crystal City TX 78839. 830/374-3451. **Contact:** Human Resources. **Description:** Del Monte Foods is an international processor and distributor of foods, operating in the following business segments: Processed Foods, Fresh Fruit, Transportation, and Institutional Services. The Processed Foods Division processes canned, frozen, dried, and chilled foods. Del Monte's operations include can manufacturing, label printing, seed production, and agricultural and scientific research. The company's products are distributed in more than 60 countries under the brand names Del Monte, Granny Goose, and Award. **Corporate headquarters location:** San Francisco CA. **Operations at this facility include:** This location cans a variety of vegetables such as spinach, carrots, peas, tomatoes, and tomato paste.

FIESTA MART INC.
5235 Katy Freeway, Houston TX 77007. 713/869-5060. **Contact:** Human Resources. **World Wide Web address:** http://www.fiestamart.com. **Description:** Operates a Houston chain of grocery stores. **Corporate headquarters location:** This location.

FREEDMAN DISTRIBUTORS
2901 Polk, Houston TX 77003. 713/229-8000. **Contact:** Personnel Manager. **World Wide Web address:** http://www.freedmanfoods.com. **Description:** Distributes boxed meat products to retail outlets. **Corporate headquarters location:** This location.

FRITO-LAY, INC.
3310 Highway 36 North, Rosenberg TX 77471. 281/232-2363. **Fax:** 281/232-1516. **Contact:** Human Resources. **World Wide Web address:** http://www.fritolay.com. **Description:** A worldwide manufacturer and wholesaler of a wide range of snack products including Fritos Corn Chips, Lays Potato Chips, Doritos Tortilla Chips, Ruffles Potato Chips, Chee-tos, and Smartfood Popcorn. **Corporate headquarters location:** Plano TX. **Other U.S. locations:** Nationwide. **Parent company:** PepsiCo, Inc. (Purchase NY) consists of Frito-Lay Company, Pepsi-Cola Company, Quaker Oats, and Tropicana Products, Inc. **Listed on:** New York Stock Exchange. **Stock exchange symbol:** PEP.

FRONTIER ENTERPRISES
8520 Crownhill Boulevard, San Antonio TX 78209-1199. 210/828-1493. **Contact:** Ms. Pat Gomez, Personnel Representative. **World Wide Web address:** http://www.jimsrestaurants.com. **Description:** Owns and operates Jim's Family Restaurants, Magic Time Machine Restaurants, and Towers of America Restaurants. Magic Time Machine Restaurants are seafood and steak dining establishments and the Towers of America Restaurants are family-style restaurants set approximately 6,000 feet in the air. **Corporate headquarters location:** This location.

GROCERS SUPPLY COMPANY, INC.
3131 East Holcombe Boulevard, Houston TX 77021. 713/747-5000. **Contact:** Human Resources. **World Wide Web address:** http://www.grocerybiz.com. **Description:** A wholesaler of a variety of goods including hardware and groceries. **Corporate headquarters location:** This location. **Operations at this facility include:** Administration; Manufacturing; Sales; Service. **Listed on:** Privately held.

FC.H. GUENTHER & SON, INC.
P.O. Box 118, San Antonio TX 78291. 210/227-1401. **Contact:** Human Resources Manager. **World Wide Web address:** http://www.chguenther.com. **Description:** A flourmill. **Positions advertised include:** Team Leader; Maintenance Mechanic. **Corporate headquarters location:** This location.

HORIZON MILLING LLC
1100 South Main Street, Galena Park TX 77547. 713/676-1100. **Contact:** Human Resources. **World Wide Web address:** http://

www.horizonmilling.com. **Description:** This facility provides a full line of flours for baking, manufacturing, and private-label applications. **Parent company:** Cargill Flour Milling & Harvest States Milling. **Other U.S. locations:** Nationwide. **Listed on:** Privately held. **Number of employees worldwide:** 90,000.

HOUSTON COCA-COLA BOTTLING COMPANY

2800 Bissonnett, Houston TX 77005. 713/664-3451. **Contact:** Regional Manager/Human Resources. **World Wide Web address:** http://www.cokecce.com. **Description:** A regional subsidiary of Coca-Cola Enterprises Inc., one of the world's largest marketers, distributors, and producers of the bottled and canned products of The Coca-Cola Company, which are among the most popular beverage brands in the world. The company also serves as a significant bottler of several other national and regional beverage brands such as Barq's and Dr. Pepper. **Parent company:** Coca-Cola Enterprises Inc. is in the liquid nonalcoholic refreshment business, which extends the company's product line beyond traditional carbonated soft drink categories to beverages such as still and sparkling waters, juices, isotonics, and teas. The company operates in 38 states, the District of Columbia, the U.S. Virgin Islands, the Islands of Tortola and Grand Cayman, and the Netherlands. **Operations at this facility include:** Administration; Manufacturing; Sales. **Listed on:** New York Stock Exchange. **Stock exchange symbol:** CCE. **Number of employees worldwide:** 72,000.

HOUSTON COCA-COLA BOTTLING COMPANY

5800 Surrey Square, Houston TX 77017-5908. 713/943-3318. **Contact:** Human Resources. **World Wide Web address:** http://www.cokecce.com. **Description:** A regional subsidiary of Coca-Cola Enterprises Inc., one of the world's largest marketers, distributors, and producers of the bottled and canned products of The Coca-Cola Company, which are among the most popular beverage brands in the world. The company also serves as a significant bottler of several other national and regional beverage brands such as Barq's and Dr. Pepper. **Parent company:** Coca-Cola Enterprises Inc. is in the liquid nonalcoholic refreshment business, which extends the company's product line beyond traditional carbonated soft drink categories to beverages such as still and sparkling waters, juices, isotonics, and teas. The company operates in 38 states, the District of Columbia, the U.S. Virgin Islands, the Islands of Tortola and Grand Cayman, and the Netherlands. **Listed on:** New York Stock Exchange. **Stock exchange symbol:** CCE. **Number of employees worldwide:** 72,000.

IMPERIAL SUGAR COMPANY

P.O. Box 9, Sugar Land TX 77487. 281/491-9181. **Contact:** Marty Thompson, Vice President of Personnel. **World Wide Web address:** http://www.imperialsugar.com. **Description:** A producer and seller of refined cane and beet sugar. Imperial Sugar Company operates four processing plants in California, two in Wyoming, two in Texas, and one in Montana. Other operations include the production and refinement of molasses, beet pulp, beet seed, and other by-products. **Subsidiaries include:** Holly Sugar.

INSTITUTIONAL SALES ASSOCIATES

3827 Promontory Point Drive, Austin TX 78744. 713/692-7213. **Contact:** Debbie Lampson. **E-mail address:** dlampson@isaonline.net. **World Web address:** http://www.isaonline.net. **Description:** Provides institutional food distribution services. **Note:** Resumes should be mailed to P.O. Box 8938, Houston Texas 77249. **Corporate headquarters location:** This location.

KING RANCH, INC.

3 Riverway, Suite 1600, Houston TX 77056. 832/681-5700. **Contact:** Human Resources. **World Wide Web address:** http://www.king-ranch.com. **Description:** One of the largest private agribusinesses in the world. The company also operates ranches and farms in Arizona, Kentucky, Florida, and Brazil. Founded in 1850. **Special programs:** Co-ops. **Office hours:** Monday - Friday, 8:00 a.m. - 5:00 p.m. **Listed on:** Privately held.

KRAFT FOODS, INC.
MAXWELL HOUSE

P.O. Box 248, Houston TX 77001-0248. 713/221-8785. **Contact:** Human Resources. **World Wide Web address:** http://www.kraftfoods.com. **Description:** Kraft Foods, Inc. is one of the largest producers of packaged grocery products in North America. Major brands include Jell-O, Post, Kool-Aid, Crystal Light, Entenmann's, Miracle Whip, Stove Top, and Shake 'n Bake. Kraft markets a number of products under the Kraft brand name including natural and processed cheeses, and dry packaged dinners. **Corporate headquarters location:** Northfield IL. **Operations at this facility include:** This location processes and markets Maxwell House brand coffee, which is supplied to more than 100 countries worldwide. **Parent company:** Philip Morris Companies is a holding company. Its principal wholly-owned subsidiaries are Philip Morris Inc. (Philip Morris U.S.A.), Philip Morris International Inc., Kraft Foods, Inc.,

Miller Brewing Company, and Philip Morris Capital Corporation. The Oscar Mayer unit markets processed meats, poultry, lunch combinations, and pickles under the Oscar Mayer, Louis Rich, Lunchables, and Claussen brand names. Kraft Foods Ingredients Corporation manufactures private-label and industrial food products for sale to other food processing companies. In the tobacco industry, Philip Morris U.S.A. and Philip Morris International together form one of the largest international cigarette operations in the world. U.S. brand names include Marlboro, Parliament, Virginia Slims, Benson & Hedges, and Merit. Miller Brewing Company brews beer under brand names including Molson Ice, Miller Genuine Draft, Miller High Life, Sharp's, Red Dog, Miller Lite, Icehouse, Foster's Lager, and Lowenbrau. Philip Morris Capital Corporation is engaged in financial services and real estate. **Listed on:** New York Stock Exchange. **Stock exchange symbol:** KFT. **Number of employees nationwide:** 114,000.

LDB CORPORATION
444 Sidney Baker Street South, Kerrville TX 78028. 830/257-2000. **Contact:** Barbara Fisher, Human Resources Manager. **Description:** Operates the Mr. Gatti's national pizza chain. **Corporate headquarters location:** This location.

LABATT FOOD SERVICE
P.O. Box 2140, San Antonio TX 78297-2140. 210/661-4216. **Physical address:** 4500 Industry Park, San Antonio TX 78218. **Fax:** 210/661-0973. **Contact:** Human Resources Department. **World Wide Web address:** http://www.labattfood.com. **Description:** A food distributor for restaurants, hospitals, military bases, schools, and other institutions.

LANCER CORPORATION
6655 Lancer Boulevard, San Antonio TX 78219. 210/310-7000. **Contact:** Human Resources Manager. **World Wide Web address:** http://www.lancercorp.com. **Description:** A manufacturer of soft drink and related food service equipment. **Corporate headquarters location:** This location. **International locations:** Worldwide. **Listed on:** American Stock Exchange. **Stock exchange symbol:** LAN. **Number of employees nationwide:** 1,300.

LANDRY'S RESTAURANTS, INC.
1510 West Loop South, Houston TX 77027. 713/850-1010. **Contact:** Human Resources. **World Wide Web address:** http://

www.landrysseafood.com. **Description:** Operates a chain of seafood restaurants. **Corporate headquarters location:** This location.

LUBY'S CAFETERIAS
P.O. Box 33069, San Antonio TX 78265. 210/654-9000. **Fax:** 210/225-5750. **Physical address:** 2211 NE Loop 410, San Antonio TX 78217. **Contact:** Human Resources. **E-mail address:** jobs@lubys.com. **World Wide Web address:** http://www.lubys.com. **Description:** A national chain restaurant that serves cafeteria-style food. **Positions advertised include:** Restaurant Manager. **Corporate headquarters location:** This location. **Listed on:** New York Stock Exchange. **Stock exchange symbol:** LUB. **Number of employees nationwide:** 11,000.

MASS MARKETING, INC.
dba SUPER S FOODS
401 Isom Road, Building 100, San Antonio TX 78216. 210/344-1960. **Contact:** Human Resources Department. **Description:** A corporate division of the retail grocery store chain Super S Foods. **Corporate headquarters location:** This location.

PABST BREWING COMPANY
312 Pearl Parkway, San Antonio TX 78215. 210/226-0231. **Contact:** Human Resources. **World Wide Web address:** http://www.pabst. com. **Description:** Produces a line of widely distributed beers and malt beverages including Pabst Blue Ribbon, Pabst Light, and Pabst Extra Light.

PEPSI-COLA COMPANY
9300 La Porte Freeway, Houston TX 77017. 713/645-4111. **Contact:** Personnel Manager. **World Wide Web address:** http://www.pepsico. com. **Description:** Bottles and distributes Pepsi-Cola beverages. **Parent company:** PepsiCo, Inc. (Purchase NY) consists of Frito-Lay Company, Gatorade/Tropicana North America, Pepsi-Cola Company, and Quaker Oats Company. **Listed on:** New York Stock Exchange. **Stock exchange symbol:** PEP.

PILGRIM'S PRIDE CORPORATION
1800 West Frank, Lufkin TX 75901. 936/639-1174. **Contact:** Human Resources. **World Wide Web address:** http://www.pilgrimspride. com. **Description:** Pilgrim's Pride Corporation is a producer of chicken products and eggs for the restaurant, institutional, food service, grocery, and wholesale markets. The company's operations

include breeding, hatching, growing, processing, packaging, and preparing poultry. Pilgrim's Pride Corporation also produces animal feed and ingredients. The company is one of the largest producers of chicken products in the United States and Mexico. The company's primary domestic distribution is handled through restaurants and retailers in central, southwestern, and western United States, and through the food service industry throughout the country. **Corporate headquarters location:** Pittsburg TX. **Other U.S. locations:** AR; AZ; OK. **Operations at this facility include:** This location is a chicken processing plant. **Listed on:** New York Stock Exchange. **Stock exchange symbol:** CHX.

RIVIANA FOODS INC.
P.O. Box 2636, Houston TX 77252. 713/529-3251. **Fax:** 713/529-1661. **Contact:** Human Resources. **E-mail address:** lpagel@ riviana.com. **World Wide Web address:** http://www.riviana. com. **Description:** Produces and distributes rice under the Mahatma, Carolina, and River brand names. **Listed on:** NASDAQ. **Stock exchange symbol:** RVFD.

SARA LEE COFFEE & TEA
235 North Norwood, Houston TX 77011. 713/928-6281. **Contact:** Human Resources. **World Wide Web address:** http://www.saralee. com. **Description:** Produces dry-roasted coffee. **Listed on:** New York Stock Exchange. **Stock exchange symbol:** SLE. **Number of employees nationwide:** 22,300.

NATHAN SEGAL AND COMPANY INC.
24 East Greenway Plaza, Suite 910, Houston TX 77046. 713/621-2000. **Contact:** Human Resources. **World Wide Web address:** http:// www.nathansegal.com. **Description:** A merchandiser of feed ingredients for livestock companies.

SPECS LIQUOR WAREHOUSE
2410 Smith Street, Houston TX 77006. 713/526-8787. **Contact:** Human Resources. **World Wide Web address:** http:// www.specsonline.com. **Description:** Operates a chain of liquor stores. **Corporate headquarters location:** This location.

STERLING FOODS INC.
1075 Arion Parkway, San Antonio TX 78216. 210/490-1669. **Contact:** Jim Keuhl, Human Resources Director. **World Wide Web address:** http://www.sterlingfoodsusa.com. **Description:**

Manufacturers of ready-to-eat foods, primarily distributed to the military.

SYSCO CORPORATION

1390 Enclave Parkway, Houston TX 77077-2099. 281/584-1390. **Contact:** Human Resources. **World Wide Web address:** http:// www.sysco.com. **Description:** Engaged principally in the wholesale distribution of food and related products and services to the food service industry. Products include a full line of frozen foods. **Positions advertised include:** Accounting Associate; Administrative Assistant; Business Analyst; Carrier Analyst. **Corporate headquarters location:** This location. **Listed on:** New York Stock Exchange. **Stock exchange symbol:** SYY.

TYSON FOODS INC.

P.O. Box 2228, Seguin TX 78155. 830/379-5151. **Contact:** Personnel Manager. **World Wide Web address:** http://www.tyson. com. **Description:** Tyson Foods Inc. is one of the world's largest fully-integrated producers, processors, and marketers of poultry-based food products. Tyson products include Tyson Holly Farms Fresh Chicken, Weaver, Louis Kemp Crab, Lobster Delights, Healthy Portion, Beef Stir Fry, Crab Delights Stir Fry, Chicken Fried Rice Kits, Pork Chops with Cinnamon Apples, Salmon Grill Kits, Fish'n Chips Kits, and Rotisserie Chicken. **Positions advertised include:** Product Manager. **Corporate headquarters location:** Springdale AR. **Operations at this facility include:** This location is a chicken processing plant. **Listed on:** New York Stock Exchange. **Stock exchange symbol:** TSN. **Number of employees nationwide:** 124,000.

WHATABURGER, INC.

4600 Parkdale Drive, Corpus Christi TX 78411. 361/878-0650. **Contact:** Director of Human Resources. **World Wide Web address:** http://www.whataburger.com. **Description:** Operates 500 restaurants in the Sunbelt area. Founded in 1950. **Positions advertised include:** General Manager. **Corporate headquarters location:** This location. **Other U.S. locations:** AZ.

WHOLE FOODS MARKET INC.

601 North Lamar Boulevard, Suite 300, Austin TX 78703. 512/477-4455. **Contact:** Human Resources. **World Wide Web address:** http:// www.wholefoods.com. **Description:** Owns and operates a chain of natural foods supermarkets. **Positions advertised include:** Business

Analyst; Project Leader; National Director of Business and Compensation; Purchasing Business Analyst; Purchasing Systems Analyst. **Other U.S. locations:** CA; LA; MA; NC; RI. **Operations at this facility include:** Regional Headquarters. **Listed on:** NASDAQ. **Stock exchange symbol:** WFMI.

GOVERNMENT

You can expect to find the following types of agencies in this chapter:
*Courts • Executive, Legislative, and General Government • Public Agencies
(Firefighters, Military, Police) • United States Postal Service*

HOUSTON, CITY OF
P.O. Box 1562, Houston TX 77251. 713/837-9300. **Contact:** Human Resources. **World Wide Web address:** http://www.ci.houston.tx.us. **Description:** As the government offices for the city of Houston, this location houses the mayor's office as well as city council offices.

NASA JOHNSON SPACE CENTER
2101 NASA Road One, Mail Code AHE, Houston TX 77058. 281/483-2135. **Contact:** Employment Specialist. **World Wide Web address:** http://www.jsc.nasa.gov. **Description:** A federal government agency responsible for developing and operating the space shuttle and a space station. **Special programs:** Internships. **Corporate headquarters location:** Washington DC.

OFFICE OF THE SECRETARY OF THE STATE OF TEXAS
1019 Brazo, Room 405, P.O. Box 12887, Austin TX 78711-2887. 512/463-5701. **Contact:** Human Resources. **World Wide Web address:** http://www.sos.state.tx.us. **Description:** A constitutional officer of the executive branch appointed by the governor with the consent of the senate. This agency is organized into five functional divisions: Executive, Elections, Information Services, Statutory Filings, and Administrative Services.

TEXAS DEPARTMENT OF HEALTH
1100 West 49th Street, Austin TX 78756-3101. 512/458-7302. **Fax:** 512/458-7409. **Contact:** Recruitment. **World Wide Web address:** http://www.tdh.state.tx.us. **Description:** Employing 6,300 people statewide, the Texas Department of Health is a government department offering health services across the state. **Positions advertised include:** Program Specialist; Director of Field Operations; Attorney; Legal Secretary; Research Specialist; Business Analyst; Program Consultant; Administrative Technician. **Special programs:** Internships. **Corporate headquarters location:** This location. **Operations at this facility include:** Administration.

TEXAS DEPARTMENT OF HUMAN SERVICES
1300 South Highway 146, Baytown TX 77520. 281/427-9480. **Contact:** Human Resources. **World Wide Web address:** http://www.dhs.state.tx.us. **Description:** This location houses the welfare office, which provides food stamps and oversees Medicaid services. **Positions advertised include:** Human Services Specialist; Director; Policy Specialist; Program Specialist; Systems Analyst; Database Administrator; Budget Analyst; Nurse; Nutritionist.

TEXAS PARKS & WILDLIFE
4200 Smith School Road, Austin TX 78744. 512/389-4800. **Contact:** Human Resources. **World Wide Web address:** http://www.tpwd.state.tx.us. **Description:** Dedicated to preserving the nature and wildlife of Austin and the surrounding Texas area. **Positions advertised include:** Clerk; Natural Resources Specialist; Park Ranger; Project Assistant; Program Administrator.

TEXAS STATE AUDITOR'S OFFICE
P.O. Box 12067, Austin TX 78711. 512/936-9500. **Fax:** 512/936-9400. **Contact:** Dennis Wilson, Human Resources Officer. **World Wide Web address:** http://www.sao.state.tx.us. **Description:** The independent auditor for the Texas state government. Texas State Auditor's Office provides legislators, agency management, and the citizens of Texas with information about the operations of state-run agencies and universities. Additional duties include the management of control audits, statewide financial and compliance audits, special investigations, classification compliance audits, briefing reports, legislative requests, and special issue areas. **Positions advertised include:** Audit Manager; Senior Information Systems Analyst; Senior Investigator. **Special programs:** Internships; Training.

U.S. DEPARTMENT OF VETERANS AFFAIRS
1615 Woodward Street, Austin TX 78772. 512/326-6052. **Contact:** Human Resources. **World Wide Web address:** http://www.va.gov. **Description:** U.S. Department of Veterans Affairs is responsible for providing federal benefits to veterans and their dependents. Headed by the Secretary of Veterans Affairs, the VA is one of the largest of the 14 cabinet departments and operates nationwide health care programs, assistance services, and national cemeteries. **Operations at this facility include:** This location performs data processing and computer programming services.

UNITED SPACE ALLIANCE COMPANY
600 Gemini Avenue, Houston TX 77058. 281/282-2000. **Contact:** Human Resources. **World Wide Web address:** http://www.unitedspacealliance.com. **Description:** A government contracted management and operations firm for the space shuttle program. **Operations at this facility include:** Administration; Service.

WEST UNIVERSITY PLACE, CITY OF
3800 University Boulevard, Houston TX 77005. 713/668-4441. **Contact:** Human Resources. **World Wide Web address:** http://www.ci.west-university-place.tx.us. **Description:** Houses administrative and government offices for city departments including public works, the city manager, parks/recreation, and senior services.

HEALTH CARE: SERVICES, EQUIPMENT, AND PRODUCTS

You can expect to find the following types of companies in this chapter:
Dental Labs and Equipment • Home Health Care Agencies • Hospitals and Medical Centers • Medical Equipment Manufacturers and Wholesalers • Offices and Clinics of Health Practitioners • Residential Treatment Centers/Nursing Homes• Veterinary Services

ABBOTT LABORATORIES
3900 Howard Lane, Austin TX 78728. 512/255-2000. **Contact:** Human Resources. **World Wide Web address:** http://www.abbott. com. **Description:** This location manufactures intravenous bags for the medical industry. Overall, Abbott Laboratories manufactures a wide range of health care products including pharmaceuticals, hospital products, diagnostic products, chemical products, and nutritional products. **Positions advertised include:** Pharmaceuticals Sales Representative; District Secretary; Account Manager; Project Manager. **Corporate headquarters location:** Abbott Park IL. **Listed on:** New York Stock Exchange. **Stock exchange symbol:** ABT.

M.D. ANDERSON CANCER CENTER
1515 Holcombe Boulevard, P.O. Box 205, Houston TX 77030. 713/792-8002. **Recorded jobline:** 713/792-8010. **Contact:** Human Resources. **World Wide Web address:** http://www.mdanderson.org. **Description:** Works to eliminate cancer and allied diseases by developing and maintaining integrated quality programs in patient care, research, education, and prevention. **NOTE:** Entry-level positions are offered. **Positions advertised include:** Receptionist; Patient Access Representative; Quality Assurance Dosimetrist; Clinical Engineer; PET Technologist; Phlebotomist; Physical Therapist; Research Assistant; Research Data Coordinator; Clinical Aide. **Special programs:** Training. **Corporate headquarters location:** This location. **Parent company:** The University of Texas System. **Operations at this facility include:** Administration; Research and Development; Service. **Number of employees at this location:** 11,000.

AUSTIN REGIONAL CLINIC
6937 North I-H 35, Suite 500, Austin TX 78752. 512/419-0707. **Contact:** Human Resources. **World Wide Web address:** http:// www.austinregionalclinic.com. **Description:** An acute care, outpatient, multispecialty facility that offers primary care for adults

and children, OB/GYN, occupational medicine, mental health services, dermatology, surgery, optometry, allergy treatment, and immunology. **Positions advertised include:** Insurance Representative; Medical Assistant; Patient Services Representative; Staff Registered Nurse.

AUSTIN STATE HOSPITAL
4110 Guadalupe Street, Austin TX 78751. 512/452-0381. **Contact:** Thomas Pozniac, Director of Human Resources. **World Wide Web address:** http://www.mhmr.state.tx.us/hospitals/austinsh/ austinsh.html. **Description:** A 350-bed, acute psychiatric hospital. Austin State Hospital has many services to offer including a Deaf Unit, Children's Unit, and the Trinity Treatment Center, which aids people with mental retardation.

BAPTIST MEDICAL CENTER
111 Dallas Street, San Antonio TX 78205-1230. 210/297-7000. **Contact:** Human Resources. **World Wide Web address:** http:// www.baptisthealthsystem.org. **Description:** A 689-bed, nonprofit, acute care hospital offering complete medical facilities for cardiac care, intensive care, emergency services, maternity, surgery, and other specialized services. **Positions advertised include:** Certified Nurse Aide; Case Manager; Patient Care Coordinator; Physical Therapist; Registered Nurse; Speech Language Pathologist. **Parent company:** Baptist Memorial Hospital System is a health care system that is comprised of five acute care, nonprofit hospitals: Baptist Medical Center, Northeast Baptist Hospital, Southeast Baptist Hospital, North Center Baptist Hospital, and St. Luke's Baptist Hospital. In total, these hospitals contain 1,700 beds.

BELLAIRE MEDICAL CENTER
5314 Dashwood Drive, Houston TX 77081-4689. 713/512-1200. **Contact:** Director of Human Resources. **Description:** A 350-bed medical center offering a range of inpatient and outpatient care including a diabetes center, an intensive care psychiatric unit, and a women's services center. Bellaire Medical Center also provides geriatric day programs and support groups for chemical dependency. **World Wide Web address:** http://www.bellairemedicalcenter.com. **Operations at this facility include:** Administration; Divisional Headquarters; Regional Headquarters; Service.

BELLVILLE GENERAL HOSPITAL
44 North Cummings, P.O. Box 977, Bellville TX 77418. 979/865-3141. **Fax:** 979/865-9631. **Contact:** Human Resources Department. **World Wide Web address:** http://www.bellvillehospital.com. **Description:** A nonprofit, rural hospital with 32 beds. Services at Bellville General Hospital include emergency room care, a nursery, obstetrics, outpatient care, and surgical procedures. Bellville General Hospital is accredited by the Joint Commission on Accreditation of Healthcare Organizations (JCAHO). **NOTE:** Second and third shifts are offered. **Positions advertised include:** Certified Nurses Aide; Certified Occupational Therapy Assistant; Dietician/Nutritionist; EEG Technologist; EKG Technician; Emergency Medical Technician; Home Health Aide; Medical Records Technician; Nuclear Medicine Technologist; Occupational Therapist; Pharmacist; Physical Therapist; Physician; Radiological Technologist; Registered Nurse; Respiratory Therapist; Social Worker; Speech-Language Pathologist. **CEO:** Michael Morris. **Facilities Manager:** Jim Stastny.

THE BROWN SCHOOLS
1407 West Stassney Lane, Austin TX 78745. 512/464-0200. **Contact:** Human Resources. **World Wide Web address:** http://www.brownschools.com. **Description:** Provides specialty services including psychiatric and behavioral services, rehabilitation services, educational services, home health services, outpatient services, residential treatment, and adoption and foster care. The Brown Schools operate more than 25 facilities in ten states. **Corporate headquarters location:** This location.

CERNER RADIOLOGY INFORMATION SYSTEMS
5 Greenway Plaza, Suite 2000, Houston TX 77046. 832/325-1500. **Contact:** Human Resources. **Description:** Engaged in the design, development, and support of hospital information systems for both clinical and business applications. **Listed on:** NASDAQ. **Stock exchange symbol:** CERN.

CHILDREN'S NUTRITION RESOURCE CENTER (CNRC)
1100 Bates Street, Houston TX 77030. 713/798-7000. **Contact:** Human Resources. **World Wide Web address:** http://www.bcm.tmc.edu/cnrc. **Description:** Researches the nutrition needs of children, pregnant women, and nursing mothers. **Positions advertised include:** Nutritionist; Research Technician; Phlebotomist; Data Collector; School Coordinator; Registered Nurse. **Parent company:** Baylor College of Medicine and the U.S. Department of Agriculture.

CHRISTUS ST. JOSEPH HOSPITAL
1404 Saint Joseph's Parkway, Houston TX 77002. 713/756-5669. **Recorded jobline:** 713/757-7433. **Contact:** Human Resources. **World Wide Web address:** http://www.christushealth.org. **Description:** A 834-bed, nonprofit medical center. Founded in 1887. **NOTE:** Entry-level positions and second and third shifts are offered. **Positions advertised include:** Administrative Assistant; Advertising Executive; Certified Nurses Aide; Clinical Lab Technician; Computer Operator; Computer Programmer; Counselor; Daycare Worker; Editor; EEG Technologist; EKG Technician; Electrician; Emergency Medical Technician; Librarian; Licensed Practical Nurse; Medical Records Technician; Nuclear Medicine Technologist; Nurse Practitioner; Occupational Therapist; Pharmacist; Physical Therapist; Physician. **Special programs:** Internships; Training; Co-ops. **Corporate headquarters location:** This location. **Operations at this facility include:** Service. **Listed on:** Privately held.

CHRISTUS SANTA ROSA HOSPITAL
333 North Santa Rosa Street, San Antonio TX 78207. 210/704-2011. **Contact:** Human Resources. **World Wide Web address:** http://www.christussantarosa.org. **Description:** Santa Rosa Hospital is an acute care hospital with 500 beds. **Positions advertised include:** Registered Nurse; Nurse Manager; Infection Control Practitioner; Occupational Therapist; Director of Risk Management; Medical Records Manager.

CHRISTUS SPOHN HOSPITAL SHORELINE
600 Elizabeth Street, Corpus Christi TX 78404. 361/881-3000. **Contact:** Human Resources. **World Wide Web address:** http://www.christushealth.org. **Description:** A 432-bed acute care medical facility. **Positions advertised include:** Registered Nurse; Nurse Manager; Infection Control Practitioner; Occupational Therapist; Director of Risk Management; Medical Records Manager. **Corporate headquarters location:** San Antonio TX. **Parent company:** CHRISTUS Health. **Operations at this facility include:** Service.

CITIZENS MEDICAL CENTER
P.O. Box 2024, Victoria TX 77902. 361/573-9181. **Physical address:** 2701 Hospital Drive, Victoria TX 77901. **Contact:** Director of Personnel. **World Wide Web address:** http://www.citizensmedicalcente.com. **Description:** A 312-bed acute care medical center. Citizens Medical Center provides many services including a Women's Pavilion and a cancer treatment floor.

Founded in 1956. **Positions advertised include:** Case Manager; Chief Nursing Executive; Clinical Dietician; Radiographer; Field Nurse; Fitness Specialist; Healthwise Safety Educator; Occupational Therapist; Physical Therapist.

CYPRESS FAIRBANKS MEDICAL CENTER HOSPITAL
10655 Steepletop Drive, Houston TX 77065-4222. 281/897-3500. **Fax:** 281/890-0236. **Recorded jobline:** 281/897-3530. **Contact:** Melanie Webb, Recruiter. **World Wide Web address:** http://www.cyfairhospital.com. **Description:** A 149-bed acute care hospital offering diagnostic services on both outpatient and inpatient bases. Founded in 1983. **NOTE:** Entry-level positions, part-time jobs, and second and third shifts are offered. **Positions advertised include:** Therapist; Director of Human Resources; Registered Nurse; Coder; Patient Account Representative; Monitor Technician. **Parent company:** Tenet Houston HealthSystem.

EDINBURG REGIONAL MEDICAL CENTER
1102 West Trenton Road, P.O. Box 2000, Edinburg TX 78539. 956/388-6000. **Contact:** Personnel. **World Wide Web address:** http://www.edinburgregional.com. **Description:** A 130-bed medical center offering a wide variety of medical and diagnostic services. **Positions advertised include:** HIM Clerk; Unit Clerk; Office Lab Clerk; Engineering Technician; Phlebotomist; Certified Nursing Assistant; Nurse Educator; Registered Nurse; Respiratory Therapist; Physical Therapist.

HCA - THE HEALTHCARE COMPANY
7400 Fannin, Suite 650, Houston TX 77054. 713/852-1500. **Contact:** Human Resources. **World Wide Web address:** http://www.hcahealthcare.com. **Description:** Columbia/HCA owns several hundred surgical centers and hospitals. Founded in 1992. **Other U.S. locations:** Nationwide. **Operations at this facility include:** This location is a regional administrative office.

HEALTHLINK, INC.
1020 Holcombe Boulevard, Suite 1650, Houston TX 77030. 713/790-0800. **Fax:** 713/852-2151. **Contact:** Human Resources. **World Wide Web address:** http://www.healthlink.com. **Description:** Offers management consulting services for the health care industry. Healthlink services are organized into three main program areas: re-engineering; strategic information systems and project planning; and implementation. IMG also designs computer-based patient records

systems for hospitals and medical centers. **Positions advertised include:** Admissions Specialist; Clinical Lab Technician; Computer Programmer; Financial Analyst; Human Resources Manager; Licensed Practical Nurse; Medical Records Technician; Radiological Technologist; Registered Nurse; Systems Analyst. **Corporate headquarters location:** St. Louis MO. **Other U.S. locations:** AR; IL; IN; IA; KY. **Number of employees nationwide:** 620.

HEALTHSOUTH
3340 Plaza 10 Boulevard, Beaumont TX 77707. 409/835-0835. **Fax:** 409/835-1401. **Contact:** Ellen Zimmerman, Director of Human Resources. **World Wide Web address:** http://www.healthsouth.com. **Description:** A physical rehabilitation hospital that also offers outpatient and home care services. **NOTE:** Part-time jobs and second and third shifts are offered. **Other U.S. locations:** Nationwide. **International locations:** Worldwide. **Listed on:** New York Stock Exchange. **Stock exchange symbol:** HRC. **CEO:** Richard Scrushy. **Number of employees worldwide:** 33,700.

HILL COUNTY MEMORIAL HOSPITAL
P.O. Box 835, Fredericksburg TX 78624-0835. 830/997-4353. **Contact:** Human Resources. **World Wide Web address:** http://www.hillcountymemorial.com. **Description:** A 77-bed, acute care hospital. Hill County Memorial Hospital offers a skilled nursing unit, medical surgery, OB/GYN, urology, and orthopedics. The hospital also has a Wellness Center that offers preventative care. Founded in 1971. **Positions advertised include:** Registered Nurse; Chief Nursing Officer; Licensed Vocational Nurse; Respiratory Therapist; Housekeeper; Coder; Switchboard Operator; Biomedical Technician.

HUNTSVILLE MEMORIAL HOSPITAL
P.O. Box 4001, Huntsville TX 77342-4001. 936/291-3411. **Contact:** Human Resources. **World Wide Web address:** http://www.huntsvillememorial.com. **Description:** A full-service hospital offering specialized outpatient facilities. **Positions advertised include:** Ultrasonographer; Registered Nurse; Radiology Technician.

IHS HOSPITAL
7310 Oak Manor Drive, San Antonio TX 78229. 210/308-0261. **Contact:** Jill Doire, Divisional Recruiter. **World Wide Web address:** http://www.ihs-inc.com. **Description:** A 138-bed acute care hospital offering a wide range of long- and short-term care services. **Positions advertised include:** Administrator.

IHS OF CORPUS CHRISTI
1314 Third Street, Corpus Christi TX 78404. 361/888-5511. **Contact:** Jill Doire, Divisional Recruiter. **World Wide Web address:** http://www.ihs-inc.com. **Description:** A 116-bed hospital. Founded in 1993. **Positions advertised include:** Administrator.

KCI (KINECTIC CONCEPTS, INC.)
P.O. Box 659508, San Antonio TX 78265-9508. 210/524-9000. **Contact:** Human Resources. **World Wide Web address:** http://www.kci1.com. **Description:** Manufactures, sells, services, and rents hospital beds for the critically ill. **Positions advertised include:** Administrative Assistant; Assembler; Billing Specialist; Biomedical Engineer; Business Analyst; Buyer/Planner; Call Center Representative; Coordinator of Patient Administration; **Corporate headquarters location:** This location.

KERRVILLE STATE HOSPITAL
721 Thompson Drive, Kerrville TX 78028. 830/896-2211. **Contact:** Human Resources. **Description:** A psychiatric hospital with 200 inpatient beds and 33 medical unit beds. Founded in 1951. **World Wide Web address:** http://www.mhmr.state.tx.us/hospitals/kerrvillesh. **Positions advertised include:** Registered Nurse; LVN; Pharmacy Technician. **Corporate headquarters location:** Austin TX.

KIMBERLY-CLARK TECNOL INC.
14 Finnegan Drive, Del Rio TX 78840. 830/774-7482. **Contact:** Human Resources. **World Wide Web address:** http://www.kchealthcare.com. **Description:** A warehouse that distributes medical products. **Parent company:** Kimberly-Clark Corporation. **Listed on:** New York Stock Exchange. **Stock exchange symbol:** KMB.

MATAGORDA GENERAL HOSPITAL
1115 Avenue G, Bay City TX 77414. 979/245-6383. **Contact:** Human Resources. **Description:** A full-service hospital offering outpatient diagnostic service facilities.

McKENNA MEMORIAL HOSPITAL
600 North Union Avenue, New Braunfels TX 78130. 830/606-9111. **Recorded jobline:** 830/606-2151. **Contact:** Human Resources Coordinator. **E-mail address:** hr@mckenna.org. **World Wide Web address:** http://www.mckenna.org. **Description:** A 116-bed, short-term care hospital. McKenna Memorial Hospital also offers an occupational health department.

McNEIL CONSUMER HEALTH CARE
4001 North Interstate Highway 35, Round Rock TX 78664. 512/255-4111. **Contact:** Human Resources. **Description:** A scientific research and development company that is also involved in the manufacturing of pharmaceutical products.

MEMORIAL HERMANN/MEMORIAL CITY
920 Frostwood, Houston TX 77024. 713/932-3470. **Fax:** 713/932-3627. **Contact:** Human Resources Representative. **World Wide Web address:** http://www.mhhs.org. **Description:** An acute care general hospital. **Positions advertised include:** Coding Manager; Dietician; Medical Technologist; OR Attendant; Pharmacist; Radiology Technologist.

MERIT MEDICAL
1111 South Velasco Street, Angleton TX 77515. 979/848-5000. **Contact:** Human Resources. **World Wide Web address:** http://www.merit.com. **Description:** Provides technologically advanced, cost-effective products and services to five medical specialties: anesthesiology, cardiology, critical care, nuclear medicine, and radiology. **Positions advertised include:** Senior Manufacturing Engineer. **Listed on:** NASDAQ. **Stock exchange symbol:** MMSI.

METHODIST SPECIALTY AND TRANSPLANT HOSPITAL
8026 Floyd Curl Drive, San Antonio TX 78229. 210/575-8110. **Recorded jobline:** 210/575-4JOB. **Contact:** Human Resources. **World Wide Web address:** http://www.mhshealth.com. **Description:** A 382-bed, licensed medical facility specializing in organ and tissue transplants, impotency treatments, incontinence treatments, gastroenteric procedures, and laparoscopic surgery.

METROPOLITAN HOSPITAL
1310 McCullough Avenue, San Antonio TX 78212. 210/208-2200. **Fax:** 210/208-2924. **Contact:** Human Resources. **World Wide Web address:** http://www.mhshealth.com. **Description:** A 263-bed hospital that offers both long-term and short-term care.

MISSION HOSPITAL, INC.
900 South Bryan Road, Mission TX 78572. 956/580-9188. **Fax:** 956/580-9430. **Contact:** Personnel. **World Wide Web address:** http://www.missionhospital.org. **Description:** A 138-bed acute care facility. **Positions advertised include:** Respiratory Therapist;

Registered Nurse; Radiology Technician; Registration Representative. **Operations at this facility include:** Health Care; Service.

MISYS HEALTHCARE SYSTEMS
2020 North Loop West, Suite 140, Houston TX 77018. 713/688-3181. **Contact:** Human Resources. **World Wide Web address:** http://www.misyshealthcare.com. **Description:** Develops health care management software. Products include +Medic Vision, +Medic PM, Auto Chart, AutoImage, and FasTracker. **NOTE:** Please send resumes to: MISYS Healthcare Systems, Human Resources, 8529 Six Forks Road, Raleigh NC 27615. **Operations at this facility include:** This location is a sales and engineering facility.

NIX HEALTH CARE SYSTEM
414 Navarro Street, San Antonio TX 78205. 210/271-1800. **Contact:** Human Resources. **World Wide Web address:** http://www.nixhealth.com. **Description:** Operates a 150-bed hospital. Nix Health Care offers such services as prenatal care, a geriatric psychiatry unit, and a skilled nursing unit.

NORTH AUSTIN MEDICAL CENTER
12221 North Mopac Expressway, Austin TX 78758. 512/901-1000. **Contact:** Human Resources. **World Wide Web address:** http://www.adclinic.com. **Description:** A 138-bed medical facility with acute, transitional, and intensive care units. Founded in 1995.

NORTHEAST BAPTIST MRI CENTER
8815 Village Drive, San Antonio TX 78217. 210/590-5822. **Contact:** Human Resources. **Description:** A medical center that performs MRIs on an outpatient basis.

SID PETERSON MEMORIAL HOSPITAL
710 Water Street, Kerrville TX 78028. 830/896-4200. **Contact:** Human Resources. **World Wide Web address:** http://www.spmh.com. **Description:** A long-term care general hospital offering centers for cardiac rehabilitation, osteoporosis, and cancer treatment. **Positions advertised include:** Charge RN; Licensed Vocational Nurse; Staff Therapist; Housekeeper; Physical Therapist; Program Nurse.

PHYSICIANS RESOURCE GROUP, INC. (PRGI)
5005 Riverway, Suite 400, Houston TX 77056. 713/629-5777. **Contact:** Human Resources. **Description:** Engaged in the operation and management of eye clinics.

PRIME MEDICAL SERVICES, INC.
1301 Capital of Texas Highway South, Suite C-300, Austin TX 78746. 512/328-2892. **Contact:** Personnel. **World Wide Web address:** http://www.primemedical.com. **Description:** Through its subsidiaries, Prime Medical Services provides nonmedical management services to lithotripsy and cardiac rehabilitation centers. Prime Medical Services operates 2 fixed-site lithotripters and 11 mobile lithotripters. **Listed on:** NASDAQ. **Stock exchange symbol:** PMSI.

THE METHODIST HOSPITAL
6600 Fannin, Suite 903, Houston TX 77030. 713/394-6614. **Fax:** 713/793-7128. **Contact:** Personnel. **World Wide Web address:** http://www.methodisthealth.com. **Description:** A nonprofit, full-service hospital. The Methodist Hospital is also the primary teaching hospital for the Baylor College of Medicine. **Positions advertised include:** Project Manager; Advanced Practice Registered Nurse; Patient Care Assistant; Dialysis Maintenance Technician; Human Resources Coordinator; Laundry Attendant. **Corporate headquarters location:** This location. **Parent company:** Methodist Health Care System.

ROUND ROCK MEDICAL CENTER
2400 Round Rock Avenue, Round Rock TX 78681. 512/341-1000. **Contact:** Personnel. **World Wide Web address:** http://www.roundrockhospital.com. **Description:** A 109-bed general hospital. Services include a 24-hour emergency room, Family Birthing Center, medical/surgical unit, six-bed intensive care unit, and a nine-bed skilled nursing unit. Founded in 1983.

POLLY RYON MEMORIAL HOSPITAL
1705 Jackson Street, Richmond TX 77469. 281/341-4831. **Fax:** 281/341-2883. **Recorded jobline:** 281/341-2852. **Contact:** Human Resources. **E-mail address:** jobs@pollyron.org. **World Wide Web address:** http://www.pollyryon.org. **Description:** A nonprofit, acute care medical facility with 185 beds. In addition to general medical and surgical procedures, Polly Ryon offers a wide range of services including active health education in the community; PROMISE, the

birthing center; imaging services such as CT scanning, mammography, and MRIs; hospice care; and STAR, the Sports Therapy and Rehabilitation service. Founded in 1949. **NOTE:** Second and third shifts are offered. **Positions advertised include:** Medical Technologist; RN Case Manager; OR Registered Nurse; Certified Coder; Sterile Processing Technician. **Corporate headquarters location:** This location. **Operations at this facility include:** Administration; Service.

ST. DAVID'S MEDICAL CENTER

1025 East 32nd Street, Austin TX 78705. 512/476-7111. **Contact:** Employment Recruiter. **World Wide Web address:** http://www.stdavids.com. **Description:** A 400-bed hospital specializing in all types of adult medical care. **Positions advertised include:** Bone Density Technician; Instrument Technician; Lab Assistant; Patient Care Technician; Physical Therapist; Social Worker; Food Service Worker; Radiology Clerk; Registered Nurse.

ST. LUKE'S EPISCOPAL HOSPITAL

P.O. Box 20269, Houston TX 77225-0269. 713/785-8537. **Physical address:** 6720 Bertner Street, Houston TX 77030. **Recorded jobline:** 800/231-1000. **Contact:** Human Resources. **World Wide Web address:** http://www.sleh.com. **Description:** A full-service hospital specializing in outpatient care. **Positions advertised include:** Director of Patient Safety; Assistant Nurse Manager; Registered Nurse; Patient Care Assistant; Administrative Assistant; Cash Applications Associate.

SAN MARCOS TREATMENT CENTER

120 Bert Brown Road, San Marcos TX 78666. 512/396-8500. **Fax:** 512/392-2212. **Contact:** Personnel Department. **E-mail address:** sanmarcos@brownschools.com. **World Wide Web address:** http://www.brownschools.com. **Description:** A 161-bed neuropsychiatric hospital that specializes in treating adolescents and young adults who have not had success in other settings. The center's patients are primarily those who experience emotional disturbances, severe impulses, aggressive behavior patterns, unprovoked mood swings, known neurological or organic disorders, seizure disorders, language problems, or severe learning complications due to substance abuse and sexual trauma. Founded in 1940. **Parent company:** The Brown Schools (Austin TX).

SETON HEALTHCARE NETWORK
1201 West 38th Street, Austin TX 78705. 512/324-4000. **Toll-free phone:** 800/880-0038. **Fax:** 512/324-1672. **Recorded jobline:** 512/324-1679. **Contact:** Human Resources Recruiters. **World Wide Web address:** http://www.seton.net. **Description:** A nonprofit, multifacility health care network. Facilities include five acute care hospitals, community clinics, home care providers, outreach programs, and physicians' offices. **NOTE:** Entry-level positions and second and third shifts are offered. **Company slogan:** Be certain it's SETON. **Positions advertised include:** Department Assistant; Medical Transcriptionist. **Corporate headquarters location:** St. Louis MO. **Parent company:** Daughters of Charity.

SHRINER'S HOSPITAL BURN INSTITUTE
815 Market Street, Galveston TX 77550. 409/770-6600. **Contact:** Human Resources. **World Wide Web address:** http://www.shrinershq.org/shc/galveston. **Description:** A 31-bed, children's burn treatment facility and research center. **Positions advertised include:** Security Guard.

SOUTH AUSTIN HOSPITAL
901 West Ben White Boulevard, Austin TX 78704. 512/447-2211. **Contact:** Human Resources. **World Wide Web address:** http://www.southaustinhospital.com. **Description:** An acute care, 162-bed hospital that provides basic care for the region. **Positions advertised include:** Respiratory Care Therapist; Licensed Vocational Nurse; Registered Nurse; Clinical Nurse Specialist; MRI Technician; Pharmacy Technician; Pharmacist; Radiology Technician.

SOUTHWEST GENERAL HOSPITAL
7400 Barlite Boulevard, San Antonio TX 78224. 210/921-3439. **Fax:** 210/921-3450. **Recorded jobline:** 210/921-3439. **Contact:** Recruiter. **World Wide Web address:** http://www.swgeneralhospital.com. **Description:** A 286-bed, acute care hospital. Southwest General Hospital offers multiple diagnostic treatment and services in the following medical specialties: general and orthopedic surgery; physical therapy and rehabilitation, the treatment of strokes and complications resulting from diabetes; plastic and oral surgery; pediatrics; cardiac and pulmonary services; treatment of infectious diseases; and diabetes treatment. Southwest General Hospital offers a full range of psychiatric services including adult inpatient, adolescent inpatient, and partial hospitalization for adults. Founded in 1979. **Positions advertised include:** Registered Nurse; Licensed

Vocational Nurse; Financial Counselor; Registered Respiratory Therapist; Nursing Supervisor; Medical Transcriptionist; Medical Technologist. **Corporate headquarters location:** Nashville TN. **Other U.S. locations:** Nationwide. **Parent company:** OrNda Healthcorp. **Operations at this facility include:** Administration; Service.

SOUTHWEST TEXAS METHODIST HOSPITAL
METHODIST WOMEN'S & CHILDREN'S HOSPITAL
7700 Floyd Curl Drive, San Antonio TX 78229. 210/575-4000. **Contact:** Human Resources. **World Wide Web address:** http://www.sahealth.com. **Description:** A 626-bed hospital that offers both short- and long-term care. Methodist Women's & Children's Hospital is a 150-bed hospital that specializes in labor, delivery, and pediatrics.

STARLITE RECOVERY CENTER
P.O. Box 317, Center Point TX 78010-0317. 830/634-2212. **Contact:** Human Resources. **World Wide Web address:** http://www.starliterecovery.com. **Description:** A residential treatment center for adults and adolescents, offering specialized care for substance abusers.

SULZER CARBOMEDICS, INC.
1300 East Anderson Lane, Austin TX 78752-1799. 512/435-3200. **Fax:** 512/435-3306. **Contact:** Glen Stedman, Director of Human Resources. **World Wide Web address:** http://www.carbomedics.com. **Description:** A manufacturer of heart valve replacement products. **Positions advertised include:** Administrative Assistant; Clinical Research Director; Senior Systems Analyst. **Parent company:** Sulzer Medica.

SULZER ORTHOPEDICS
9900 Spectrum Drive, Austin TX 78717. 512/432-9900. **Fax:** 512/432-9200. **Recorded jobline:** 512/432-9283. **Contact:** Employment Recruiter. **World Wide Web address:** http://www.sulzerorthopedics.com. **Description:** A worldwide leader in the manufacture and distribution of orthopedic implants for knees, hips, and shoulders. **Positions advertised include:** Engineering Drafter (Temporary); Library Assistant (Temporary). **Parent company:** Sulzer Medica.

TENET MID-JEFFERSON HOSPITAL
P.O. Box 1917, Nederland TX 77627-1917. 409/727-2321. **Contact:** Human Resources. **World Wide Web address:** http://www.tenethealth.com. **Description:** A full-service hospital with specialized outpatient facilities. **Positions advertised include:** Registered Nurse; Licensed Vocational Nurse; Case Manager; Phlebotomist. **Listed on:** New York Stock Exchange. **Stock exchange symbol:** THC.

TEXAS CENTER FOR INFECTIOUS DISEASE
TEXAS DEPARTMENT OF HEALTH
2303 SE Military Drive, San Antonio TX 78223. 210/534-8857x2255. **Fax:** 210/531-4504. **Contact:** Director of Human Resources. **World Wide Web address:** http://www.tdh.state.tx.us/tcid. **Description:** A hospital that provides acute and chronic care to all patients referred for evaluation. **NOTE:** Texas Center for Infectious Disease offers career opportunities in the following areas: Chronic Respiratory Disease Services, which allows individuals to work with inpatient respiratory disease patients with a concentration on physical rehabilitation, patient education, and lifestyle adaptations; Diabetic Services, in which care includes medical evaluation and patient teaching; Chest Disease Services, through which the hospital treats diseases such as lung cancer, fungal disease, and tuberculosis; and Ambulatory Services, which offers an opportunity to work in a variety of clinics to include chest, Hansen's Disease, diabetes, and infectious diseases. The Texas Center for Infectious Disease also has a Tuberculosis Education Center. **Special programs:** Internships. **Corporate headquarters location:** Austin TX. **Operations at this facility include:** Administration; Research and Development; Service.

TEXAS CHILDREN'S HOSPITAL
P.O. Box 300630, Mail Code 4-4230, Houston TX 77230-0630. 832/824-2020. **Recorded jobline:** 832/824-2022. **Contact:** Human Resources. **World Wide Web address:** http://www.txchildrens.org. **Description:** A pediatric hospital. **Positions advertised include:** Assistant Director of Nursing; Clinical Training and Development Specialist; Clinical Nurse Coordinator; Education Coordinator; Licensed Vocational Nurse; Medical Assistant; Patient Care Assistant; Service Coordinator. **Operations at this facility include:** Administration; Research and Development; Service.

TEXAS MEDICAL CENTER
2151 West Holcombe Boulevard, Houston TX 77030-3303. 713/791-6400. **Contact:** Christy Clark, Director of Human Resources. **Fax:** 713/791-6402. **World Wide Web address:** http://www.tmc.edu. **Description:** A private, nonprofit medical center.

TEXAS ORTHOPEDIC HOSPITAL
7401 South Main, Houston TX 77030. 713/799-8600. **Toll-free phone:** 800/678-4501. **Contact:** Personnel. **World Wide Web address:** http://www.texasorthopedic.com. **Description:** An orthopedic hospital offering specialty surgery, sports medicine, and rehabilitation services. Texas Orthopedic Hospital is an affiliate of Columbia/HCA Healthcare Corporation. Founded in 1995. **Positions advertised include:** Cardiovascular Technician; Critical Care Educator; Director of Women's Services; Licensed Vocational Nurse; Patient Care Technician; Phlebotomist.

TOMBALL REGIONAL HOSPITAL
P.O. Box 889, Tomball TX 77375. 281/351-1623. **Physical address:** 605 Holderrietch Road, Tomball TX 77375. **Jobline:** 281/351-3739. **Contact:** Carrol Adolph. **E-mail address:** jobs@tomballhospital.org. **World Wide Web address:** http://www.tomballhospital.org. **Description:** A full-service hospital employing over 300 physicians. Founded in 1976. **Positions advertised include:** Nuclear Medical Technician; Registered Nurse; Licensed Vocational Nurse; Case Manager; Respiratory Therapist; Physical Therapist; Occupational Therapist; Certified Coding Analyst; Medical Records Clerk; Housekeeper; Cook.

TWELVE OAKS MEDICAL CENTER
6700 Bellaire Boulevard, Houston TX 77074. 713/774-7611. **Contact:** Gary Griffin, Director of Human Resources Department. **World Wide Web address:** http://www.twelveoaksmedicalcenter.com. **Description:** A general hospital. **Positions advertised include:** MRI Technician; Nursing Supervisor; Phlebotomist; Coding Specialist; Social Worker; Assistant Occupational Therapist; Registered Nurse; Registration Associate.

U.S. DEPARTMENT OF VETERANS AFFAIRS
HOUSTON VETERANS ADMINISTRATION MEDICAL CENTER
2002 Holcombe Boulevard, Houston TX 77030. 713/791-1414. **Contact:** Human Resources. **World Wide Web address:** http://www.va.gov. **Description:** A medical center. From 54 hospitals in

1930, the health care system has grown to include 171 medical centers; more than 364 outpatient, community, and outreach clinics; 130 nursing home care units; and 37 domiciliary residences. The department operates at least one medical center in each of the 48 contiguous states, Puerto Rico, and the District of Columbia. With approximately 76,000 medical center beds, the VA treats nearly one million patients in hospitals; 75,000 in nursing home care units; and 25,000 in domiciliary residences. The medical center's outpatient clinics register approximately 24 million visits per year. **NOTE:** The VA Medical Center is seeking to hire current or former federal employees, veterans, and disabled veterans. The VA Medical Center is currently under hiring constraints. Applications from the general public are not accepted. **Parent company:** U.S. Department of Veterans Affairs.

U.S. DEPARTMENT OF VETERANS AFFAIRS
VETERANS ADMINISTRATION MEDICAL CENTER
3600 Memorial Boulevard, Kerrville TX 78028. 830/896-2020. **Contact:** Human Resources. **World Wide Web address:** http://www.va.gov. **Description:** A medical center operated by the U.S. Department of Veterans Affairs. From 54 hospitals in 1930, the VA health care system has grown to include 171 medical centers; more than 364 outpatient, community, and outreach clinics; 130 nursing home care units; and 37 domiciliary residences. The VA operates at least one medical center in each of the 48 contiguous states, Puerto Rico, and the District of Columbia. With approximately 76,000 medical center beds, the VA treats nearly 1 million patients in VA hospitals; 75,000 in nursing home care units; and 25,000 in domiciliary residences. The VA's outpatient clinics register approximately 24 million visits per year. **NOTE:** South Texas Veterans Healthcare System hires current or former federal employees, veterans, and disabled veterans. South Texas Veterans Healthcare System is currently under hiring constraints. Applications from the general public are not accepted. **Corporate headquarters location:** Washington DC.

VALLEY BAPTIST MEDICAL CENTER
P.O. Drawer 2588, Harlingen TX 78550. 956/389-1100. **Contact:** Personnel Manager. **E-mail address:** humanresources@valleybaptist. net. **World Wide Web address:** http://www.vbmc.org. **Description:** A 588-bed, nonprofit, acute care, medical center. **NOTE:** Second and third shifts are offered. **Positions advertised include:** Mammography Technician; Licensed Physical Therapy Assistant;

Physical Therapist; Application Specialist; Phlebotomist; Clinical Laboratory Scientist; Nurse Manager; Pharmacist. **Special programs:** Internships; Co-ops; Summer Jobs. **Corporate headquarters location:** This location.

VALLEY REGIONAL MEDICAL CENTER
100A Alton Gloor Boulevard, Brownsville TX 78526. 956/350-7000. **Contact:** Human Resources. **World Wide Web address:** http://www.valleyregionalmedicalcenter.com. **Description:** This 171-bed, acute care medical center offers services such as skilled nursing, rehabilitation, and various medical specialties. **Positions advertised include:** Director of Food and Nutrition Services; Perinatal Educator; Director of Human Resources; RN Case Manager; Speech Therapist.

WEST OAKS HOSPITAL
6500 Hornwood Drive, Houston TX 77074. 713/995-0909. **Fax:** 713/995-5249. **Recorded jobline:** 713/778-5276. **Contact:** Human Resources. **Description:** A freestanding psychiatric hospital that provides care on inpatient, day treatment, residential treatment, and outpatient bases to children, adolescents, and adults. **Special programs:** Summer Jobs. **Corporate headquarters location:** Austin TX.

HOTELS AND RESTAURANTS

You can expect to find the following types of companies in this chapter:
Casinos • Dinner Theaters • Hotel/Motel Operators • Resorts • Restaurants

ALAMO CAFE
P.O. BOX 790721, San Antonio TX 78279. 210/341-1336. **Fax:** 210/341-3036. **Contact:** Human Resources. **World Wide Web address:** http://www.alamocafe.com. **Description:** A family-style restaurant that serves both American and Mexican foods. **Corporate headquarters location:** This location. **Other U.S. locations:** Dallas TX. **Parent company:** Alamo Restaurants Inc.

DOUBLETREE GUEST SUITES HOTEL
303 West 15th Street, Austin TX 78701. 512/478-7000. **Contact:** Monica D'Richards, Human Resources Director. **World Wide Web address:** http://www.doubletree.com. **Description:** A 189-room hotel.

EMBASSY SUITES HOTEL
300 South Congress Avenue, Austin TX 78704. 512/469-9000. **Contact:** Human Resources Department. **World Wide Web address:** http://www.embassy-suites.com. **Description:** A 262-room hotel.

FLAGSHIP HOTEL OVER THE WATER
2501 Seawall Boulevard, Galveston TX 77550. **Toll-free phone:** 800/392-6542. **Fax:** 409/762-1619. **Contact:** Human Resources. **World Wide Web address:** http://www.galveston.com/accom/flagship. **Description:** A hotel and resort.

FOUR SEASONS HOTEL HOUSTON
1300 Lamar Street, Houston TX 77010. 713/650-1300. **Contact:** Human Resources. **World Wide Web address:** http://www.fshr.com. **Description:** A 399-room hotel that also houses the DeVille Restaurant. Four Seasons Hotels & Resorts operates approximately 55 luxury hotels and resorts in 25 countries. Founded in 1960. **Corporate headquarters location:** Toronto, Canada.

GOLDEN CORRAL
4610 Garth Road, Baytown TX 77522. 281/422-3455. **Contact:** Hiring Manager. **World Wide Web address:** http://www.goldencorralrest.com. **Description:** One location of a chain of family steakhouses. **Corporate headquarters location:** Raleigh NC.

HOFFBRAU STEAKS

5075 Garth Road, Baytown TX 77520. 281/421-1998. **Contact:** Human Resources. **World Wide Web address:** http://www.hoffbrausteaks.com. **Description:** A casual-dining steak house and beer garden. Hoffbrau Steaks operates through 26 locations. Founded in 1939. **Corporate headquarters location:** Austin TX.

HOFFBRAU STEAKS

2310 North 11th Street, Beaumont TX 77703. 409/892-6911. **Contact:** Human Resources. **World Wide Web address:** http://www.hoffbrausteaks.com. **Description:** A casual-dining steak house and beer garden. Hoffbrau Steaks operates through 26 locations. Founded in 1939. **Corporate headquarters location:** Austin TX.

HOLIDAY INN BEAUMONT PLAZA

3950 Interstate 10 South, Beaumont TX 77705. 409/842-5995. **Fax:** 409/842-0315. **Contact:** Human Resources Department. **World Wide Web address:** http://www.sixcontinentshotels.com/holiday-inn. **Description:** This is a franchise location of the national hotel chain. Holiday Inn Beaumont Plaza offers 235 guest rooms and has one of the largest hotel conference centers in Texas. **Other U.S. locations:** Nationwide. **Parent company:** Six Continents Hotels.

HOLIDAY INN EXPRESS

5222 Interstate 10 East, Baytown TX 77521. 281/421-7200. **Fax:** 281/421-7209. **Contact:** Human Resources Department. **World Wide Web address:** http://www.sixcontinentshotels.com/hiexpress. **Description:** One location of the national hotel chain. **Other U.S. locations:** Nationwide. **Parent company:** Six Continents Hotels.

HOLIDAY INN MIDTOWN

2095 North 11th Street, Beaumont TX 77703. 409/892-2222. **Contact:** Human Resources. **World Wide Web address:** http://www.sixcontinentshotels.com/holiday-inn. **Description:** One location of the national hotel chain. Holiday Inn Midtown offers 190 guest rooms, as well as meeting and banquet facilities. **Other U.S. locations:** Nationwide. **Parent company:** Six Continents Hotels.

HOLIDAY INN NORTH

6911 North Interstate Highway 35, Austin TX 78752. 512/459-4251. **Contact:** Human Resources. **World Wide Web address:** http://www.sixcontinentshotels.com/holiday-inn. **Description:** One location of the nationwide hotel chain. **Parent company:** Six Continents Hotels.

HYATT REGENCY HILL COUNTRY RESORT
9800 Hyatt Resort Drive, San Antonio TX 78251. 210/647-1234. **Contact:** Penny Nichols Bowden, Human Resources Director. **World Wide Web address:** http://www.hyatt.com. **Description:** Operates as a unit of the nationwide chain of hotels. Hyatt Regency Hill Country Resort has six locations throughout Texas. **Parent company:** Hyatt Hotels Corporation.

HYATT REGENCY HOUSTON
1200 Louisiana Street, Houston TX 77002. 713/646-6922. **Contact:** LaTanya Hunter, Employment Manager. **World Wide Web address:** http://houstonregency.hyatt.com. **Description:** A 963-room hotel with meeting and banquet facilities. **Positions advertised include:** Assistant Restaurant Manager; Housekeeper/Room Attendant; Restaurant Manager. **Corporate headquarters location:** Chicago IL. **Other U.S. locations:** Nationwide. **International locations:** Worldwide. **Parent company:** Hyatt Hotels Corporation.

JACK IN THE BOX
1111 North Loop West, Suite 600, Houston TX 77008. 713/293-6200. **Contact:** Human Resources. **World Wide Web address:** http://www.jackinthebox.com. **Description:** Operates and franchises more than 1,730 Jack in the Box restaurants, which are primarily in the western and southwestern United States. International operations currently include restaurants in Hong Kong and Mexico. **Positions advertised include:** C-Store/Fuel Operations Manager; Restaurant Manager; Assistant Facility Service Manager; Assistant Restaurant Manager. **Listed on:** New York Stock Exchange. **Stock exchange symbol:** JBX.

LA QUINTA INNS, INC.
909 Hidden Ridge, Suite 600, Irving TX 75038. 210/302-6000. **Contact:** Human Resources. **World Wide Web address:** http://www.laquinta.com. **Description:** Develops, owns, and operates a nationwide chain of lodging inns. La Quinta Inns has more than 330 locations in 32 states. Founded in 1964. **Positions advertised include:** Executive Assistant. **Corporate headquarters location:** This location. **Parent company:** Meditrust. **Listed on:** New York Stock Exchange. **Stock exchange symbol:** LQI. **Number of employees nationwide:** More than 7,000.

QUALITY INN BAYTOWN
300 South Highway 146 Business Road, Baytown TX 77520. 281/427-7481. **Contact:** Human Resources. **World Wide Web address:** http://www4.choicehotels.com. **Description:** A full-service hotel, operating as part of the national chain. **Other U.S. locations:** Nationwide. **Parent company:** Choice Hotels International. **Listed on:** NYSE. **Stock exchange symbol:** CHH.

TACO CABANA, INC.
8918 Tesoro Drive, Suite 200, San Antonio TX 78217. 210/804-0990. **Fax:** 210/804-2425. **Contact:** Personnel. **World Wide Web address:** http://www.tacocabana.com. **Description:** Taco Cabana operates a chain of Mexican restaurants. Founded in 1978. **Corporate headquarters location:** This location. **Parent company:** Carrols Corporation.

VICTORIAN CONDO HOTEL & CONFERENCE CENTER
6300 Seawall Boulevard, Galveston TX 77550. **Toll-free phone:** 800/231-6363. **Contact:** Personnel. **World Wide Web address:** http://www.galveston.com/victorian. **Description:** A full-service hotel and conference center.

INSURANCE

You can expect to find the following types of companies in this chapter:
Commercial and Industrial Property/Casualty Insurers • Health Maintenance Organizations (HMOs) • Medical/Life Insurance Companies

ACAP GROUP
P.O. Box 42814, Houston TX 77242-2814. 713/974-2242. **Toll-free phone:** 800/527-2567. **Fax:** 713/953-7920. **Contact:** Personnel Director. **Description:** A holding company for life insurance subsidiaries. **NOTE:** Entry-level positions are offered. **Corporate headquarters location:** This location. **Subsidiaries include:** American Capitol Insurance Company; Imperial Plan; Statesman National Life Insurance Company; Texas Imperial Life Insurance Company.

AMERICAN GENERAL CORPORATION
P.O. Box 3247, Houston TX 77253. 713/522-1111. **Contact:** Human Resources. **World Wide Web address:** http://www.agc.com. **Description:** One of the largest public insurance companies in the United States. Other services include mortgage loans, real estate investment and development, investment counseling, and management and distribution of mutual funds. **Corporate headquarters location:** This location. **Subsidiaries include:** American General Annuities; American General Life Company. **Parent company:** AIG. **Listed on:** New York Stock Exchange. **Stock exchange symbol:** AIG.

AMERICAN NATIONAL INSURANCE COMPANY
One Moody Plaza, Galveston TX 77550. 409/763-4661. **Fax:** 409/766-6417. **Contact:** Human Resources. **World Wide Web address:** http://www.american-national.com. **Description:** A leading insurance company that, directly and through its subsidiaries, offers a broad line of insurance coverage including individual life, health, and annuities; group life and health; and credit insurance. **Positions advertised include:** Actuarial; Compliance Informational Professional. **Corporate headquarters location:** This location. **Subsidiaries include:** American National Property and Casualty Insurance Company; Securities Management and Research, Inc. **Listed on:** NASDAQ. **Stock exchange symbol:** ANAT.

CHICAGO TITLE INSURANCE COMPANY
909 Fannon, Suite 200, Houston TX 77010. 713/659-1411. **Fax:** 713/653-6190. **Contact:** Administrative Services Office. **World Wide**

Web address: http://www.houston.ctic.com. **Description:** Provides title insurance. **Corporate headquarters location:** Chicago IL. **Other U.S. locations:** Nationwide. **Subsidiaries include:** Ticor Title Security Union. **Operations at this facility include:** Administration; Divisional Headquarters; Sales; Service. **Listed on:** New York Stock Exchange. **Stock exchange symbol:** FNF.

CITIZENS, INC.
P.O. Box 149151, Austin TX 78714-9151. 512/837-7100. **Fax:** 512/836-9785. **Contact:** Human Resources. **World Wide Web address:** http://www.citizensinc.com. **Description:** A life insurance holding company. **Positions advertised include:** Executive Assistant; Accounting Manager; Commissions Technician; Actuarial Manager; Operations Manager; Claims Processor; Customer Relations Manager. **Corporate headquarters location:** This location. **Subsidiaries include:** Citizens Insurance Company of America (CICA) is a Colorado life insurance company that provides ordinary whole-life products on an international basis. **Listed on:** American Stock Exchange. **Stock exchange symbol:** CIA.

FIC INSURANCE GROUP
P.O. Box 149138, Austin TX 78714-9138. 512/404-5000. **Contact:** Human Resources. **World Wide Web address:** http://www.ficgroup.com. **Description:** An insurance company that specializes in life insurance. **Corporate headquarters location:** This location. **Other U.S. locations:** Seattle WA.

FARMERS INSURANCE GROUP
P.O. Box 149044, Austin TX 78714-9044. 512/238-4400. **Contact:** Human Resources. **World Wide Web address:** http://www.farmersinsurance.com. **Description:** Operates as the center for applications and payments for processing auto, home, boat, and life insurance.

THE NATIONAL ALLIANCE FOR INSURANCE EDUCATION & RESEARCH
P.O. Box 27027, Austin TX 78755-1027. 512/345-7932. **Fax:** 512/343-2167. **Contact:** Amy Schott, Human Resources Director. **World Wide Web address:** http://www.scic.com. **Description:** A nonprofit insurance education organization offering the Certified Insurance Counselors (CIC) designation, the Certified Insurance Service Representatives (CISR) designation, and the Certified Risk

Manager (CRM) designation. The Academy of Producers Insurance Studies is the research arm of The National Alliance.

PROGRESSIVE COUNTY MUTUAL INSURANCE COMPANY
1124 South IH 35, Austin TX 78704. 512/441-2000. **Fax:** 512/464-1136. **Recorded jobline:** 512/464-1164. **Contact:** Human Resources. **World Wide Web address:** http://www.progressive.com. **Description:** An automobile insurance company. **Listed on:** New York Stock Exchange. **Stock exchange symbol:** PGR.

RANGER INSURANCE COMPANY
P.O. Box 2807, Houston TX 77252-2807. 713/954-8100. **Contact:** Human Resources. **World Wide Web address:** http://www.rangerinsurance.com. **Description:** Markets specialty lines of commercial property and casualty insurance as well as nonstandard automobile insurance. **Corporate headquarters location:** This location.

STATE FARM INSURANCE
8900 Amberglen Boulevard, Austin TX 78729. 512/918-4000. **Contact:** Human Resources. **World Wide Web address:** http://www.statefarm.com. **Description:** An insurance company that processes home, life, and health insurance policies through its various agents. **Corporate headquarters location:** Bloomington IL.

STATE FARM INSURANCE
6707 North Gessner Drive, Houston TX 77040. 713/895-2200. **Contact:** Human Resources. **World Wide Web address:** http://www.statefarm.com. **Description:** Provides home, life, and health insurance policies. **Corporate headquarters location:** Bloomington IL.

LEGAL SERVICES

You can expect to find the following types of companies in this chapter:
Law Firms • Legal Service Agencies

BOBBIT, HALTER & WATSON
8700 Groundhill Boulevard, Suite 300, San Antonio TX 78209. 210/824-1555. **Contact:** Richard Halter, Managing Partner. **Description:** A law firm involved in many different areas including real estate, litigation, wills, and probates.

ANDREWS & KURTH L.L.P.
600 Travis Street, Suite 4200, Houston TX 77002. 713/220-4200. **Contact:** Deborah Ganjavi, Human Resources Director. **World Wide Web address:** http://www.andrews-kurth.com. **Description:** A law firm. **Corporate headquarters location:** This location. **Other area locations:** Dallas TX. **Other U.S. locations:** Los Angeles CA; Washington DC; New York NY. **Operations at this facility include:** Administration.

ARMBRUST & BROWN L.L.P.
100 Congress Avenue, Suite 1300, Austin TX 78701-4042. 512/435-2300. **Fax:** 512/435-2360. **Contact:** Human Resources Department. **World Wide Web address:** http://www.abaustin.com. **Description:** A law firm specializing in real estate and product liability law.

BAKER BOTTS LLP
One Shell Plaza, 910 Louisiana Street, Houston TX 77002. 713/229-1234. **Fax:** 713/229-1522. **Contact:** Annette M. Schlaf, Manager of Legal Assistants. **E-mail address:** annette.schlaf@bakerbotts.com. **World Wide Web address:** http://www.bakerbotts.com. **Description:** A law firm providing services in almost all areas of civil law. Baker Botts, LLP is one of the nation's oldest and largest law firms. **Positions advertised include:** Legal Assistant; Paralegal. **Corporate headquarters location:** This location. **Other U.S. locations:** DC; NY. **International locations:** Azerbaijan; England; Russia; Saudi Arabia. **Operations at this facility include:** Service.

BRACEWELL AND PATTERSON LLP
711 Louisiana Street, Suite 2900, Houston TX 77002-2781. 713/223-2900. **Contact:** Helen Lilienstern, Director of Human Resources. **World Wide Web address:** http://www.bracepatt.com. **Description:** A law firm divided into a litigation group and a business group. The

litigation group specialties include trial, bankruptcy, and appellate law. The business group specialties include corporate, energy, and real estate law. **Other U.S. locations:** Austin TX; Dallas TX.

BROWN SIMS, P.C.
1177 West Loop South, 10th Floor, Houston TX 77027. 713/629-1580. **Fax:** 713/629-5027. **Contact:** Administrator. **World Wide Web address:** http://www.brownsims.com. **Description:** A law firm specializing in shipping law. **Positions advertised include:** Legal Secretary. **Corporate headquarters location:** This location.

CLARK, THOMAS & WINTERS
P.O. Box 1148, Austin TX 78767. 512/472-8800. **Contact:** Jean Atkisslin, Assistant to the President. **World Wide Web address:** http://www.ctw.com. **Description:** A law firm specializing in a variety of areas including antitrust, environmental, and product liability law.

FULBRIGHT AND JAWORSKI LLP
1301 McKinney Street, Suite 5100, Houston TX 77010-3095. 713/651-5151. **Contact:** Director of Human Resources. **World Wide Web address:** http://www.fulbright.com. **Description:** A national legal services firm. **Positions advertised include:** Contracts Held Desk Specialist; Legal Assistant; Technical Advisor. **Special programs:** Internships. **Corporate headquarters location:** This location. **Operations at this facility include:** Administration.

GRISSOM, RICHARDS, AND FEATHERSTON
3700 Montrose Boulevard, Houston TX 77006. 713/526-4773. **Contact:** Human Resources. **Description:** A law firm specializing in personal injury and worker's compensation.

HOWREY, SIMON, ARNOLD & WHITE
750 Bering Drive, Houston TX 77057. 713/787-1400. **Contact:** Human Resources. **World Wide Web address:** http://www.howrey.com. **Description:** A law firm specializing in antitrust matters.

JACKSON WALKER L.L.P.
1401 McKinney Street, Suite 1900, Houston TX 77010. 713/752-4347. **Fax:** 713/752-4435. **Contact:** Bette Moore, Administrator. **E-mail address:** bmoore@iw.com. **World Wide Web address:** http://www.jw.com. **Description:** A full-service law firm with a worldwide client base. Jackson Walker specializes in corporate, trust, and estate

law. **Special programs:** Internships. **Corporate headquarters location:** Dallas TX.

LOCKE LIDDELL & SAPP LLP
3400 J.P. Morgan Chase Tower, 600 Travis, Houston TX 77002. 713/226-1200. **Contact:** Stanley Wells, Human Resources. **World Wide Web address:** http://www.lockeliddell.com. **Description:** A firm practicing in all segments of corporate law.

NATHAN, SOMMERS, LIPPMAN, JACOBS & GORMAN
2800 Post Oak Boulevard, 61st Floor, Houston TX 77056. 713/960-0303. **Contact:** Kristie Ratliff, Financial Administrator. **Description:** A corporate law firm specializing in bankruptcy law, litigation, and real estate law. **Special programs:** Internships. **Corporate headquarters location:** This location.

PLUNKETT & GIBSON, INC.
P.O. Box BH002, San Antonio TX 78201. 210/734-7092. **Physical address:** 6243 IH 10 West, Suite 600, San Antonio TX 78201. **Contact:** Human Resources. **World Wide Web address:** http://www.plunkett-gibson.com. **Description:** A defense law firm specializing in a variety of areas including insurance, medical malpractice, bankruptcy, and litigation.

SUSMAN GODFREY L.L.P.
1000 Louisiana Street, Suite 5100, Houston TX 77002-5096. 713/651-9366. **Contact:** Personnel. **World Wide Web address:** http://www.susmangodfrey.com. **Description:** A law firm specializing in antitrust, energy and natural resources, libel, negligence, litigation, intellectual property, and product liability law.

THOMPSON & KNIGHT LLP
2 Allen Center, 1200 Smith Street, Suite 3600, Houston TX 77002. 713/654-8111. **Contact:** Human Resources. **World Wide Web address:** http://www.tklaw.com. **Description:** A law firm providing services in a variety of disciplines including corporate, bankruptcy, employment, and international law.

U.S. LEGAL SUPPORT, INC.
519 North Sam Houston Parkway East, Houston TX 77060. 713/653-7100. **Toll-free phone:** 800/622-1107. **Fax:** 713/653-7171. **Contact:** Human Resources Manager. **World Wide Web address:** http://www.uslegalsupport.com. **Description:** Provides support services in

the areas of certified depositions and trial reporters, specialized video services, and records retrieval.

MANUFACTURING: MISCELLANEOUS CONSUMER

You can expect to find the following types of companies in this chapter:
Art Supplies • Batteries • Cosmetics and Related Products • Household Appliances and Audio/Video Equipment • Jewelry, Silverware, and Plated Ware • Miscellaneous Household Furniture and Fixtures • Musical Instruments • Tools • Toys and Sporting Goods

ADT SECURITY SERVICES

11500 Metric Boulevard, Suite 430, Austin TX 78758. 512/832-0122. **Contact:** Human Resources. **World Wide Web address:** http://www.adtsecurityservices.com. **Description:** Designs, installs, sells, and monitors fire and burglar alarm systems for commercial and industrial retail customers. ADT Security also offers armed and unarmed security guards. **Corporate headquarters location:** Boca Raton FL. **Parent company:** Tyco International, Ltd. **Listed on:** New York Stock Exchange. **Stock exchange symbol:** TYC.

ADT SECURITY SERVICES

140 Heimer Road, Suite 100, San Antonio TX 78232. 210/491-0300. **Contact:** Human Resources. **World Wide Web address:** http://www.adtsecurityservices.com. **Description:** Designs, installs, sells, and monitors fire and burglar alarm systems for commercial and industrial retail customers. ADT Security also offers armed and unarmed security guards. **Corporate headquarters location:** Boca Raton FL. **Parent company:** Tyco International, Ltd. **Listed on:** New York Stock Exchange. **Stock exchange symbol:** TYC.

ADTEC DETENTION SYSTEMS

10700 Sentinel Street, San Antonio TX 78217. 210/829-7951. **Fax:** 210/829-0010. **Contact:** Personnel. **Description:** Manufactures locks and sliding devices for security within prison and jail systems. **Number of employees at this location:** 40.

ALLIED SECURITY INC.

9800 North Lamar Boulevard, Suite 206, Austin TX 78753. 512/836-8599. **Contact:** Human Resources. **World Wide Web address:** http://www.alliedsecurity.com. **Description:** One of the largest contract security officer companies in the nation. Allied Security provides loss prevention services to private businesses and government agencies. **Corporate headquarters location:** King of Prussia PA.

ALLIED SECURITY INC.

1635 NE Loop 410, Suite 206, San Antonio TX 78209. 210/829-1711. **Contact:** Human Resources. **World Wide Web address:** http://www.alliedsecurity.com. **Description:** One of the largest contract security officer companies in the nation. Allied Security provides loss prevention services to private businesses and government agencies. **Corporate headquarters location:** King of Prussia PA.

ALLIED VAUGHN

3694 Westchase Drive, Houston TX 77042. 713/266-4269. **Contact:** Human Resources. **World Wide Web address:** http://www.allied-digital.com. **Description:** One of the nation's leading independent, multimedia manufacturing companies, offering CD-audio and CD-ROM mastering and replication; videocassette and audiocassette duplication; laser video disc recording; off-line and online video editing; motion picture film processing; film-to-tape and tape-to-film transfers; and complete finishing, packaging, warehousing, and fulfillment services. **Listed on:** Privately held.

COMMEMORATIVE BRANDS

P.O. Box 149207, Austin TX 78714-9207. 512/444-0577. **Contact:** Human Resources. **World Wide Web address:** http://www.artcarved.com. **Description:** Manufactures custom jewelry for schools, sports, and businesses. Other areas of activity include service award programs and the printing of announcements. **Operations at this facility include:** Administration; Divisional Headquarters; Manufacturing; Sales; Service.

FAROUK SYSTEMS

250 Pennbright Drive, Houston TX 77090. 281/876-2000. **Contact:** Human Resources. **World Wide Web address:** http://www.farouk.com. **Description:** Manufactures a wide variety of consumer hair care products.

IGLOO PRODUCTS CORPORATION

1001 West Sam Houston Parkway North, Houston TX 77013. 713/465-2571. **Contact:** Human Resources. **World Wide Web address:** http://www.igloocoolers.com. **Description:** Manufactures beverage coolers, ice chests, and similar products. Igloo Products Corporation is a division of Coca-Cola Company.

IMMUDYNE, INC.

11200 Wilcrest Green Drive, Houston TX 77042. 713/783-7034. **Contact:** Human Resources. **World Wide Web address:** http://www.immudyne.com. **Description:** Develops, manufactures, and markets dietary supplements and skin care products. **Corporate headquarters location:** This location.

TRICO TECHNOLOGIES

1995 Billy Mitchell Boulevard, Brownsville TX 78521. 956/544-2722. **Contact:** Human Resources. **World Wide Web address:** http://www.tricoproducts.com. **Description:** A manufacturer of windshield wipers. **Special programs:** Training. **Corporate headquarters location:** Rochester Hills MI.

MANUFACTURING:
MISCELLANEOUS INDUSTRIAL

You can expect to find the following types of companies in this chapter:
Ball and Roller Bearings • Commercial Furniture and Fixtures • Fans, Blowers, and Purification Equipment • Industrial Machinery and Equipment • Motors and Generators/Compressors and Engine Parts • Vending Machines

AERIFORM CORPORATION
4201 FM 1960 West, Suite 590, Houston TX 77068. 281/631-0667. **Contact:** Human Resources. **World Wide Web address:** http://www.aeriform.com. **Description:** Aeriform ranks among the nation's largest independent suppliers of specialty gases, medical gases, welding equipment, and cryogenic products. **Positions advertised include:** Driver; Inside/Counter Sales Representative; Branch Manager; Customer Service Manager. **Corporate headquarters location:** This location.

AIR PRODUCTS & CHEMICALS, INC.
1423 Highway 225, P.O. Box 3326, Pasadena TX 77501. 713/477-6841. **Contact:** Human Resources. **World Wide Web address:** http://www.airproducts.com. **Description:** Manufactures specialty chemicals, industrial gases, and related equipment. **Operations at this facility include:** This location manufactures polyurethane intermediates. **Listed on:** New York Stock Exchange. **Stock Exchange Symbol:** APD.

AKZO NOBEL CATALYSTS
13000 Bay Park Road, Pasadena TX 77507. 281/474-2864. **Contact:** Human Resources. **World Wide Web address:** http://www.akzonobel-catalysts.com. **Description:** Akzo Nobel is a worldwide manufacturer of chemicals, coatings, health care products, and fibers. Business activities are conducted in four units: The Chemicals Group produces polymer chemicals, rubber chemicals, catalysts, detergents, surfactants, functional chemicals, chlor-alkali, and industrial chemicals. The Coatings Group produces decorative coatings, car refinishes, industrial coatings, industrial wood finishes, aerospace finishes, automotive finishes, and resins. The Pharma Group includes ethical drugs, hospital supplies, nonprescription products, raw materials for the pharmaceuticals industry, generics, and veterinary products. The Fibers Group produces textile, industrial, and high-performance fibers, industrial

nonwovens, and membranes for medical, technical, and industrial uses. **Corporate headquarters location:** Chicago IL. **International locations:** Worldwide. **Operations at this facility include:** This location manufactures catalysts.

CSI INTERNATIONAL
P.O. Box 266307, Houston TX 77207-6724. 713/644-5353. **Fax:** 713/845-1515. **Contact:** Human Resources. **E-mail address:** hr@csiionline.com. **World Wide Web address:** http://www.csiionline.com. **Description:** Manufactures control valves. **Positions advertised include:** Sales Professional; Engineer. **Corporate headquarters location:** This location.

CAPITAL CITY CONTAINER CORP.
P.O. Box 870, Buda TX 78610-0870. 512/312-1222. **Physical address:** 150 Precision Drive, Buda TX. **Fax:** 512/312-1349. **Contact:** Human Resources. **World Wide Web address:** http://www.capitalcitycontainer.com. **Description:** Manufactures corrugated containers and provides die cut, direct print, and four-color process services.

CONTINENTAL MANUFACTURING COMPANY
9797 Old Galveston Road, Houston TX 77034. 713/947-2600. **Contact:** Human Resources. **World Wide Web address:** http://www.cbmwmixers.com. **Description:** Manufactures automotive drums, drum brakes, and related accessories.

DANIEL INDUSTRIES, INC.
9720 Oldkaty Road, Houston TX 77055. 713/467-6000. **Contact:** Human Resources. **World Wide Web address:** http://www.danielind.com. **Description:** A manufacturer of fluid measurement products, primarily for the oil and natural gas industries. **Corporate headquarters location:** This location. **Parent company:** Emerson Electric. **Listed on:** New York Stock Exchange. **Stock exchange symbol:** EMR. **Number of employees nationwide:** 1,600.

E.I. DUPONT DE NEMOURS & COMPANY
P.O. Box 347, La Porte TX 77572-0347. 281/471-2771. **Physical address:** 12501 Strang Road, La Porte TX 77571. **Contact:** Human Resources. **World Wide Web address:** http://www.dupont.com. **Description:** E.I. DuPont de Nemours & Company's activities include the manufacturing of biomedical, industrial, and consumer

products (such as photographic, data-recording, and video devices); the production of man-made fiber products (with applications in a variety of consumer and commercial industries), polymer products (such as plastic resins, elastomers, and films), and agricultural and industrial chemicals (such as herbicides and insecticides, pigments, fluorochemicals, petroleum additives, and mineral acids); the exploration and production of crude oil and natural gas; the refining, marketing, and downstream transportation of petroleum; and the mining and distribution of steam and metallurgical coals. The company supplies the aerospace, agriculture, apparel, transportation, health care, and printing and publishing industries. **Corporate headquarters location:** Wilmington DE. **Operations at this facility include:** This location manufactures specialty chemicals such as titanium dioxide, fluorochemicals, and polymer intermediates used in coatings, paper, plastic, textile, and other industries; manufactures specialty fibers for textile, apparel, and other markets; produces engineering polymers, elastomers, fluoropolymers, ethylene polymers, and other polymers for packaging, construction, electrical, paper, and other industries; explores for, produces, refines, markets, supplies, and transports crude oil; produces and transports natural gas and natural gas products; produces agricultural chemicals; and owns and operates refineries. **Listed on:** New York Stock Exchange. **Stock exchange symbol:** DD.

E.I. DUPONT DE NEMOURS & COMPANY
P.O. Box 2626, Victoria TX 77902-2626. 361/572-1111. **Physical address:** 2695 Old Bloomington Road North, Victoria TX 77905. **Contact:** Human Resources. **World Wide Web address:** http://www.dupont.com. **Description:** E.I. DuPont de Nemours & Company's activities include the manufacturing of biomedical, industrial, and consumer products (such as photographic, data-recording, and video devices); the production of man-made fiber products (with applications in a variety of consumer and commercial industries); polymer products (such as plastic resins, elastomers, and films); agricultural and industrial chemicals (such as herbicides and insecticides, pigments, fluorochemicals, petroleum additives, and mineral acids); the exploration and production of crude oil and natural gas; the refining, marketing, and downstream transportation of petroleum; and the mining and distribution of steam and metallurgical coals. The company supplies the aerospace, agricultural, apparel, transportation, health care, and printing and publishing industries. **Corporate headquarters location:** Wilmington DE. **Operations at this facility include:** This location is a chemical

processing plant. **Listed on:** New York Stock Exchange. **Listed on:** New York Stock Exchange. **Stock exchange symbol:** DD.

ETS LINDGREN
1301 Arrow Point Drive, Cedar Park TX 78613. 512/835-4684. **Fax:** 512/835-4729. **Contact:** Kristen Kobierowski, Human Resources Manager. **World Wide Web address:** http://www.ets-lindgren.com. **Description:** Designs, manufactures, and maintains products that measure, contain, and suppress electromagnetic, RF, and microwave energy. The company markets its products under the names Rantec, EMCO, Rayproof, and Enroshield. Founded in 1995. **NOTE:** Second and third shifts are offered. **Special programs:** Internships. **Other U.S. locations:** IL; OK; WI. **International locations:** Finland; Singapore. **Parent company:** ESCO Technologies Corporation is a diversified producer of commercial products. ESCO's products include electronic equipment, valves and filters, filtration and fluid flow components, automatic test equipment, utility load management equipment, and anechoic/shielding systems. ESCO's other operating subsidiaries include PTI Technologies, Inc.; VACCO Industries; Distribution Control Systems, Inc.; Rantec Microwave & Electronics; Lindgren RF Enclosures; Comtrak Technologies, Inc.; and Filtertek Inc. **Listed on:** New York Stock Exchange. **Stock exchange symbol:** ESE.

EAGLE TRAFFIC CONTROL SYSTEMS
8004 Cameron Road, Austin TX 78754. 512/837-8310. **Fax:** 512/837-8470. **Contact:** Jan Sannes, Human Resources Manager. **World Wide Web address:** http://www.eagletcs.com. **Description:** Manufactures traffic control systems and lights. **Parent company:** Siemens Energy & Automation, Inc.

ENGINE COMPONENTS INC.
9503 Middlex Drive, San Antonio TX 78217. 210/820-8100. **Contact:** Human Resources. **World Wide Web address:** http://www.eci2fly.com. **Description:** Manufactures and repairs engine components for aircraft. **Corporate headquarters location:** This location. **Other U.S. locations:** Bradenton FL; Aurora OR.

FLEXITALLIC GASKET COMPANY
6915 Highway 225, Deer Park TX 77536. 713/356-3600. **Contact:** Human Resources. **E-mail address:** hr@flexitallic.com. **World Wide Web address:** http://www.flexitallic.com. **Description:** Manufactures

spiral gaskets. **Corporate headquarters location:** Houston TX. **Other U.S. locations:** NJ.

FLOW PRODUCTS INCORPORATED
800 Koomey Road, Brookshire TX 77423. 281/934-6014. **Fax:** 281/934-6052. **Contact:** Human Resources. **World Wide Web address:** http://www.paco-pumps.com. **Description:** Manufactures industrial pumps and valves through its subsidiaries. **Positions advertised include:** Regional Sales Representative; Manual Machinist; Application Engineer; Design Engineer; Order Entry Coordinator. **Corporate headquarters location:** This location. **Other U.S. locations:** AL; CA; OR; TN; UT; VA; WA. **Subsidiaries include:** Johnston Pump; PACO Pumps; General Valve. All three companies are also at this location.

GAYLORD CONTAINER CORPORATION
1111 Coliseum Road, San Antonio TX 78219. 210/225-2901. **Contact:** Human Resources. **World Wide Web address:** http://www.gaylordcontainer.com. **Description:** Gaylord Container Corporation makes and distributes corrugated containers, containerboard, unbleached kraft paper, specialty chemicals, multiwall bags, grocery bags, and sacks to manufacturing end users and converters. The company operates through two grocery bag and sack conversion plants, three paper mills, nineteen corrugated container plants, two multiwall bag plants, and four other facilities. By-products of container production include dimethyl sulfide and dimethyl sulfoxide, which the company also markets. **Corporate headquarters location:** Deerfield IL. **Listed on:** American Stock Exchange. **Stock exchange symbol:** GCR.

W.W. GRAINGER
430 Sun Belt Drive, Corpus Christi TX 78408. 361/289-9201. **Fax:** 361/289-7943. **Contact:** Human Resources. **World Wide Web address:** http://www.grainger.com. **Description:** W.W. Grainger is a national supplier of industrial equipment such as motors, pumps, and safety maintenance equipment. The company distributes a variety of equipment and components to the industrial, commercial, contracting, and institutional markets. Products are sold through local branches and include equipment and components for motors, air tools, hydraulic products, refrigeration items, power and hand tools, office equipment, computer supplies, replacement parts, industrial products, safety items, cold weather clothing, and storage

equipment. Founded in 1927. **Operations at this facility include:** This location sells industrial supplies.

GROTH CORPORATION
13650 North Promenade Boulevard, Stafford TX 77477. 713/675-6151. **Contact:** Human Resources Manager. **E-mail address:** hr@growthcorp.com. **World Wide Web address:** http://www.grothcorp.com. **Description:** Engaged in the manufacture, sale, and service of valves and related instrumentation products. The company's customer base includes petrochemical and paper/pulp plants, and municipalities. **Corporate headquarters location:** This location. **Operations at this facility include:** Manufacturing; Sales; Service.

GULF STATES ASPHALT COMPANY
P.O. Box 508, South Houston TX 77587-0508. 713/941-4410. **Physical address:** 300 Christi Place, South Houston TX 77587-5165. **Contact:** Human Resources. **World Wide Web address:** http://www.gsac.net. **Description:** An asphalt manufacturing plant.

HUGHES CHRISTENSEN COMPANY
P.O. Box 2539, Houston TX 77252. 281/363-6000. **Physical address:** 9110 Grogans Mill Road, The Woodlands TX 77380. **Fax:** 281/363-6025. **Contact:** Human Resources. **World Wide Web address:** http://www.hugheschris.com. **Description:** A manufacturer of rock bits and diamond bits for the oil and gas industries. **Positions advertised include:** Financial Analyst; Drafter; Process Analyst; Electrical Engineer; Senior Legal Assistant; Critical Well Project Manager; Accounts Payable Supervisor. **Corporate headquarters location:** This location. **Parent company:** Baker Hughes, Inc. **Listed on:** New York Stock Exchange. **Stock exchange symbol:** BHI.

HYDRIL COMPANY
3300 North Sam Houston Parkway East, Houston TX 77032. 281/449-2000. **Fax:** 281/985-3295. **Contact:** Mike Danford, Director of Human Resources. **World Wide Web address:** http://www.hydril.com. **Description:** Manufactures oil field machinery and petroleum equipment. Founded in 1933. **Positions advertised include:** Engineer; Senior CNC Programmer; Sales Representative. **Corporate headquarters location:** This location. **Listed on:** NASDAQ. **Stock exchange symbol:** HYDL. **Number of employees worldwide:** 1,500.

INDUSTRIAL PROFILE SYSTEMS

6703 Theall Road, Houston TX 77066. 281/893-0100. **Contact:** Human Resources. **World Wide Web address:** http://www.ips-i.com. **Description:** Manufactures aluminum work centers for industrial automation and machine building. **Parent company:** Parker-Hannifin. **Listed on:** New York Stock Exchange. **Stock exchange symbol:** PH.

INLAND CONTAINER CORPORATION

1750 Inland Road, Orange TX 77632. 409/746-2441. **Contact:** Human Resources. **World Wide Web address:** http://www.inlandonline.com. **Description:** Manufactures corrugated shipping containers and boxes. **Corporate headquarters location:** Indianapolis IN.

INPUT/OUTPUT, INC.

12300 Parc Crest Drive, Stafford TX 77477. 281/933-3339. **Contact:** Human Resources. **World Wide Web address:** http://www.i-o.com. **Description:** Designs, manufactures, and markets seismic data acquisition systems and related equipment. **Positions advertised include:** Senior Digital Design Engineer; Development Engineer; Senior MEMS Development Engineer; Financial Manager; National Sales Account Manager. **Corporate headquarters location:** This location. **Subsidiaries include:** Output Exploration Company conducts geophysical operations and acquires oil and gas leases. Founded in 1968. **Listed on:** New York Stock Exchange. **Stock exchange symbol:** IO.

INTERCRAFT-BURNES COMPANY

One Intercraft Plaza, P.O. Box 1130, Taylor TX 76574. 512/352-8500. **Contact:** Human Resources. **E-mail address:** human.resources @connoisseurframes.com. **World Wide Web address:** http://www.intercraft.com. **Description:** A manufacturer of picture frames sold to volume purchasers. **Positions advertised include:** Accounts Payable Supervisor; Senior Financial Analyst; Senior Cost Analyst; Product Manager; Product Designer; Import Sourcing Manager; Forecast Analyst. **Corporate headquarters location:** This location. **Other U.S. locations:** NC; NH; RI; TN. **International locations:** Canada; France; Mexico. **Parent company:** Newell Rubbermaid Company. **Operations at this facility include:** Administration; Manufacturing; Sales. **Listed on:** New York Stock Exchange. **Stock exchange symbol:** NWL. **Number of employees worldwide:** 3,600.

KEWAUNEE SCIENTIFIC CORPORATION

1300 SM 20 East, Lockhart TX 78644. 512/398-5292. **Contact:** Human Resources. **E-mail address:** humanresources@ kewaunee.com. **World Wide Web address:** http://www.kewaunee. com. **Description:** Manufactures laboratory and technical workstations, furniture, and related accessories for industrial and commercial markets. **Corporate headquarters location:** Statesville NC. **Listed on:** NASDAQ. **Stock exchange symbol:** KEQU.

KONE & CRANE

7300 Chippewa Boulevard, Houston TX 77086. 281/445-2225. **Contact:** Human Resources. **Description:** Manufactures and services industrial cranes and hoists. **Other U.S. locations:** Nationwide. **Operations at this facility include:** Administration; Divisional Headquarters; Manufacturing; Research and Development; Sales; Service.

LEPCO

5204 North Expressway, Brownsville TX 78597. 956/350-5650. **Contact:** Office Manager. **World Wide Web address:** http:// www.ies.net/lepco. **Description:** A manufacturer of transformers and conductors. **Corporate headquarters location:** This location.

LONG REACH MANUFACTURING COMPANY

P.O. Box 450069, Houston TX 77245-0069. **Physical address:** 12300 Amelia Drive, Houston TX 77045. **Toll-free phone:** 800/285-7000. **Contact:** Carol Gilder, Human Resources Manager. **World Wide Web address:** http://www.long-reach.com. **Description:** Engaged in the manufacture of hydraulic forklift attachments. **Positions advertised include:** Design Attachment Engineer; Manufacturing Engineer. **Corporate headquarters location:** This location. **Parent company:** TBM Holdings, Inc. **Operations at this facility include:** Administration; Manufacturing; Research and Development; Service; Wholesaling.

LONZA INC.

9700 Bayport Boulevard, Pasadena TX 77507. 281/291-2300. **Contact:** Human Resources. **World Wide Web address:** http:// www.lonza.com. **Description:** Manufactures organic intermediates that are used to produce paints, dyes, and pharmaceuticals.

MKS INSTRUMENTS
ENI SOUTHWEST
4150 Freidrich Lane, Suite J, Austin TX 78744. 512/339-8949. **Contact:** Human Resources. **World Wide Web address:** http://www.mksinst.com. **Description:** Manufactures, sells, and services RS generators used in the semiconductor industry. **NOTE:** Send resumes to: ENI, Human Resources, 100 Highpower Road, Rochester NY 14623. **Parent company:** MKS Instruments. **Listed on:** New York Stock Exchange. **Stock exchange symbol:** MKSI.

MENSOR CORPORATION
201 Barnes Drive, San Marcos TX 78666-5917. 512/396-4200. **Fax:** 512/396-1820. **Contact:** Human Resources. **World Wide Web address:** http://www.mensor.com. **Description:** Manufactures precision instruments and pressure systems.

MONARCH PAINT COMPANY
4220 Lock Field, Houston TX 77092. 713/680-2799. **Contact:** Personnel. **World Wide Web address:** http://www.monarchpaint.com. **Description:** Manufactures and distributes paints, resins, and spray equipment.

NATIONAL INSTRUMENT CORPORATION
11500 North Mopac Expressway, Austin TX 78759-3504. 512/794-0100. **Fax:** 512/683-8745. **Contact:** Human Resources. **World Wide Web address:** http://www.ni.com. **Description:** Manufactures interface boards for the test measurement industry. **Corporate headquarters location:** This location.

NEWPARK SHIPBUILDING & REPAIR INC.
P.O. Box 16198, Galveston TX 77552. 409/740-2818. **Contact:** Human Resources. **World Wide Web address:** http://www.fwav.com. **Description:** Manufactures barges, towboats, and riverboats for a wide range of customers. **Parent company:** Firstwave Marine.

NEWPARK SHIPBUILDING & REPAIR INC.
8502 Cypress, Houston TX 77012. 713/967-6300. **Contact:** Human Resources. **World Wide Web address:** http://www.fwav.com. **Description:** Manufactures barges, towboats, and riverboats for a wide range of customers. **Parent company:** Firstwave Marine. **Operations at this facility include:** Service.

OPTIVELO CORPORATION
211 Highland Cross, Suite 114, Houston TX 77073. 281/209-3900. **Fax:** 281/209-3901. **Contact:** Van Wilson, Human Resources Manager. **World Wide Web address:** http://www.optivelo.com. **Description:** Uses hardware and software components to provide open automation system solutions to the industrial manufacturing and process industries. Applications include custom solutions for data acquisition, control, relational database, and network computing needs. **Office hours:** Monday - Friday, 8:00 a.m. - 5:00 p.m. **Corporate headquarters location:** This location. **Listed on:** Privately held.

OWENS-CORNING FIBERGLAS CORPORATION
8360 Market Street, Houston TX 77029-2498. 713/672-8338. **Contact:** Human Resources Director. **World Wide Web address:** http://www.owenscorning.com. **Description:** Owens-Corning Fiberglas Corporation manufactures and sells thermal and acoustical insulation products including insulation for appliances, glass fiber roofing shingles, roof insulation and industrial asphalt. Other products include windows, glass fiber textile yarns, wet process chopped strands and specialty mats, and polyester resins. **Subsidiaries include:** Barbcorp, Inc.; Dansk-Svensk Glasfiber AS; Eric Co.; European Owens-Corning Fiberglas SA; IPM Inc.; Kitsons Insulations Products Ltd.; Owens-Corning AS; Owens-Corning Building Products; Owens-Corning Finance; Owens-Corning FSC, Inc. **Operations at this facility include:** This location manufactures roofing and asphalt shingles. **Listed on:** New York Stock Exchange. **Stock exchange symbol:** OWC.

PAK-MOR MANUFACTURING CO.
P.O. Box 14147, San Antonio TX 78214. 210/923-4317. **Contact:** Personnel Director. **Description:** A manufacturer of refuse trucking equipment. **Corporate headquarters location:** This location.

POWELL INDUSTRIES, INC.
P.O. Box 12818, Houston TX 77217-2818. 713/944-6900. **Contact:** Human Resources. **World Wide Web address:** http://www.powellind.com. **Description:** Manufactures a wide variety of power distribution equipment including switchgear and power breakers, switchboards, instrument panels, and portable control houses. **Corporate headquarters location:** This location. **Operations at this facility include:** Administration; Manufacturing; Research and

Development; Sales; Service. **Listed on:** NASDAQ. **Stock exchange symbol:** POWL.

IQ PRODUCTS COMPANY
P.O. Box 690347, Houston TX 77269. 281/444-6454. **Contact:** Human Resources. **E-mail address:** mailtohr@iqproducts.com. **World Wide Web address:** http://www.iqproducts.com. **Description:** Manufactures and packages personal care products, insecticides, and automotive products. **Positions advertised include:** Sales Project Coordinator; Project Specialist; Industrial Engineer; Chemistry Product Coordinator.

REYNOLDS INTERNATIONAL INC.
P.O. Box 550, McAllen TX 78505-0550. 956/687-7500. **Contact:** Human Resources. **World Wide Web address:** http://www.reynoldsinternational.com. **Description:** Manufactures tractor equipment. **Corporate headquarters location:** This location.

SASOL NORTH AMERICA, INC.
900 Threadneedle Street, Houston TX 77079. 281/588-3000. **Contact:** Personnel. **World Wide Web address:** http://www.sasolnorthamerica.com. **Description:** Manufactures specialty and commodity chemicals for domestic and international markets. **Corporate headquarters location:** This location.

SCHLUMBERGER
P.O. Box 14484, Houston TX 77054. 713/747-4000. **Contact:** Sarah Pierce, Personnel Manager. **World Wide Web address:** http://www.slb.com. **Description:** Engaged in manufacturing, selling, and servicing a broad range of oil tool equipment. Principal products are gas lift equipment, well completion and safety equipment, wireline units and tools, and energy measurement and control equipment. The company also supplies solid and conductor wireline services and maintains a wireline fleet comprised of hydraulically operated reels mounted on barges, trucks, and skid units. **NOTE:** Jobseekers are encouraged to submit their resume via the Website: http://www.careers.slb.com. **Listed on:** New York Stock Exchange. **Stock exchange symbol:** SLB.

SCHLUMBERGER OILFIELD SERVICES
GEO QUEST
5599 San Felipe, Suite 1700, Houston TX 77056. 713/513-2000. **Contact:** Human Resources. **World Wide Web address:** http://

www.slb.com. **Description:** Develops and sells advanced scientific and engineering software to major oil companies and governments. The company helps find and produce oil and gas, manage environmental concerns, and plan regional and urban development. **Parent company:** Schlumberger Limited. **Listed on:** New York Stock Exchange. **Stock exchange symbol:** SLB.

SCHLUMBERGER PCS

P.O. Box 40262, Houston TX 77240-0262. 713/466-0980. **Contact:** Human Resources. **World Wide Web address:** http://www.slb.com. **Description:** Schlumberger is engaged in manufacturing, selling, and servicing a broad range of oil tool equipment. Principal products are gas lift equipment, well completion and safety equipment, wireline units and tools, and energy measurement and control equipment. The company also supplies solid and conductor wireline services and maintains a wireline fleet comprised of hydraulically operated reels mounted on barges, trucks, and skid units. **NOTE:** Jobseekers are encouraged to submit their resume via the Website: http://www.careers.slb.com. **Operations at this facility include:** This location manufactures and leases gas-handling equipment. **Listed on:** New York Stock Exchange. **Stock exchange symbol:** SLB.

SERCEL INC.

10502 Fallstone Road, Houston TX 77099. 281/498-0600. **Contact:** Human Resources. **World Wide Web address:** http://www.sercel. com. **Description:** Manufactures and markets a wide range of geophysical data acquisition equipment and specialized cable for the energy industry. Sercel is a leading international supplier of geophones, cable, and connectors to the oil and gas exploration industry. **Operations at this facility include:** Administration.

SOLVAY POLYMERS

1230 Battleground Road, Deer Park TX 77536. 713/307-3000. **Contact:** Human Resources. **World Wide Web address:** http:// www.solvayamerica.com. **Description:** Manufactures hydrogen peroxide, polyethylene, and polypropylene. **Parent company:** Solvay America.

STEWART & STEVENSON INC.

4516 Harrisburg Boulevard, Houston TX 77011. 713/923-2161. **Contact:** Mark Ross, Personnel Director. **World Wide Web address:** http://www.ssss.com. **Description:** Manufactures a broad line of products, primarily diesel or gas turbine powered, serving a multitude of industries and markets. Stewart & Stevenson Inc. has three principal divisions. Engine Operations engineers and builds power systems utilizing diesel or gas turbine engines for such uses as irrigation systems, oil well drilling rigs, and generators. Electric Operations produces a line of switchgear and control systems for numerous industries. Other Operations include materials handling equipment and refrigeration equipment for the transportation industry. **Corporate headquarters location:** This location. **Listed on:** NASDAQ. **Stock exchange symbol:** SSSS.

TEMPLE-INLAND, INC.
P.O. Drawer N, Diboll TX 75941. 936/829-1313. **Contact:** Human Resources. **World Wide Web address:** http://www.templeinland. com. **Description:** A holding company offering corrugated packaging, bleached paperboard, building products, and financial services. **Positions advertised include:** IT Senior Auditor; Process Engineer; Senior Internal Auditor. **Corporate headquarters location:** This location. **Listed on:** New York Stock Exchange. **Stock exchange symbol:** TIN.

THERMON MANUFACTURING COMPANY
P.O. Box 609, San Marcos TX 78667-0609. 512/396-5801. **Physical address:** 100 Thermon Drive, San Marcos TX 78666. **Contact:** Personnel Manager. **World Wide Web address:** http:// www.thermon.com. **Description:** A manufacturer of heat tracings.

TYCO INTERNATIONAL INC.
P.O. Box 40010, Houston TX 77240. 713/466-1176. **Contact:** Human Resources. **World Wide Web address:** http://www.tycoint. com. **Description:** Manufactures valves for industrial, marine, and municipal end uses. **Positions advertised include:** New Business Territory Manager; Process Optimization Leader; Receptionist; Application Engineer. **Listed on:** New York Stock Exchange. **Stock exchange symbol:** TYC.

TYCO VALVES AND CONTROLS
3950 Greenbriar, Stafford TX 77477. 281/274-4400. **Contact:** Beverly Martinez, Payroll Manager. **World Wide Web address:** http://www.tycovalves.com. **Description:** Engaged in the designing, engineering, manufacturing, and marketing of special purpose and conventional precision valves for use in the petroleum, chemical, natural gas transmission, and power generation industries. Product lines include safety relief valves used for overpressure protection;

hand valves and instrument manifolds used in conjunction with pressure and flow measuring devices; and a variety of other valve and valve-related products.

U.S. ZINC CORPORATION
P.O. Box 611, Houston TX 77001. 713/926-1705. **Contact:** Human Resources. **World Wide Web address:** http://www.uszinc.com. **Description:** A multistate manufacturer of secondary zinc. Products include zinc dust (powder), zinc oxide, and zinc metal. The company is also a primary recycler of industrial scrap. Customers include tire makers, galvanizers, and chemical process facilities. **Corporate headquarters location:** This location. **Other U.S. locations:** GA; IL; TN. **Operations at this facility include:** Administration; Manufacturing; Sales. **Listed on:** Privately held.

USFILTER
4415 East Greenwood Street, Baytown TX 77520. 281/383-7033. **Fax:** 281/383-3273. **Contact:** Human Resources. **World Wide Web address:** http://www.usfilter.com. **Description:** Produces filters, filtration equipment, strainers, and related items. USFilter also operates related research facilities. **Positions advertised include:** Field Service Supervisor; Process Engineer; Contract Accountant; Installer; Strategic Account Manager. **Corporate headquarters location:** Palm Desert CA. **Other U.S. locations:** Nationwide.

VALLEN CORPORATION
521 North Sam Houston Parkway East, Suite 300, Houston TX 77060. 713/462-8700. **Fax:** 281/272-8242. **Contact:** Human Resources. **World Wide Web address:** http://www.vallen.com. **Description:** Manufactures and distributes safety products. Founded in 1947. **Corporate headquarters location:** This location. **Other U.S. locations:** Nationwide. **International locations:** Canada; Mexico. **Subsidiaries include:** Vallen Safety Supply Company. **Parent company:** Hagemeyer N.V. Company. **Number of employees nationwide:** 1,000.

VARCO
TUBOSCOPE, INC.
P.O. Box 808, Houston TX 77001. 713/799-5100. **Contact:** Human Resources. **World Wide Web address:** http://www.tuboscope.com. **Description:** Manufactures and distributes coatings for pipes. **Listed on:** New York Stock Exchange. **Stock exchange symbol:** VRC.

MINING/GAS/PETROLEUM/ENERGY RELATED

You can expect to find the following types of companies in this chapter:
*Anthracite, Coal, and Ore Mining • Mining Machinery and Equipment •
Oil and Gas Field Services • Petroleum and Natural Gas*

ABRAXAS PETROLEUM CORPORATION

P.O. Box 701007, San Antonio TX 78270-1007. 210/490-4788. **Fax:**
210/490-8816. **Contact:** Personnel. **World Wide Web address:**
http://www.abraxaspetroleum.com. **Description:** An independent
crude oil and natural gas exploration and production company with
operations concentrated in western Canada, Texas, and Wyoming.
The company has participated in the drilling of over 500 wells in 17
states. Abraxas Petroleum Corporation owns interests in over 450 oil
wells, 120 gas wells, and 170 service wells. The company operates
the following three centralized production facilities in Texas:
Abraxas Production Corporation (Midland TX), Abraxas Production
Corporation (Ira TX), and Portilla Gas Plant (Sinton TX). Founded in
1977. **Corporate headquarters location:** This location. **Listed on:**
American Stock Exchange. **Stock exchange symbol:** ABP.

ADAMS RESOURCES AND ENERGY

P.O. Box 844, Suite 2700, Houston TX 77001. 713/881-3600.
Contact: Human Resources. **Description:** A petroleum exploration
and production company. **Corporate headquarters location:** This
location.

ANADARKO PETROLEUM CORPORATION

P.O. Box 1330, Houston TX 77251. 281/875-1101. **Contact:** Human
Resources Department. **World Wide Web address:** http://
www.anadarko.com. **Description:** Involved in the exploration and
recovery of petroleum. **Listed on:** New York Stock Exchange. **Stock
exchange symbol:** APC.

APACHE CORPORATION

2000 Post Oak Boulevard, Suite 100, Houston TX 77056. 713/296-
6000. **Contact:** Human Resources. **World Wide Web address:** http://
www.apachecorp.com. **Description:** An independent oil and gas
exploration and production company that owns large reserves of oil
and natural gas. Apache Corporation's domestic operations are
located primarily in the Gulf of Mexico; the Gulf Coast of Texas and
Louisiana; the Permian Basin of West Texas and New Mexico
(almost half of the company's daily crude oil production comes from

this region); the Anadarko Basin of Oklahoma; and in the Green River Basin of the Rocky Mountains. Founded in 1954. **Positions advertised include:** Senior International Tax Accountant; Administrative Assistant; Records Manager; Senior Staff Reservoir Engineer; Drilling Technician; Staff Systems Analyst. **Corporate headquarters location:** This location. **International locations:** Africa; Australia; China; Egypt; Indonesia. **Listed on:** New York Stock Exchange. **Stock exchange symbol:** APA.

AQUILA GAS PIPELINE CORPORATION
800 East Sonterra Boulevard, Suite 400, San Antonio TX 78258. 210/403-7300. **Fax:** 210/403-7533. **Contact:** Human Resources. **World Wide Web address:** http://www.aquila.com. **Description:** Purchases, gathers, transports, processes, and markets natural gas and natural gas liquids. Aquila Gas Pipeline Corporation also purchases, markets, and arranges for the delivery of natural gas outside of its pipeline system. The company has over 2,000 miles of pipe and over 2,000 connected wells. **Positions advertised include:** Permissions Coordinator; Products Artist; Art Buyer; Web Developer; Traffic Manager. **Corporate headquarters location:** This location. **Listed on:** New York Stock Exchange. **Stock exchange symbol:** ILA.

ARAMCO SERVICES COMPANY
9009 West Loop South, Houston TX 77002. 713/432-4000. **Fax:** 713/432-4600. **Contact:** Personnel. **World Wide Web address:** http://www.aramcoservices.com. **Description:** Provides support services to its parent company, Saudi Aramco, one of the world's leading producers and exporters of oil and gas. **Parent company:** Saudi Aramco. **Operations at this facility include:** Service. **Listed on:** Privately held.

BHP MINERALS INC.
1360 Post Oak Boulevard, Suite 150, Houston TX 77056. 713/961-8500. **Contact:** Personnel Supervisor. **World Wide Web address:** http://www.bhp.com. **Description:** Mines coal and other minerals. **Positions advertised include:** Drilling Engineering Supervisor; Completions Engineering Supervisor; Finance Advisor; Senior Accountant; Payroll Specialist; Fixed Asset Accountant; Facilities Manager. **Listed on:** New York Stock Exchange. **Stock exchange symbol:** BHP.

B.J. SERVICES COMPANY

5500 NW Central Drive, Houston TX 77092. 713/462-4239. **Contact:** Human Resources. **World Wide Web address:** http://www.bjservices.com. **Description:** An energy consulting firm offering technical services such as cementing, stimulation (including acidizing), and nitrogen services. B.J. Services Company is a division of Hughes Tool Company (Houston TX) and Dresser Industries (Dallas TX). **Listed on:** New York Stock Exchange. **Stock exchange symbol:** BJS.

BP AMOCO PLC

501 Westlake Park Boulevard, Houston TX 77079. 281/366-2000. **Contact:** Employment Office. **World Wide Web address:** http://www.bp.com. **Description:** Engaged in exploratory and developmental drilling and in advanced recovery techniques. **Operations at this facility include:** Administration; Service. **Listed on:** New York Stock Exchange. **Stock exchange symbol:** BP.

BAKER ENERGY

16340 Park Ten Place, Suite 320, Houston TX 77084. 281/579-7850. **Contact:** Human Resources. **World Wide Web address:** http://www.mbakercorp.com. **Description:** Maintains and operates oilrig platforms. **Positions advertised include:** Operator; Civil Associate; GIS Associate; Instrument Technician; Technical Specialist; Water Resources Engineer. **Listed on:** American Stock Exchange. **Stock Exchange symbol:** BKR.

BAKER HUGHES INC.

3900 Essex Lane, Suite 1200, Houston TX 77027. 713/439-8600. **Contact:** Human Resources. **World Wide Web address:** http://www.bakerhughes.com. **Description:** Provides vital information to many segments of the energy industry through high-technology data acquisition operations. **Positions advertised include:** Mechanical QC Inspector; Drafter; Senior Mechanical Drafter; Process Analyst; NC Programmer; Electrical Engineer; Senior Project Engineer. **Corporate headquarters location:** This location. **Other U.S. locations:** Nationwide. **International locations:** Worldwide. **Operations at this facility include:** Administration; Divisional Headquarters; Manufacturing; Regional Headquarters; Research and Development; Sales. **Listed on:** New York Stock Exchange. **Stock exchange symbol:** BHI.

BAY, INC.
401 Corn Products Road, Corpus Christi TX 78409. 361/289-2400. **Contact:** Manager of Personnel. **Description:** Provides construction and fabrication services to the petroleum industry.

BLUE DOLPHIN ENERGY COMPANY
801 Travis Street, Suite 2100, Houston TX 77002. 713/227-7660. **Contact:** Human Resources. **World Wide Web address:** http://www.blue-dolphin.com. **Description:** Engaged in the acquisition, exploration, and development of oil and gas properties. **Listed on:** NASDAQ. **Stock exchange symbol:** BDCO.

BREDERO PRICE COMPANY
2350 North Sam Houston Parkway East, Suite 500, Houston TX 77032. 281/886-2350. **Contact:** Human Resources. **World Wide Web address:** http://www.brederoshaw.com. **Description:** Produces corrosion coatings, weight coatings, and insulation coatings for pipelines. **Office hours:** Monday - Friday, 8:00 a.m. - 5:00 p.m. **Parent company:** Haliburton Company (Dallas TX) & ShawCor Ltd. (Toronto Canada).

BURLINGTON RESOURCES
5051 Westheimer, Suite 1400, Houston TX 77056-5604. 713/624-9000. **Contact:** Human Resources. **World Wide Web address:** http://www.br-inc.com. **Description:** Explores for, develops, and manufactures petroleum and natural gas products. **Corporate headquarters location:** This location. **Subsidiaries include:** Meridian Oil Holdings operates pipelines and sells natural gas liquids. **Listed on:** New York Stock Exchange. **Stock exchange symbol:** BR.

CABOT OIL & GAS CORPORATION
P.O. Box 4544, Houston TX 77210-4544. 281/589-4600. **Recorded jobline:** 281/589-5700. **Contact:** Human Resources Department. **World Wide Web address:** http://www.cabotog.com. **Description:** Involved in all facets of oil and gas, from production and drilling to the selling of refined products. **Listed on:** New York Stock Exchange. **Stock exchange symbol:** COG.

CACTUS PIPE & SUPPLY COMPANY
One Greenway Plaza, Suite 450, Houston TX 77046. 713/877-1948. **Fax:** 713/877-8204. **Contact:** Controller. **Description:** A distributor of oil field pipes. **Corporate headquarters location:** This location. **Other U.S. locations:** Duson LA.

CHEVRONTEXACO CORPORATION
4800 Furnace, Bellaire TX 77401. 713/752-6000. **Contact:** Employment Office. **World Wide Web address:** http://www.texaco. com. **Description:** A global energy company engaged in all aspects of the oil and gas industry, including exploration and production; refining, marketing and transportation; chemicals manufacturing and sales; and power generation. **Positions advertised include:** Administrative Assistant. **Corporate headquarters location:** San Francisco CA. **Listed on:** New York Stock Exchange. **Stock exchange symbol:** CVX. **Number of employees worldwide:** 55,700.

CHEVRONTEXACO CORPORATION
1301 McKinney, Houston TX 77010. 713/754-2000. **Contact:** Human Resources Department. **World Wide Web address:** http://www.chevrontexaco.com. **Description:** Produces petrochemicals. Chevron Texaco is a global energy company engaged in all aspects of the oil and gas industry, including exploration and production; refining, marketing and transportation; chemicals manufacturing and sales; and power generation. **Positions advertised include:** Senior Flow Assurance Specialist; Flow Assurance Specialist. **Corporate headquarters location:** San Francisco CA. **Operations at this facility include:** Administration; Divisional Headquarters; Sales. **Listed on:** New York Stock Exchange. **Stock exchange symbol:** CVX. **Number of employees worldwide:** 55,700.

COLUMBIA GULF TRANSMISSION
P.O. Box 683, Houston TX 77001. 713/267-4100. **Contact:** Shirley McCollum, Personnel Director. **World Wide Web address:** http://www.columbiagastrans.com. **Description:** Engaged in the transmission and distribution of natural gas.

CONOCO INC.
P.O. Box 2197, Houston TX 77252. 281/293-1000. **Physical address:** 600 North Dairy Ashford, Houston TX 77079. **Contact:** Human Resources. **World Wide Web address:** http://www.conoco. com. **Description:** Engaged in the development and production of crude oil, natural gas, and natural gas liquids. Exploration and production operations currently include exploration activity in 15 countries on six continents. Conoco produces more than 453,000 barrels of petroleum liquids and 1.2 billion cubic feet of gas each day. Downstream operations comprise refining crude oil and other feedstock into petroleum products, trading crude oil and products, distributing, and marketing petroleum products. Marketing activities

include selling gasoline, diesel, and motor oils mainly under the Conoco, Jet, and Seca brand names through more than 7,900 retail outlets in the United States, Europe, and the Asia Pacific region. The company also manufactures and markets a wide range of industrial lubricants and specialty products. It is one of the world's leading suppliers of graphite coke, a premium product used to make electrodes for the steel manufacturing industry. **Corporate headquarters location:** This location. **International locations:** Worldwide. **Listed on:** New York Stock Exchange. **Stock exchange symbol:** COC. **Number of employees worldwide:** 20,000.

CONTOUR ENERGY
1001 McKinney, Suite 900, Houston TX 77002. 713/652-5200. **Contact:** Human Resources Department. **World Wide Web address:** http://www.contourenergy.com. **Description:** Engaged in oil and gas development, acquisition, exploration, and production. **Corporate headquarters location:** This location.

COOPER CAMERON BELL
16500 South Main Street, Missouri City TX 77489-1300. 281/499-8511. **Contact:** Human Resources. **World Wide Web address:** http://www.ccvalve.com. **Description:** Manufactures valves, well heads, actuators, and safety systems for oil field markets worldwide, as well as valves for use in chemical, plastics, food-processing, and paper-making plants, and conventional and geothermal steam power-producing facilities. **Corporate headquarters location:** This location. **Parent company:** Cooper Cameron Corporation. **Operations at this facility include:** Administration; Manufacturing; Research and Development; Sales; Service.

CORAL ENERGY, LLC
909 Fannin Street, Suite 700, Houston TX 77010. 713/230-3000. **Contact:** Human Resources. **World Wide Web address:** http://www.coral-energy.com. **Description:** Operates a natural gas pipeline and purchases, gathers, processes, treats, transports, and markets natural gas. Gathering and transportation operations are situated mainly in the gas-producing areas of southern Texas, eastern Texas, and the Texas-Louisiana Gulf Coast regions. **Other U.S. locations:** OK; WV. **Parent company:** Shell Trading. **Listed on:** Privately held.

CROWN CENTRAL PETROLEUM CORPORATION
111 Red Bluff Road, Pasadena TX 77506. 713/664-4133. **Contact:** Human Resources. **E-mail address:** recruiter@crowncentral.com.

World Wide Web address: http://www.crowncentral.com. **Description:** An independent refiner and marketer of petroleum products. Crown Central Petroleum and its La Gloria Oil and Gas Company subsidiary operate two refineries in Texas with a combined capacity of 152,000 barrels per day. Crown Central Petroleum markets its refined products at 376 retail gasoline stations and convenience stores in seven Mid-Atlantic and Southeastern states. The company's wholesale operations extend from its Texas refineries into the Southeastern, Mid-Atlantic, and Midwestern regions of the United States. **Corporate headquarters location:** Baltimore MD.

CROWN CENTRAL PETROLEUM CORPORATION
P.O. Box 1759, Houston TX 77251. 713/472-2461. **Contact:** Human Resources. **E-mail address:** recruiter@crowncentral.com. **World Wide Web address:** http://www.crowncentral.com. **Description:** An independent refiner and marketer of petroleum products. Crown Central Petroleum and its La Gloria Oil and Gas Company subsidiary operate two refineries in Texas with a combined capacity of 152,000 barrels per day. Crown Central Petroleum markets its refined products at 376 retail gasoline stations and convenience stores in seven Mid-Atlantic and Southeastern states. The company's wholesale operations extend from its Texas refineries into the Southeastern, Mid-Atlantic, and Midwestern regions of the United States. **NOTE:** Send resumes to: Crown Central Petroleum Corporation, 111 Red Bluff Road, Pasadena TX 77506. **Corporate headquarters location:** Baltimore MD.

DEVON ENERGY CORPORATION
2001 Timberloch, The Woodlands TX 77380. 713/377-5500. **Fax:** 713/377-5680. **Contact:** Personnel. **World Wide Web address:** http://www.devonenergy.com. **Description:** Engaged in oil and gas exploration, production, and property acquisitions. **Listed on:** American Stock Exchange. **Stock exchange symbol:** DVN.

DIAMOND OFFSHORE DRILLING, INC.
P.O. Box 4558, Houston TX 77210. 281/492-5300. **Contact:** Human Resources. **World Wide Web address:** http://www.diamondoffshore.com. **Description:** A drilling contractor for oil and gas companies. **Corporate headquarters location:** This location. **Listed on:** New York Stock Exchange. **Stock exchange symbol:** DO.

DUKE ENERGY CORPORATION
P.O. Box 1642, Houston TX 77251-1642. 713/627-5400. **Physical address:** 5400 Westheimer Court, Houston TX 77056-5310. **Contact:** Human Resources. **World Wide Web address:** http://www.duke-energy.com. **Description:** Involved in natural gas pipeline operations. The company owns and operates an interstate natural gas transmission system that consists of more than 4,300 miles of pipeline. **Positions advertised include:** Business Continuity Planner; Lead IT Audit Consultant; Senior Audit Consultant; Senior Corporate Tax Analyst; Senior IM Telecommunications Analyst.

DYNEGY, INC.
P.O. Box 4777, Houston TX 77210. 713/507-6400. **Physical address:** 1000 Louisiana, Suite 5800, Houston TX 77002. **Contact:** Human Resources. **World Wide Web address:** http://www.dynegy.com. **Description:** Produces gas, oil, and electric power. **Corporate headquarters location:** This location. **Listed on:** New York Stock Exchange. **Stock exchange symbol:** DYN.

EOG RESOURCES
P.O. Box 4362, Houston TX 77210. 713/651-7000. **Contact:** Human Resources. **World Wide Web address:** http://www.eogresources.com. **Description:** Engaged in the exploration, development, and production of natural gas and crude oil. **Position advertised include:** Petrophysical Specialist; Environmental/Safety Representative; Geological Specialist; Senior Engineering Technician. **Listed on:** New York Stock Exchange. **Stock exchange symbol:** EOG.

EL PASO CORPORATION
Coastal Tower, 9 Greenway Plaza, Houston TX 77046-0995. 713/420-2600. **Contact:** Human Resources. **World Wide Web address:** http://www.elpaso.com. **Description:** Engaged in oil extraction, marketing, and transmission, with over 20,000 miles of pipeline. El Paso Corporation also refines, markets, and distributes petroleum and related products; conducts oil and gas exploration; mines for coal; manufactures chemicals; and operates trucking facilities. **Positions advertised include:** Accountant; Network Operations Center Technician. **Listed on:** New York Stock Exchange. **Stock exchange symbol:** EP.

EL PASO ENERGY CORPORATION
1001 Louisiana Street, Suite W1419B, Houston TX 77002. 713/420-2131. **Contact:** Human Resources. **World Wide Web address:** http://

www.epenergy.com. **Description:** A holding company with subsidiaries engaged in transporting and selling natural gas, mining and selling minerals, and manufacturing industrial products. **Positions advertised include:** Accountant; Network Operations Center Technician. **Corporate headquarters location:** This location. **Operations at this facility include:** Administration; Research and Development. **Listed on:** New York Stock Exchange. **Stock exchange symbol:** EPG.

ETHYL CORPORATION
P.O. Box 472, Pasadena TX 77501. 713/740-8300. **Contact:** Human Resources. **World Wide Web address:** http://www.ethyl.com. **Description:** Manufactures fuel and lubricant additives including products for gas and diesel fuels, engine oils, automatic transmission fluids, gear oils, hydraulic fluids, and industrial oils. **Subsidiaries include:** Whitby, Inc. markets over-the-counter drugs such as analgesics, bronchodilators, and nutritional supplements.

EVANS SYSTEMS, INC. (ESI)
P.O. Box 2480, Bay City TX 77404-2480. 979/245-2424. **Fax:** 979/244-5070. **Contact:** Human Resources. **Description:** A holding company. **Corporate headquarters location:** This location. **Subsidiaries include:** Way Energy distributes wholesale and retail refined petroleum products and lubricants and owns and operates convenience stores in southern Texas and Louisiana; Chem-Way Systems, Inc. produces, packages, and markets automotive aftermarket chemical products in 23 states; EDCO Environmental Systems, Inc. provides environmental remediation services and installations of underground storage tanks; Distributor Information Systems Corporation provides information systems and software for distributors and convenience store owners and operators.

THE EXPLORATION COMPANY
500 North Loop 1604 East, Suite 250, San Antonio TX 78232. 210/496-5300. **Fax:** 210/496-3232. **Contact:** Human Resources. **World Wide Web address:** http://www.txco.com. **Description:** Acquires, explores, and develops oil and gas properties. The Exploration Company operates through three divisions: Oil and Gas Operations, ExproFuels Operations, and Mineral Properties. The company also converts vehicle engines that use gasoline for combustion to propane or natural gas, supplies alternative fuels to customers, and constructs alternative fuels refueling facilities. **Listed on:** NASDAQ. **Stock exchange symbol:** TXCO.

EXPLORATION CONSULTANTS LTD. INC.
9801 Westheimer, Suite 1060, Houston TX 77042. 713/784-5800. **Contact:** Human Resources. **World Wide Web address:** http://www.ecqc.com. **Description:** Provides consulting services for exploration in the oil and gas industries.

EXXONMOBIL COAL AND MINERALS COMPANY
P.O. Box 1314, Houston TX 77251-1314. 713/978-5333. **Contact:** Employment Coordinator. **World Wide Web address:** http://www.exxon.mobil.com. **Description:** ExxonMobil is an integrated oil company engaged in petroleum and chemical products marketing, refining, manufacturing, exploration, production, transportation, and research and development worldwide. Other products include fabricated plastics, films, food bags, housewares, garbage bags, and building materials. The company also has subsidiaries involved in real estate development and mining operations. **Corporate headquarters location:** Irving TX. **Operations at this facility include:** This location is engaged in the exploration, mining, and marketing of coal and minerals. **Listed on:** New York Stock Exchange. **Stock exchange symbol:** XOM.

EXXONMOBIL CORPORATION
P.O. Box 2180, Houston TX 77252-2180. 713/656-3636. **Physical address:** 800 Bell Street, Houston TX 77002. **Contact:** Human Resources. **World Wide Web address:** http://www.exxon.mobil.com. **Description:** An integrated oil company engaged in petroleum and chemical products marketing, refining, manufacturing, exploration, production, transportation, and research and development worldwide. Other products include fabricated plastics, films, food bags, housewares, garbage bags, and building materials. The company also has subsidiaries involved in real estate development and mining operations. **Corporate headquarters location:** Irving TX. **Listed on:** New York Stock Exchange. **Stock exchange symbol:** XOM.

FRONTIER OIL CORPORATION
10000 Memorial, Suite 600, Houston TX 77024-3341. 713/688-9600. **Fax:** 713/688-0616. **Contact:** Personnel. **World Wide Web address:** http://www.frontieroil.com. **Description:** Engaged in oil and gas exploration and production. **Listed on:** New York Stock Exchange. **Stock exchange symbol:** FTO.

GLOBAL INDUSTRIES, LTD.
5151 San Felipe, Suite 900, Houston TX 77056. 713/952-3483. **Contact:** Human Resources. **World Wide Web address:** http://www.globalind.com. **Description:** Provides construction and diving services to the offshore oil and gas industry. **Corporate headquarters location:** Lafayette LA. **Subsidiaries include:** Global Pipeline PLUS's fleet of seven multipurpose barges is one of the largest and most diverse in the Gulf. The barges have various combinations of pipelay, pipebury, and derrick capabilities, which offer a wide range of services including deepwater installation, pipelay by the reel method, and pipeline maintenance and repair. Global Movable Offshore's three derrick barges provide offshore lifting services, including installation and removal of platforms and associated components, drilling and workover rigs, and other equipment. Global Divers' fleet of four dive support vessels (DSV) provides diving services for virtually every phase of offshore oil and gas development and production. Global Divers has one of the largest DSVs with a dedicated saturation system in the Gulf and is a leader in deepwater diving, underwater welding technology, subsea completions, and nuclear power plant diving services. A full service trucking company, Pelican transports general commodities as well as oil field equipment, pipe, and supplies. The Red Adair Company is a worldwide leader in wild well control. In addition to fire fighting, the company offers contingency planning and training, engineering, well plug and abandonment, and rig inspection services.

GLOBAL SANTA FE CORPORATION
P.O. Box 4379, Houston TX 77210-4379. 281/596-5100. **Contact:** Human Resources Department. **World Wide Web address:** http://www.glsfdrill.com. **Description:** An oil and gas offshore drilling contractor. **Listed on:** New York Stock Exchange. **Stock exchange symbol:** GSF.

GOODRICH PETROLEUM COMPANY
815 Walker Street, Suite 1040, Houston TX 77002. 713/780-9494. **Fax:** 713/780-9254. **Contact:** Robert C. Turnham, Jr., Chief Operating Officer. **World Wide Web address:** http://www.goodrichpetroleum.com. **Description:** A petroleum and natural gas exploration and production company. **Listed on:** New York Stock Exchange. **Stock exchange symbol:** GDP.

GRANT GEOPHYSICAL, INC.
P.O. Box 219950, Houston TX 77218-9950. 281/398-9503. **Fax:** 281/647-9464. **Contact:** Human Resources Manager. **E-mail address:** hr@grantgeo.com. **World Wide Web address:** http://www.grantgeo. com. **Description:** Plans and conducts 3-D and 2-D land and transition zone seismic data acquisition surveys for oil companies worldwide. **Special programs:** Internships. **Corporate headquarters location:** This location. **Other U.S. locations:** LA; OK. **International locations:** Indonesia; South America. **Operations at this facility include:** Administration; Research and Development; Sales.

GREYWOLF DRILLING
1907 East Main Street, Alice TX 78332. 361/668-8364. **Contact:** Mike Flores, Human Resources Manager. **World Wide Web address:** http://www.gwdrilling.com. **Description:** Engaged in gas and oil drilling. The company's primary drilling sites are located throughout southern Texas. **Listed on:** American Stock Exchange. **Stock exchange symbol:** GW.

GULF MARINE FABRICATORS
P.O. Box 3000, Aransas Pass TX 78335. 361/776-7551. **Fax:** 361/776-5406. **Contact:** Human Resources. **Description:** Manufactures off-shore rigs. **Corporate headquarters location:** This location.

GULF PUBLISHING/PIPE LINE & GAS INDUSTRY MAGAZINE
3 East Greenwood Plaza, Suit 900, Houston TX 77046. 713/529-4301. **Contact:** Editor. **World Wide Web address:** http://www.gulfpub.com. **Description:** A magazine dealing primarily with pipeline transportation of crude oil, refined petroleum products, natural gas, and gas distribution. **Positions advertised include:** Editor.

GULFMARK OFFSHORE
4400 Post Oak Parkway, 5 Post Oak Park Building, Suite 1170, Houston TX 77027. 713/963-9522. **Contact:** Human Resources. **World Wide Web address:** http://www.gulfmark.com. **Description:** Provides marine transportation and erosion control services. **Listed on:** NASDAQ. **Stock exchange symbol:** GMRK.

HALLIBURTON COMPANY
P.O. Box 60087, Houston TX 77205. 281/871-4000. **Physical address:** 3000 North Sam Houston Parkway East, Houston TX 77032. **Contact:** Human Resources. **World Wide Web address:**

http://www.halliburton.com. **Description:** A leading supplier of engineered products and services used in hydrocarbon energy-related utilities worldwide. **Positions advertised include:** Mechanical Engineer; Chemical Engineer. **Listed on:** New York Stock Exchange. **Stock exchange symbol:** HAL.

THE HOWELL COMPANIES
1111 Fannin Street, Suite 1500, Houston TX 77002. 713/658-4000. **Fax:** 713/658-4007. **Contact:** Rick Robinson, Administration Manager. **Description:** Engaged in oil and gas exploration and production, crude oil transportation and marketing, specialty hydrocarbons manufacturing and marketing, and custom chemical processing. **Corporate headquarters location:** This location. **Operations at this facility include:** Manufacturing; Research and Development; Sales.

HUNT PETROLEUM
P.O. Box 1350, Houston TX 77251-1350. 713/871-3400. **Contact:** Human Resources. **E-mail address:** recruitment@ huntpetroleum.com. **World Wide Web address:** http:// www.huntpetroleum.com. **Description:** Conducts onshore and offshore exploration and development activities in the Gulf Coast and Rocky Mountain areas and supplies its parent company with natural gas via exploration, production, and acquisition activities. **Positions advertised include:** Geoscientist System Administrator.

ICO, INC.
5333 Westheimer, Suite 600, Houston TX 77056. 713/351-4100. **Contact:** Kathy Barnett, Director of Corporate Administration. **World Wide Web address:** http://www.icoinc.com. **Description:** An oil field service company that also inspects and coats field tubular goods. **Corporate headquarters location:** This location. **Operations at this facility include:** Service. **Listed on:** NASDAQ. **Stock exchange symbol:** ICOC.

KINDER MORGAN
500 Dallas Street, Suite 1000, Houston TX 77002. 713/369-9000. **Contact:** Human Resources. **World Wide Web address:** http:// www.kindermorgan.com. **Description:** Distributes natural gas. **Corporate headquarters location:** This location. **Listed on:** New York Stock Exchange. **Stock exchange symbol:** KMI.

KOCH INDUSTRIES, INC.
P.O. Box 1478, Houston TX 77251-1478. 713/544-4123. **Contact:** Selection Supervisor. **World Wide Web address:** http://www.kochind.com. **Description:** Koch Industries, Inc. is involved in virtually all phases of the oil and gas industry, as well as in chemicals, chemical technology products, agriculture, hard minerals, trading, and financial investments. **Positions advertised include:** Business Process Analyst; Credit/Equity Associate; Financial Trader; Quantitative Analyst; Senior Accountant. **Corporate headquarters location:** Wichita KS. **Other U.S. locations:** Nationwide. **Operations at this facility include:** Administration; Sales. **Listed on:** Privately held.

KVAERNER PROCESS SYSTEMS
7909 Parkwood Circle Drive, 6th Floor, Houston TX 77036. 713/271-7086. **Contact:** Human Resources. **World Wide Web address:** http://www.kvaerner.com. **Description:** Engaged in the engineering and manufacturing of hydraulic and electrohydraulic control systems for subsea oil production and drilling operations, as well as system engineering, integration, and analysis for subsea production completion.

M.I. DRILLING FLUIDS
P.O. Box 42842, Houston TX 77242-2842. 713/739-0222. **Contact:** Billy Berryhill, Manager of Employment. **World Wide Web address:** http://www.midf.com. **Description:** Manufactures drilling fluid systems and oil field production chemicals.

MISSION RESOURCES
1331 Lamar, Suite 1455, Houston TX 77010. 713/650-1025. **Contact:** Human Resources. **World Wide Web address:** http://www.mrcorp.com. **Description:** Engaged in the development, exploration, and production of oil and gas properties in the Gulf Coast region. **Listed on:** NASDAQ. **Stock exchange symbol:** MSSN.

MOTIVA ENTERPRISES
1100 Louisiana, P.O. Box 4453, Houston TX 77002. 713/277-8000. **Contact:** Human Resources. **World Wide Web address:** http://www.shellus.com. **Description:** Engaged in the offshore drilling of oil off the Gulf and East Coasts of the United States. **Parent company:** Shell Company.

NABORS INDUSTRIES

515 West Greens Road, Suite 1200, Houston TX 77067. 281/874-0035. **Contact:** Human Resources. **World Wide Web address:** http://www.nabors.com. **Description:** Provides contract drilling and oil field services worldwide. Services include comprehensive oilfield management, logistics, and engineering. Nabors Industries is active in the United States, Canada, Gulf of Mexico, United Kingdom, North Sea, Middle East, and other locations around the globe. **Number of employees worldwide:** 16,800.

NATIONAL OILWELL

500 Industrial Boulevard, Sugar Land TX 77478. 281/240-6111. **Contact:** Human Resources. **World Wide Web address:** http://www.natoil.com. **Description:** Manufactures electromechanical equipment such as brake systems and generators. Founded in 1954. **Corporate headquarters location:** Houston TX. **Listed on:** New York Stock Exchange. **Stock exchange symbol:** NOI. **Number of employees at nationwide:** 6,200.

NATIONAL OILWELL

P.O. Box 4638, Houston TX 77210. 713/467-9888. **Contact:** Human Resources. **World Wide Web address:** http://www.natoil.com. **Description:** Designs and develops electronic control systems for industrial applications. The company is a world leader in the field of power conversion equipment. It is one of the largest suppliers of variable speed drives to the oil industry and one of the world's largest users of large thyristor devices. **Corporate headquarters location:** This location. **Listed on:** New York Stock Exchange. **Stock exchange symbol:** NOI. **Number of employees at nationwide:** 6,200.

NATIONAL OILWELL

P.O. Box 4638, Houston TX 77210-4638. 713/960-5100. **Contact:** Human Resources. **World Wide Web address:** http://www.natoil.com. **Description:** A manufacturer and distributor of oil field machinery. **Listed on:** New York Stock Exchange. **Stock exchange symbol:** NOI. **Number of employees at nationwide:** 6,200.

NEWFIELD EXPLORATION

363 North Sam Houston Parkway East, Suite 2020, Houston TX 77060. 281/847-6000. **Contact:** Human Resources. **World Wide Web address:** http://www.newfld.com. **Description:** Engaged in oil

and gas exploration. **Listed on:** New York Stock Exchange. **Stock exchange symbol:** NFX.

NOBLE DRILLING CORPORATION
13135 South Dairy Ashford, Suite 800, Sugar Land TX 77478. 281/276-6100. **Fax:** 281/491-2092. **Contact:** Human Resources. **World Wide Web address:** http://www.noblecorp.com. **Description:** Provides offshore drilling services. **Corporate headquarters location:** This location. **Listed on:** New York Stock Exchange. **Stock exchange symbol:** NE.

NUEVO ENERGY COMPANY
1021 Main Street, Suite 2100, Houston TX 77002. 713/652-0706. **Contact:** Human Resources. **World Wide Web address:** http://www.nuevoenergy.com. **Description:** Engaged in the exploration, development, and acquisition of crude oil and natural gas. **Corporate headquarters location:** This location. **Listed on:** New York Stock Exchange. **Stock exchange symbol:** NEV.

OPTIMIZED PROCESS DESIGNS (OPD)
P.O. Box 810, Katy TX 77493. 281/371-7500. **Physical address:** 25610 Clay Road, Katy TX 77493. **Fax:** 281/371-0132. **Contact:** Human Resources. **World Wide Web address:** http://www.opd-inc.com. **Description:** Designs, engineers, and constructs natural gas treatment facilities. **Parent company:** Koch Industries, Inc. **Listed on:** Privately held.

PENNZOIL COMPANY
P.O. Box 2967, Houston TX 77252-2967. 713/546-4000. **Contact:** Supervisor of Human Resources. **World Wide Web address:** http://www.pennzoil.com. **Description:** Engaged in oil and gas exploration and production; processing, refining, and marketing oil, gas, and refined petroleum products; and mining and marketing sulfur. **Corporate headquarters location:** This location. **Parent company:** Pennzoil-Quakerstate Company. **Listed on:** New York Stock Exchange. **Stock exchange symbol:** PZL.

PLAINS RESOURCES
500 Dallas Street, Suite 700, Houston TX 77002. 713/654-1414. **Fax:** 713/654-1523. **Contact:** Human Resources. **E-mail address:** careers@plainsresources.com. **World Wide Web address:** http://www.plainsresources.com. **Description:** A *Fortune* 500 energy company that is involved in the acquisition, development,

exploitation, exploration, and production of crude oil. **Corporate headquarters location:** This location. **Listed on:** New York Stock Exchange. **Stock exchange symbol:** PLX.

POGO PRODUCING COMPANY
P.O. Box 2504, Houston TX 77252-2504. 713/297-5000. **Contact:** Human Resources. **E-mail address:** humanresources@ pogoproducing.com. **World Wide Web address:** http:// www.pogoproducing.com. **Description:** Engaged in the exploration, development, and production of oil and natural gas. **Listed on:** New York Stock Exchange. **Stock exchange symbol:** PPP.

PORTA-KAMP MANUFACTURING COMPANY INC.
555 Gelhorn Drive, Houston TX 77029. 713/674-3163. **Contact:** Human Resources. **World Wide Web address:** http:// www.portakamp.com. **Description:** Manufactures offshore drilling equipment and metal portable buildings. **Corporate headquarters location:** This location.

REED-HYZALOG COMPANY
6501 Navigation, Houston TX 77011. 713/924-5200. **Contact:** Human Resources. **Description:** Manufactures rock bits and other machinery for use in offshore drilling.

RELIANT ENERGY HL&P
P.O. Box 4567, Houston TX 77210. 713/207-3000. **Physical address:** 1111 Louisiana Street, Suite 1328B, Houston TX 77002. **Fax:** 713/207-9993. **Recorded jobline:** 713/207-7373. **Contact:** Human Resources. **E-mail address:** hr@reliantenergy.com. **World Wide Web address:** http://www.reliantenergy.com. **Description:** Generates, transmits, distributes, and sells electric energy to over 1.6 million customers. **Positions advertised include:** Senior Secretary; Legal Secretary; Director of Supply Settlements; Senior Business Operations Systems Analyst; Energy Sales Representative; Credit Representative; Head Operator. **Corporate headquarters location:** This location. **Subsidiaries include:** Reliant Energy, Inc. (also at this location); Reliant Energy Resources Corporation. **Parent company:** Houston Industries Inc. **Listed on:** New York Stock Exchange. **Stock exchange symbol:** REI. **Number of employees nationwide:** 16,500.

SMITH INTERNATIONAL, INC.
P.O. Box 60068, Houston TX 77205. 281/443-3370. **Contact:** Human Resources. **World Wide Web address:** http://www.smith-

intl.com. **Description:** Smith International, Inc. is a worldwide supplier of products and services to the oil and gas drilling, completion and production, and mining industries. **Positions advertised include:** Turbine Technician. **Corporate headquarters location:** This location. **Operations at this facility include:** Administration; Divisional Headquarters; Manufacturing; Regional Headquarters; Research and Development; Sales; Service.

SOLVAY MINERALS, INC.
P.O. Box 27328, Houston TX 77227-7328. 713/525-6800. **Toll-free phone:** 800/443-2785. **Contact:** Human Resources Department. **World Wide Web address:** http://www.solvayamerica.com. **Description:** A manufacturer of sodium-based products through the mining and processing of trona. Solvay Minerals produces soda ash, caustic soda, sodium sulfite, and trona products. The company offers mechanically refined sodium sesquicarbonate to the merchant market. Coarse product is exclusively marketed and sold to the animal feed market by an outside company. Other products are marketed directly by Solvay Minerals for acid gas and acid neutralization applications. **Parent company:** Solvay America.

SOUTHERN CLAY PRODUCTS INC.
1212 Church Street, Gonzales TX 78629. 830/672-2891. **Fax:** 830/672-1908. **Contact:** Human Resources. **World Wide Web address:** http://www.scprod.com. **Description:** Mines and processes clay minerals for use in a variety of products including paint. **Corporate headquarters location:** This location.

SOUTHERN UNION COMPANY
504 Lavaca, Suite 800, Austin TX 78701. 512/370-8321. **Fax:** 512/370-8380. **Contact:** Human Resources. **World Wide Web address:** http://www.southernunionco.com. **Description:** A natural gas distribution utility company serving approximately 976,000 customers in Missouri, Texas, and Oklahom. **Special programs:** Internships. **Corporate headquarters location:** This location. **Other U.S. locations:** FL; MA; MO; PA; OK; RI. **Subsidiaries include:** Southern Union Gas (Austin TX) serves about 498,000 residential, commercial, industrial, agricultural, and other customers in Texas and Oklahoma. Missouri Gas Energy (Kansas City MO) serves approximately 478,000 customers in central and western Missouri. **Operations at this facility include:** Administration; Sales. **Listed on:** New York Stock Exchange. **Stock exchange symbol:** SUG. **Number of employees nationwide:** 3,100.

SWIFT ENERGY COMPANY
16825 Northchase Drive, Suite 400, Houston TX 77060. 281/874-2700. **Fax:** 281/874-2164. **Contact:** Charles Lopez, Manager of Human Resources. **World Wide Web address:** http://www.swiftenergy.com. **Description:** Sells oil and gas to industrial customers. **Listed on:** New York Stock Exchange. **Stock exchange symbol:** SFY. **Number of employees at this location:** 209.

TPC CORPORATION
2603 Augusta Drive, Suite 1400, Houston TX 77057. 281/597-6200. **Toll-free phone:** 800/568-3527. **Fax:** 713/369-9501. **Contact:** Human Resources. **Description:** Markets and trades natural gas through facilities in Texas, Louisiana, Mississippi, and other locations throughout the Gulf Coast. **Corporate headquarters location:** This location. **Parent company:** PacifiCorp.

TESORO PETROLEUM CORPORATION
300 Concord Plaza Drive, San Antonio TX 78216. 210/828-8484. **Recorded jobline:** 210/283-2600. **Contact:** Human Resources Manager. **World Wide Web address:** http://www.tesoropetroleum.com. **Description:** Engaged in the refining, transportation, and marketing of natural gas, crude oil, and related products. Other operations include exploration and oil field services such as supplying lubricants, fuels, and specialty products to the U.S. drilling industry. Tesoro Petroleum has refining facilities in Alaska, exploration and production facilities in Texas, and sells its products to customers primarily in Alaska, the Far East, and the Rocky Mountain region. **Positions advertised include:** Receptionist; PBX Operator. **Corporate headquarters location:** This location. **Listed on:** New York Stock Exchange. **Stock exchange symbol:** TSO.

TEXOIL, INC.
110 Cypress Station Drive, Suite 220, Houston TX 77090. 281/537-9920. **Fax:** 281/537-8324. **Contact:** Human Resources. **World Wide Web address:** http://www.texoil.com. **Description:** Engaged in oil and gas exploration and development. **Corporate headquarters location:** This location.

UTEX INDUSTRIES INC.
P.O. Box 901, Weimar TX 78962. 979/725-8503. **Physical address:** 605 Utex Drive, Weimar TX 78962. **Contact:** Human Resources. **World Wide Web address:** http://www.utexind.com. **Description:**

Manufactures gaskets, o-rings, and related products for the oil industry.

VALERO ENERGY CORPORATION

P.O. Box 500, San Antonio TX 78292. 210/370-2000. **Physical address:** One Valero Place, San Antonio TX 78212. **Contact:** Human Resources. **World Wide Web address:** http://www.valero.com. **Description:** Valero Energy Corporation has an extensive refining system with a throughput capacity of nearly 2 million barrels per day. The company's geographically diverse refining network stretches from Canada to the U.S. Gulf Coast, and West Coast. Valero has almost 5,000 retail sites in the United States and Canada, branded as Valero, Diamond Shamrock, Ultramar, Beacon, and Total. Valero is a leading producer of premium environmentally clean products, such as reformulated gasoline, (CARB) Phase II gasoline, low-sulfur diesel and oxygenates. The company also operates a credit card program with over 500,000 active accounts. **Positions advertised include:** Associate Accountant; Associate Commercial Analyst; Benefits Administration Supervisor; Compensation Analyst; Foreign Trade Zone Analyst; Lead Systems Specialist; Planning Engineer; Systems Analyst; Technical Specialist. **Corporate headquarters location:** This location. **Listed on:** New York Stock Exchange. **Stock exchange symbol:** VLO. **Number of employees worldwide:** 22,000.

VALERO ENERGY CORPORATION

P.O. Box 696000, San Antonio TX 78269. 210/592-2000. **Contact:** Human Resources. **World Wide Web address:** http://www.valero. com. **Description:** Owns and operates refineries that manufacture diesel, gasoline, and petroleum products. **Positions advertised include:** Associate Accountant; Associate Commercial Analyst; Benefits Administration Supervisor; Compensation Analyst; Foreign Trade Zone Analyst; Lead Systems Specialist; Planning Engineer; Systems Analyst; Technical Specialist. **Corporate headquarters location:** San Antonio TX. **Operations at this facility include:** Administration; Manufacturing. **Listed on:** New York Stock Exchange. **Stock exchange symbol:** VLO. **Number of employees worldwide:** 22,000.

VALERO ENERGY CORPORATION
THREE RIVERS REFINERY

P.O. Box 490, Three Rivers TX 78071. 361/786-2536. **Physical address:** 301 Leroy Street, Three Rivers TX 78071. **Contact:** Human

Resources. **Description:** Valero Energy Corporation has an extensive refining system with a throughput capacity of nearly 2 million barrels per day. The company's geographically diverse refining network stretches from Canada to the U.S. Gulf Coast, and West Coast. Valero has almost 5,000 retail sites in the United States and Canada, branded as Valero, Diamond Shamrock, Ultramar, Beacon, and Total. Valero is a leading producer of premium environmentally clean products, such as reformulated gasoline, (CARB) Phase II gasoline, low-sulfur diesel and oxygenates. The company also operates a credit card program with over 500,000 active accounts. **Corporate headquarters location:** San Antonio TX. **Operations at this facility include:** This location is an oil refinery. **Listed on:** New York Stock Exchange. **Stock exchange symbol:** VLO. **Number of employees worldwide:** 22,000.

WESTERN GEOPHYSICAL COMPANY
P.O. Box 2469, Houston TX 77252. 713/789-9600. **Contact:** Human Resources. **Description:** Provides a full range of geophysical services for oil and gas exploration. Services include land and marine seismic surveys, geophysical programming, and data processing and interpretation. **Corporate headquarters location:** This location. **Other U.S. locations:** AK; CA; CO. **International locations:** Australia; Bolivia; Brazil; Colombia; Egypt; England; Guatemala; Italy; Pakistan; Saudi Arabia; Singapore; Tunisia. **Operations at this facility include:** Administration; Manufacturing; Research and Development; Sales; Service.

WILLIAMS GAS PIPELINES-TRANSCO
P.O. Box 1396, Houston TX 77251. 713/215-2000. **Physical address:** 2800 Post Oak Boulevard, Houston TX 77056. **Contact:** Human Resources. **World Wide Web address:** http://www.williams. com. **Description:** Transports natural gas to the southeastern and northeastern United States. **Corporate headquarters location:** This location. **Parent company:** Williams Energy. **Listed on:** New York Stock Exchange. **Stock exchange symbol:** WMB.

WOOD GROUP PRESSURE CONTROL
P.O. Box 82, Houston TX 77001-0082. 281/847-9990. **Contact:** Human Resources. **E-mail address:** corporate@woodgroup.com. **World Wide Web address:** http://www.woodgroup.co.uk. **Description:** Manufactures and remanufactures wellheads and other oil field equipment.

PAPER AND WOOD PRODUCTS

You can expect to find the following types of companies in this chapter:
*Forest and Wood Products and Services • Lumber and Wood Wholesale •
Millwork, Plywood, and Structural Members • Paper and Wood Mills*

LOUISIANA-PACIFIC CORPORATION

P.O. Box 268, New Waverly TX 77358. 936/295-5471. **Contact:**
Human Resources. **World Wide Web address:** http://www.lpcorp.
com. **Description:** Louisiana-Pacific Corporation is a forest products
firm that harvests timber and converts it into a wide range of wood
products including lumber, panel products, doors, and other goods.
Louisiana-Pacific Corporation operates more than 100 manufacturing
facilities and 20 distribution centers in the United States and Canada.
Operations at this facility include: This location is a sales office.
Listed on: New York Stock Exchange. **Stock exchange symbol:** LPX.

LOUISIANA-PACIFIC CORPORATION

100 Interstate 45 North, Conroe TX 77305. 936/756-0541. **Contact:**
Human Resources. **World Wide Web address:** http://www.lpcorp.
com. **Description:** A forest products firm that harvests timber and
converts it into a wide range of wood products including lumber,
panel products, doors, and other goods. Louisiana-Pacific **Listed on:**
New York Stock Exchange. **Stock exchange symbol:** LPX.

WEYERHAEUSER COMPANY

P.O. Box 1209, Sealy TX 77474. 979/885-4191. **Contact:** Human
Resources   Manager.   **World   Wide   Web   address:**   http://
www.weyerhaeuser.com. **Description:** Weyerhaeuser Company's
principal businesses are the growing and harvesting of timber; the
manufacture, distribution, and sale of forest products including logs,
wood chips, and building products; real estate development and
construction; and financial services. Weyerhaeuser is one of the
world's largest private owners of marketable softwood timber and
one of the largest producers of softwood lumber and pulp. The
company is also one of North America's largest producers of forest
products and recyclers of office wastepaper, newspaper, and
corrugated boxes. Weyerhaeuser Company also sells electricity to
utility companies generated from its 15 trash-to-energy plants and six
small cogeneration and recycling plants. The Water Division
manufactures   and   operates   facilities   and   systems   for   water
purification, water treatment, and managed by-products. The Air
Division designs, manufactures, and integrates air pollution emission

control and measurement systems and related equipment. Founded in 1900. **Corporate headquarters location:** Federal Way WA. **Other U.S. locations:** Nationwide. **International locations:** Worldwide. **Listed on:** New York Stock Exchange. **Stock exchange symbol:** WY. **Number of employees worldwide:** 47,000.

PRINTING AND PUBLISHING

You can expect to find the following types of companies in this chapter:
Book, Newspaper, and Periodical Publishers • Commercial Photographers •
Commercial Printing Services • Graphic Designers

AUSTIN AMERICAN-STATESMAN
305 South Congress Avenue, Austin TX 78704. 512/445-3500. **Fax:**
512/445-3883. **Contact:** Personnel Director. **World Wide Web
address:** http://www.austin360.com. **Description:** Publishes the
Austin American-Statesman, a daily newspaper.

THE BAYTOWN SUN
P.O. Box 90, Baytown TX 77520. 281/422-8302. **Contact:** Human
Resources. **World Wide Web address:** http://www.baytownsun.com.
Description: A daily newspaper. **Positions advertised include:**
General Assignment Reporter; Classified Telemarketer; Copy Editor;
Circulation Manager; News Editor.

BRAZOSPORT FACTS
P.O. Box 549, Clute TX 77531. 979/265-7411. **Contact:** Bill
Cornwell, Publisher. **World Wide Web address:** http://
www.thefacts.com. **Description:** A daily newspaper.

CALLER-TIMES PUBLISHING COMPANY
P.O. Box 9136, Corpus Christi TX 78469. 361/884-2011. **Fax:**
361/884-5357. **Contact:** Kristin Millet, Vice President of Human
Resources. **World Wide Web address:** http://www.caller.com.
Description: A daily newspaper delivered throughout southwestern
Texas. Founded in 1883.

CONSOLIDATED GRAPHICS, INC.
5858 Westheimer Road, Suite 200, Houston TX 77057. 713/787-
0977. **Contact:** Human Resources. **World Wide Web address:** http://
www.consolidatedgraphics.com. **Description:** Operates commercial
printing companies nationwide. **Corporate headquarters location:**
This location. **Other U.S. locations:** Nationwide. **Subsidiaries
include:** Apple Graphics, Inc. (Los Angeles CA); Automated Graphics
Systems (Washington DC and Cleveland OH); Bridgetown Printing
Company (Portland OR); Byrum Lithographing Company (Columbus
OH); CMI (Chicago IL); Emerald City Graphics (Seattle WA)
produces technical and training manuals; Everett Graphics, Inc.
(Oakland CA); Graphtec, Inc. (Washington DC); McKay Press, Inc.

(Midland MI); Maryland Comp.com (Baltimore MD); Metropolitan Printing Service, Inc. (Bloomington IN); Mount Vernon Printing Company (Washington DC); Multiple Images Printing, Inc. (Chicago IL); Piccari Press, Inc. (Philadelphia PA); Precision Litho (Vista CA); Superior Colour Graphics (Kalamazoo MI); Wentworth Printing Corp. (Columbia SC). **Listed on:** New York Stock Exchange. **Stock exchange symbol:** CGX.

CONSTRUCTION DATA CORPORATION
11940 Jollyville Road, Suite 305-S, Austin TX 78759. 512/219-5150. **Toll-free phone:** 800/872-7878. **Fax:** 772/299-0818. **Contact:** Richard M. Griffin, Senior Editor. **E-mail address:** jobs@ cdcnews.com. **World Wide Web address:** http://www.cdcnews. com. **Description:** A construction trade publication that provides planning news and bidding opportunities. CDC produces 29 editions from Maine to California. Founded in 1977. **NOTE:** Entry-level positions and part-time jobs are offered. **Positions advertised include:** Reporter/Editor; Inside Sales Representative. **Special programs:** Internships. **Corporate headquarters location:** Vero Beach FL. **Listed on:** Privately held.

GALVESTON COUNTY DAILY NEWS
P.O. Box 628, Galveston TX 77553. 409/744-3611. **Fax:** 409/744-6268. **Contact:** Rosetta Bonnin, Business Office Manager. **World Wide Web address:** http://www.galvnews.com. **Description:** A daily newspaper with a circulation of 24,000. **Parent company:** Southern Newspapers Inc. **Listed on:** Privately held.

GALVESTON POLICE DEPARTMENT
5303 Avenue S, Galveston TX 77550. 409/741-0068. **Contact:** Human Resources. **World Wide Web address:** http:// www.galpd.org/emp.html. **Description:** Provides law enforcement services to the Galveston area.

THE HOUSTON BUSINESS JOURNAL
1001 West Loop South, Suite 650, Houston TX 77027. 713/688-8811. **Fax:** 713/963-0482. **Contact:** Human Resources Department. **World Wide Web address:** http://www.bizjournals.com/houston. **Description:** A daily business journal. **Corporate headquarters location:** This location. **Parent company:** American City Business Journal.

HOUSTON CHRONICLE
801 Texas Avenue, Houston TX 77002. 713/220-7171. **Contact:** Ann Turnbach, Personnel Director. **World Wide Web address:** http://www.houstonchronicle.com. **Description:** A daily newspaper. **Corporate headquarters location:** This location.

THE JEWISH HERALD-VOICE
P.O. Box 153, Houston TX 77001. 713/630-0391. **Contact:** Mrs. Jeanne Samuels, Editor. **World Wide Web address:** http://jewishheraldvoice.com. **Description:** A weekly newspaper for the Jewish community.

THE PSYCHOLOGICAL CORPORATION
19500 Bulverde, San Antonio TX 78259. 800/872-1726. **Contact:** Human Resources. **World Wide Web address:** http://www.psychcorp.com. **Description:** One of the oldest and largest commercial test publishers in the nation. The company provides tests (e.g. the Stanford Achievement Test Series, the Metropolitan Achievement Tests, and Wechsler Intelligence Scales for Children and Adults) and related services to schools and colleges, clinicians and professional organizations, businesses, and public entities. The company's services include test research and development, printing, marketing, distribution, administration, and scoring. Psychological Corporation has three divisions: an educational measurement division; a psychological measurement and communications division; and a division that awards licenses and credentials. **NOTE:** Entry-level positions and second and third shifts are offered. **Positions advertised include:** Administrative Assistant; Assessment Specialist; Cost Accountant; Revenue Accounting Manager; Sales Administrator; Sampling Associate. **Corporate headquarters location:** This location. **Parent company:** Reed Elsevier.

SAN ANTONIO EXPRESS NEWS
P.O. Box 2171, San Antonio TX 78297-2171. 210/225-7411. **Contact:** Human Resources. **World Wide Web address:** http://www.express-news.net. **Description:** A newspaper with a circulation of approximately 250,000 daily and 390,000 on Sundays.

TEXAS MONTHLY
P.O. Box 1569, Austin TX 78767. 512/320-6900. **Fax:** 512/476-9007. **Contact:** Angela Hollinsworth, Office Manager. **E-mail address:** humanresources@texasmonthly.com. **World Wide Web address:** http://www.texasmonthly.com. **Description:** *Texas Monthly*

is a regional, general interest magazine. Articles range from health and travel to true crime. The magazine has a circulation of approximately 300,000. Founded in 1972. **Positions advertised include:** Associate Art Director; National Account Manager; Account Executive. **Special programs:** Internships. **Corporate headquarters location:** This location.

REAL ESTATE

You can expect to find the following types of companies in this chapter:
Land Subdividers and Developers • Real Estate Agents, Managers,
and Operators • Real Estate Investment Trusts

COLDWELL BANKER
8610 Seawall Boulevard, Site 230, Galveston TX 77554. 409/740-4040. **Toll-free phone:** 800/701-1016. **Fax:** 409/740-3586. **Contact:** Personnel. **World Wide Web address:** http://www.coldwellbanker.com. **Description:** One of the largest residential real estate companies in the United States and Canada in terms of total home sales transactions. Coldwell Banker is also a leader in corporate relocation services. **Corporate headquarters location:** Parsippany NJ. **Other U.S. locations:** Nationwide. **Parent company:** Cendant Corporation. **Listed on:** New York Stock Exchange. **Stock exchange symbol:** CD.

COLDWELL BANKER
3100 Padre Boulevard, South Padre Island TX 78597-3469. 956/761-7801. **Contact:** Personnel. **World Wide Web address:** http://www.coldwellbanker.com. **Description:** Coldwell Banker is one of the largest residential real estate companies in the United States and Canada in terms of total home sales transactions. Coldwell Banker is also a leader in corporate relocation services. **Corporate headquarters location:** Parsippany NJ. **Other U.S. locations:** Nationwide. **Parent company:** Cendant Corporation. **Listed on:** New York Stock Exchange. **Stock exchange symbol:** CD.

BEELER PROPERTIES, INC.
7500 San Felipe, Suite 750, Houston TX 77063. 713/785-8200. **Fax:** 713/785-4143. **Contact:** Human Resources. **Description:** Specializes in the development, construction, and management of apartment buildings. **Corporate headquarters location:** This location. **Parent company:** Beeler-Sanders, Inc.

BOUDREAUX & LEONARD, P.C.
1100 Louisiana Street, Suite 1400, Houston TX 77002. 713/757-0000. **Fax:** 713/757-0178. **Contact:** Human Resources Manager. **World Wide Web address:** http://www.boudreauxleonard.com. **Description:** A law office. Founded in 1981. **NOTE:** Entry-level positions are offered. **Special programs:** Summer Jobs. **Corporate headquarters location:** This location. **Listed on:** Privately held.

BRADFIELD PROPERTIES INC.
18830 Stone Oak Parkway, San Antonio TX 78258-4113. 210/496-4949. **Contact:** Human Resources. **World Wide Web address:** http://www.bradfieldproperties.com. **Description:** A real estate company specializing in residential, commercial, and multifamily property management.

CAMDEN PROPERTY TRUST
3 Greenway Plaza, Suite 1300, Houston TX 77046. 713/354-2500. **Contact:** Recruiting Manager. **World Wide Web address:** http://www.camdenprop.com. **Description:** A real estate investment trust that buys, sells, builds, and manages apartment communities throughout the Southwest. **NOTE:** Entry-level positions are offered. **Corporate headquarters location:** This location. **Other area locations:** Austin TX; Corpus Christi TX; Dallas TX; El Paso TX; Fort Worth TX; San Antonio TX. **Other U.S. locations:** AZ; CA; CO; FL; MO; NC; NV. **Operations at this facility include:** Administration. **Listed on:** New York Stock Exchange. **Stock exchange symbol:** CPT. **Number of employees nationwide:** 1,750.

CAPSTONE REAL ESTATE SERVICES
210 Baron Springs Road, Suite 300, Austin TX 78704. 512/646-6700. **Contact:** Human Resources. **World Wide Web address:** http://www.capstonerealestate.com. **Description:** Sells, rents, and leases apartments and commercial properties.

DMC MANAGEMENT
6363 Woodway, Suite 1000, Houston TX 77057. 713/977-4844. **Contact:** Human Resources. **Description:** A real estate management firm specializing in multifamily properties.

FINSA INDUSTRIAL PARKS
973 South Minnesota, Brownsville TX 78521. 956/550-9017. **Contact:** Human Resources. **World Wide Web address:** http://www.finsa.net. **Description:** A company that constructs, owns, sells, and leases industrial park property.

FIRST AMERICAN FLOOD DATA SERVICES
11902 Burnet Road, Suite 400, Austin TX 78758. 512/834-9595. **Contact:** Judy Ellison, Personnel Director. **World Wide Web address:** http://www.firstam.com. **Description:** Determines whether properties are in a flood zone for mortgage companies and banks.

HINES PROPERTIES INC.

2800 Post Oak Boulevard, 48th Floor, Houston TX 77056. 713/966-2629. **Contact:** David LeVrier, Director of Human Resources. **World Wide Web address:** http://www.hines.com. **Description:** Engaged in commercial real estate development and property management. The company has properties in 39 U.S. cities. **Positions advertised include:** Controller; Senior Project Manager; Senior Project Accountant; Staff Accountant; Bookkeeper; Receptionist; Senior Construction Manager; Construction Manager; Assistant Construction Manager. **Corporate headquarters location:** This location. **Operations at this facility include:** Administration.

THE HOUSE COMPANY

2615 Broadway, Galveston TX 77550. 409/763-8030. **Contact:** Human Resources. **World Wide Web address:** http://www.thehousecompany.com. **Description:** A real estate agency dealing with residential properties and specializing in relocation services.

KAUFMAN AND BROAD

9990 Richmond Avenue, Suite 400, Houston TX 77042. 713/977-6633. **Contact:** Human Resources. **World Wide Web address:** http://www.kaufmanandbroad.com. **Description:** A single-family residential homebuilder. **Positions advertised include:** Bilingual Sales Consultant; Director of Land Acquisition; New Home Sales Counselor; Customer Service Coordinator; Data Entry Coordinator; Financial Analyst; Studio Consultant.

KUPER REALTY CORPORATION

6606 North New Braunfels Avenue, San Antonio TX 78209. 210/822-8602. **Contact:** Manager. **World Wide Web address:** http://www.kuperrealty.com. **Description:** A real estate agency engaged in the sale of residential and commercial properties as well as ranches and land.

PALM HARBOR HOMES INC.

P.O. Box 19529, Austin TX 78760. 512/385-5880. **Fax:** 512/385-2910. **Contact:** Personnel Manager. **World Wide Web address:** http://www.palmharbor.com. **Description:** Produces manufactured houses. Founded in 1978. **Positions advertised include:** Retail Sales Associate. **Corporate headquarters location:** Addison TX. **Other U.S. locations:** AL; AZ; FL; GA; NC; OH; OR. **Listed on:** NASDAQ.

Stock exchange symbol: PHHM. **Number of employees nationwide:** 4,100.

USAA REAL ESTATE COMPANY
9830 Colonnade Boulevard, Suite 600, San Antonio TX 78230-2239. 210/498-3222. **Fax:** 210/498-8986. **Contact:** Human Resources. **World Wide Web address:** http://www.realco.usaa.com. **Description:** Engaged in commercial real estate services for corporate, institutional, and private investors.

DAVID WEEKLEY HOMES
1111 North Post Oak Road, Houston TX 77055. 713/963-0500. **Contact:** Personnel Director. **World Wide Web address:** http://www.davidweekleyhomes.com. **Description:** Builds energy-efficient homes and offers multilevel warranties. **Positions advertised include:** Residential Sales Associate; Construction Manager; Builder Services Representative.

WEINGARTEN REALTY INVESTORS
P.O. Box 924133, Houston TX 77292-4133. 713/866-6000. **Physical address:** 2600 Citadel Plaza Drive, Suite 300, Houston TX 77008. **Fax:** 713/866-6993. **Contact:** Human Resources. **E-mail address:** jobs@weingarten.com. **World Wide Web address:** http://www.weingarten.com. **Description:** Buys, sells, and manages shopping centers and industrial properties. **Positions advertised include:** Senior Leasing Executive. **Listed on:** New York Stock Exchange. **Stock exchange symbol:** WRI.

WILDWOOD MANAGEMENT GROUP
18585 Sigimi, Suite 101, San Antonio TX 78258. 210/403-9785. **Contact:** Human Resources. **Description:** Engaged in property management for apartments and condominiums.

WUKASCH COMPANY
1810 Guadalupe Street, Austin TX 78701. 512/472-4700. **Contact:** Don C. Wukasch, President. **Description:** A diversified real estate and securities investment company providing real estate property management and securities portfolio management. **Special programs:** Internships. **Corporate headquarters location:** This location. **Listed on:** Privately held.

RETAIL

You can expect to find the following types of companies in this chapter:
Catalog Retailers • Department Stores; Specialty Stores•
Retail Bakeries • Supermarkets

BARNES & NOBLE BOOKSTORES
2545 Town Center Boulevard, Sugar Land TX 77479. 281/265-4620.
Contact: Manager. **World Wide Web address:** http://www.bn.com.
Description: A discount bookstore chain operating nationwide.
Corporate headquarters location: New York NY.

BARNES & NOBLE BOOKSTORES
7626 Westheimer, Houston TX 77063. 713/783-6016. **Contact:**
Manager. **World Wide Web address:** http://www.bn.com.
Description: A discount bookstore chain operating nationwide.
Corporate headquarters location: New York NY.

BIG KMART
3500 Garth Road, Baytown TX 77521. 281/422-6886. **Contact:**
Hiring Manager. **World Wide Web address:** http://www.kmart.com.
Description: One location of the national chain of general
merchandise stores. **Corporate headquarters location:** Troy MI.
Parent company: Kmart Corporation operates 2,100 Kmart discount
stores worldwide. **Listed on:** New York Stock Exchange. **Stock
exchange symbol:** KM.

FOLEY'S
1110 Main Street, Houston TX 77002. 713/405-7035. **Contact:**
Human Resources. **World Wide Web address:** http://www.foleys.
com. **Description:** One location of the department store chain
operating through over 50 stores. **Parent company:** The May
Department Stores Company.

HEB GROCERY COMPANY
P.O. Box 839999, San Antonio TX 78283. 210/938-8000. **Recorded
jobline:** 210/938-5222. **Contact:** Human Resources. **E-mail address:**
careers@heb.com. **World Wide Web address:** http://www.heb.com.
Description: Operates a chain of retail grocery stores. Founded in
1905. **NOTE:** Interested jobseekers should contact the jobline before
sending a resume. **Office hours:** Monday - Friday, 8:00 a.m. - 5:00
p.m. **Corporate headquarters location:** This location. **Listed on:**
Privately held. **President:** Charles Butt.

HOLLAND PHOTO IMAGING

1221 South Lamar Boulevard, Austin TX 78704. 512/442-4274. **Fax:** 512/442-5898. **Contact:** Personnel. **World Wide Web address:** http://www.hollandphoto.com. **Description:** A photo processing company. Founded in 1982.

JCPENNEY COMPANY, INC.

2000 San Jacinto Mall, Baytown TX 77521. 281/421-2354. **Contact:** Hiring Manager. **World Wide Web address:** http://www.jcpenney. net. **Description:** One location of the department store chain that sells apparel, home furnishings, and leisure lines. **Corporate headquarters location:** Dallas TX. **Other U.S. locations:** Nationwide. **Listed on:** New York Stock Exchange. **Stock exchange symbol:** JCP. **Number of employees worldwide:** 267,000.

MEN'S WEARHOUSE

5803 Glenmont Drive, Houston TX 77081. 713/664-3692. **Contact:** Human Resources Department. **World Wide Web address:** http:// www.menswearhouse.com. **Description:** One of the largest off-price retailers of men's tailored business attire in the United States. The stores offer designer brand-name and private-label suits, sports jackets, slacks, dress shirts, and accessories at discount prices. **Corporate headquarters location:** This location. **Listed on:** New York Stock Exchange. **Stock exchange symbol:** MW.

MOORE SUPPLY COMPANY

P.O. Box 448, Conroe TX 77305. 936/756-4445. **Contact:** Human Resources. **World Wide Web address:** http://www.mooresupply. com. **Description:** Engaged in the retail and wholesale of plumbing supplies, lavatory supplies, tubs, and toilets.

OFFICE DEPOT, INC.

2209 Rutland Drive, Suite A100, Austin TX 78758. 512/837-8999. **Fax:** 512/837-1221. **Contact:** Human Resources. **World Wide Web address:** http://www.officedepot.com. **Description:** One of the nation's leading office products dealers. The company offers over 11,000 business products including furniture; desk accessories; office essentials; computer products; business machines; visual communications; safety and maintenance supplies; personalized organizers and dated goods; writing instruments; business cases and binders; filing and storage; paper, envelopes, and business forms; and labels and mailing supplies. **Corporate headquarters location:** Delray Beach FL. **Subsidiaries include:** Viking Office Products is a direct mail marketer. **Listed on:** New York Stock Exchange. **Stock exchange symbol:** ODP.

OFFICE DEPOT, INC.
6225 West by Northwest Boulevard, Houston TX 77040. 713/996-3200. **Contact:** Human Resources. **World Wide Web address:** http://www.officedepot.com. **Description:** One of the nation's leading office products dealers. The company offers over 11,000 different business products including furniture; desk accessories; office essentials; computer products; business machines; visual communications; safety and maintenance supplies; personalized organizers and dated goods; writing instruments; business cases and binders; filing and storage; paper, envelopes, and business forms; and labels and mailing supplies. **Corporate headquarters location:** Delray Beach FL. **Subsidiaries include:** Viking Office Products is a direct mail marketer. **Listed on:** New York Stock Exchange. **Stock exchange symbol:** ODP.

RALSTON DRUG AND DISCOUNT LIQUOR
3147 Southmore Boulevard, Houston TX 77004. 713/524-3045. **Contact:** Human Resources. **Description:** Operates discount liquor and drug stores with 18 local outlets.

RANDALLS FOOD MARKETS
P.O. Box 4506, Houston TX 77210-4506. 713/435-2400. **Fax:** 713/435-2499. **Recorded jobline:** 713/268-3404. **Contact:** Employment Manager. **World Wide Web address:** http://www.randalls.com. **Description:** Operates 1,782 retail grocery stores throughout the United States and Canada. **Corporate headquarters location:** This location. **Listed on:** New York Stock Exchange. **Stock exchange symbol:** SWY.

RICE EPICUREAN MARKETS INC.
P.O. Box 159, Belair TX 77402. 713/662-7700. **Contact:** Personnel Director. **E-mail address:** employment@riceepicurean.com. **World Wide Web address:** http://www.riceepicurean.com. **Description:** Operates and manages a chain of food stores. **Positions advertised include:** Deli Cook; Baker; Cake Decorator; Office Manager. **Office hours:** Monday - Friday, 8:00 a.m. - 5:00 p.m. **Corporate headquarters location:** This location. **Operations at this facility include:** Administration.

STAR FURNITURE COMPANY
P.O. Box 219169, Houston TX 77218-9169. 281/492-5445. **Fax:** 281/579-5909. **Contact:** Paige Olson, Director of Human Resources. **World Wide Web address:** http://www.starfurniture.com. **Description:** Engaged in the retail sale of home furnishings. **Positions advertised include:** Sales Consultant; Assistant Manager; Retail Office Assistant; Service Assistant; Warehouse Worker; Driver's Helper. **Corporate headquarters location:** This location. **Other U.S. locations:** College Station TX. **Parent company:** Berkshire Hathaway Inc. **Operations at this facility include:** Administration; Sales; Service. **Listed on:** Privately held.

VF FACTORY OUTLET
805 Factory Outlet Drive, Hempstead TX 77445-5604. 979/826-8277. **Contact:** Human Resources. **World Wide Web address:** http://www.vffo.com. **Description:** A discount retailer of jeanswear, sportswear, activewear, intimate apparel, and occupational apparel. **Positions advertised include:** Store Management Trainee. **Other U.S. locations:** Nationwide.

WALGREEN COMPANY
8110 Kempwood, Houston TX 77055. 713/973-5800. **Contact:** Human Resources. **World Wide Web address:** http://www.walgreens.com. **Description:** Walgreen is a retail drug store chain with more than 3,600 stores nationwide. The company sells prescription and proprietary drugs and also carries cosmetics, toiletries, tobacco, and general merchandise. **Corporate headquarters location:** Deerfield IL. **Operations at this facility include:** This location is a district office and warehouse. **Listed on:** New York Stock Exchange. **Stock exchange symbol:** WAG.

WOLF CAMERA
3264 Westheimer, Houston TX 77098. 713/528-3332. **Contact:** Manager. **World Wide Web address:** http://www.wolfcamera.com. **Description:** A one-hour photo development lab. The company also sells film, frames, and other photography products.

WOLF CAMERA AND VIDEO
607 Congress Avenue, Austin TX 78701. 512/476-3977. **Contact:** Human Resources. **World Wide Web address:** http://www.wolfcamera.com. **Description:** A retail distributor of photographic equipment and supplies that also offers photofinishing

services. The company operates through more than 700 retail stores.
Other U.S. locations: Nationwide.

STONE, CLAY, GLASS, AND CONCRETE PRODUCTS

You can expect to find the following types of companies in this chapter:
Cement, Tile, Sand, and Gravel • Crushed and Broken Stone •
Glass and Glass Products • Mineral Products

AMERICAN FLAT GLASS DISTRIBUTORS, INC. (AFGD)
3822 Airport Boulevard, Austin TX 78722. 512/474-2375. **Fax:** 512/474-5821. **Contact:** Branch Manager. **World Wide Web address:** http://www.afgd.com. **Description:** Specializes in architectural insulated glass units and custom tempering. AFGD manufactures a complete line of insulated glass units for commercial and residential applications. The product line includes clear, tint, and reflective glass; wire glass; and equipment for the handling, storage, and transportation of glass. There are 50 AFGD locations throughout North America. **Positions advertised include:** Inside Sales Representative. **Corporate headquarters location:** Atlanta GA. **Subsidiaries include:** AFGD Canada. **Parent company:** AFG Industries, Inc. **Operations at this facility include:** Manufacturing; Sales. **Listed on:** Privately held.

AMERICAN FLAT GLASS DISTRIBUTORS, INC. (AFGD)
10750 Sentinel Drive, San Antonio TX 78217. 210/653-7790. **Fax:** 210/655-3945. **Contact:** Mr. Scott Dunbar, Plant Manager. **World Wide Web address:** http://www.afgd.com. **Description:** Specializes in architectural insulated glass units and custom tempering. AFGD manufactures a complete line of insulated glass units for commercial and residential applications. The product line includes clear, tint, and reflective glass; wire glass; and equipment for the handling, storage, and transportation of glass. There are 50 AFGD locations throughout North America. **Positions advertised include:** Inside Sales Representative. **Corporate headquarters location:** Atlanta GA. **Subsidiaries include:** AFGD Canada. **Parent company:** AFG Industries, Inc. **Operations at this facility include:** Manufacturing; Sales. **Listed on:** Privately held.

AMERICAN FLAT GLASS DISTRIBUTORS, INC. (AFGD)
5901 Milwee, Houston TX 77292-4767. 713/686-2509. **Contact:** Mike Russell, Branch Manager. **World Wide Web address:** http://www.afgd.com. **Description:** Specializes in architectural insulated glass units and custom tempering. AFGD manufactures a complete line of insulated glass units for commercial and residential

applications. The product line includes clear, tint, and reflective glass; wire glass; and equipment for the handling, storage, and transportation of glass. There are 50 AFGD locations throughout North America. **Positions advertised include:** Inside Sales Representative. **Corporate headquarters location:** Atlanta GA. **Subsidiaries include:** AFGD Canada. **Parent company:** AFG Industries, Inc. **Operations at this facility include:** Manufacturing; Sales. **Listed on:** Privately held.

DAL-TILE INTERNATIONAL
143 West Bay Area Boulevard, Webster TX 77598. 281/554-4575. **Contact:** Human Resources. **World Wide Web address:** http://www.daltile.com. **Description:** Manufactures and distributes ceramic tiles. **Positions advertised include:** Staff Accountant. **Parent company:** Mohawk Industries. **Listed on:** New York Stock Exchange. **Stock exchange symbol:** MHK.

FORDYCE COMPANY
P.O. Box 1417, Victoria TX 77902. 361/573-4309. **Physical address:** 120 South Main Place, Suite 500, Victoria TX 77901. **Contact:** Personnel Director. **Description:** Produces sand and gravel. **Corporate headquarters location:** This location. **Number of employees at this location:** 120.

SHEPLER'S
9103 East Almeda Road, Houston TX 77054. 713/799-1150. **Toll-free phone:** 800/729-1150. **Fax:** 713/799-8431. **Contact:** Anna Olizares, Human Resources Coordinator. **World Wide Web address:** http://www.cmcsheplers.com. **Description:** A supplier of concrete accessories, highway products, and form systems. **NOTE:** Entry-level positions are offered. **Special programs:** Internships; Training. **Corporate headquarters location:** This location. **Parent company:** CMC Steel Group. **Operations at this facility include:** Administration; Sales.

VULCAN MATERIALS
P.O. Box 791550, San Antonio TX 78279. 210/349-3311. **Contact:** Human Resources Manager. **World Wide Web address:** http://www.vulcanmaterials.com. **Description:** Fabricators of concrete, asphalt, and other stone products. **Corporate headquarters location:** Birmingham AL. **Listed on:** New York Stock Exchange. **Stock exchange symbol:** VMC.

TRANSPORTATION/TRAVEL

You can expect to find the following types of companies in this chapter:
Air, Railroad, and Water Transportation Services • Courier Services • Local and Interurban Passenger Transit • Ship Building and Repair • Transportation Equipment Travel Agencies • Trucking • Warehousing and Storage

BLUE WHALE MOVING COMPANY
8291 Springdale Road, Suite 100, Austin TX 78724. 512/328-6688. **Contact:** Human Resources. **World Wide Web address:** http://www.bluewhale.com. **Description:** Provides both furniture storage and moving services throughout Texas. Founded in 1985.

CAPITAL METRO
2910 East Fifth Street, Austin TX 78702. 512/389-7400. **Fax:** 512/369-6010. **Contact:** Human Resources. **World Wide Web address:** http://www.capmetro.austin.tx.us. **Description:** Operates the public bus system for the metropolitan Austin area. **Positions advertised include:** Fleet Mechanic; Project Manager; DBE Coordinator; DBE Program Specialist; Data Analyst; Internal Auditor; Budget Analyst. **Corporate headquarters location:** This location.

CENTRAL FREIGHT LINES, INC.
6315 Highway 347, Beaumont TX 77705. 409/722-8371. **Contact:** Human Resources. **World Wide Web address:** http://www.centralfreight.com. **Description:** One of the largest regional motor carriers in the United States operating through 77 terminals. Founded in 1925. **Corporate headquarters location:** Waco TX. **Other U.S. locations:** Nationwide.

FEDERAL EXPRESS CORPORATION (FEDEX)
1220 Riverbend, Dallas TX 75247. 800/GOF-EDEX. **Contact:** Recruiting. **World Wide Web address:** http://www.fedex.com. **Description:** One of the world's largest express transportation companies serving 212 countries worldwide. FedEx ships approximately 3.2 million packages daily. FedEx operates more than 45,000 drop-off locations, and has a fleet that consists of more than 640 aircraft and 44,5000 vehicles. **Corporate headquarters location:** Memphis TN. **Other U.S. locations:** Nationwide. **International locations:** Worldwide. **Listed on:** New York Stock Exchange. **Stock exchange symbol:** FDS.

PORT OF HOUSTON AUTHORITY

P.O. Box 2562, Houston TX 77252-2562. 713/670-2400. **Contact:** Human Resources. **World Wide Web address:** http://www.portofhouston.com. **Description:** Administers and regulates the Port of Houston Authority. Responsibilities include fire and safety protection along the 50-mile Houston Ship Channel. The Port Authority owns 43 general cargo wharves, two liquid-cargo wharves, and many other facilities.

RAILAMERICA, INC

4040 Broadway, Suite 200, San Antonio TX 78209. 210/841-7600. **Fax:** 561/226-1627. **Contact:** Human Resources. **World Wide Web address:** http://www.railamerica.com. **Description:** A leading operator of short line railroads nationwide. **Positions advertised include:** Electrician. **NOTE:** Send resumes to: RailAmerica, Inc., Employment, 5300 Broken Sound Boulevard Northwest, Boca Raton FL 33487.

THAI AIRWAYS INTERNATIONAL LTD.

8700 North Stemmons Freeway, Suite 133, Dallas TX 75247. 800/426-5204. **Contact:** Human Resources. **World Wide Web address:** http://www.thaiair.com. **Description:** One of Asia's leading airlines, offering flights to 72 cities in 37 countries.

TIDEWATER

7815 Harborside Drive, Galveston TX 77554. 409/744-9500. **Contact:** Human Resources. **World Wide Web address:** http://www.tidewater-construction.com. **Description:** Provides offshore marine transportation services.

VIA METROPOLITAN TRANSIT

1021 San Pedro, San Antonio TX 78212. 210/362-2240. **Contact:** Human Resources. **E-mail address:** hr.emp@viainfo.net. **World Wide Web address:** http://www.viainfo.net. **Description:** A bus line for the city of San Antonio. **Positions advertised include:** Shop Attendant; Bus Operator; Paratransit Operator; Substitute Teacher. **Corporate headquarters location:** This location.

UTILITIES: ELECTRIC/GAS/WATER

You can expect to find the following types of companies in this chapter:
*Gas, Electric, and Fuel Companies; Other Energy-Producing Companies •
Public Utility Holding Companies • Water Utilities*

TEXAS-NEW MEXICO POWER COMPANY
702 36th Street North, Texas City TX 77590-6639. 409/948-8451.
Contact: Human Resources. **Wide Web address:** http://www.tnpe.
com. **Description:** Generates, transmits, distributes, and sells electric
energy. **Parent company:** TNP Enterprises Inc.

MISCELLANEOUS WHOLESALING

You can expect to find the following types of companies in this chapter:
Exporters and Importers • General Wholesale Distribution Companies

ACR GROUP, INC.
3200 Wilcrest Drive, Suite 440, Houston TX 77042-6019. 713/780-8532. **Fax:** 713/780-4067. **Contact:** Human Resources. **World Wide Web address:** http://www.acrgroup.com. **Description:** A wholesale distributor of heating, ventilation, air conditioning, and refrigeration equipment, parts, and supplies. ACR Group's products include motors, fiberglass air handling products, sheet metal products, copper tubing, flexible duct, controls, grilles, registers, and pipe vents. The company has 18 distribution outlets in the United States. Founded in 1990. **Corporate headquarters location:** This location. **Other U.S. locations:** Nationwide. **Subsidiaries include:** ACR Supply, Inc. (TX and LA); Beaumont A/C Supply, Inc. (TX); Contractors Heating & Supply, Inc. (CO and NM); Ener-Tech Industries, Inc. (TN); Florida Cooling Supply, Inc. (FL); Heating and Cooling Supply, Inc. (NV); Lifetime Filter, Inc. (TX); Total Supply, Inc. (GA); Valley Supply, Inc. (TN); West Coast HVAC Supply, Inc. (CA). **President/CEO:** Alex Trevino, Jr.

AMC INDUSTRIES
3535 Metro Parkway, San Antonio TX 78247. 210/545-2566. **Fax:** 210/545-2977. **Contact:** Patsy Hester, Human Resources. **Description:** A wholesale distributor of water well parts. **Corporate headquarters location:** This location. **Other U.S. locations:** Austin TX; Houston TX.

CONTI WINDOW FASHIONS
408 Arlington Street, Houston TX 77007-2696. 713/863-7761. **Contact:** Human Resources. **Description:** A manufacturer and wholesaler of window coverings for retailers.

FERGUSON ENTERPRISES, INC.
19 Burwood Lane, San Antonio TX 78216. 210/344-4950. **Fax:** 210/344-1253. **Contact:** Manager. **World Wide Web address:** http://www.ferguson.com. **Description:** A retail and wholesale distributor of plumbing supplies. **Positions advertised include:** Sales/Management Trainee; Controller Trainee. **Corporate headquarters location:** This location.

JOHNSON SUPPLY AND EQUIPMENT
10151 Stella Link, Houston TX 77025. 713/661-6666. **Contact:** Human Resources. **World Wide Web address:** http:// www.johnsonsupply.com. **Description:** A supplier of air conditioning systems and equipment.

O&M SALES, INC.
8705 Shoal Creek Boulevard, Suite 103, Austin TX 78757-6839. 512/453-0275. **Contact:** Human Resources. **World Wide Web address:** http://www.o-m-sales.com. **Description:** A wholesaler of semiconductors and other electronic components.

PRIME SERVICE
16225 Park Ten Place, Suite 200, Houston TX 77084. 281/578-5600. **Contact:** Human Resources. **World Wide Web address:** http:// www.rentalservice.com. **Description:** Wholesales and rents a wide variety of construction and industrial equipment for industrial users and homeowners. **Corporate headquarters location:** This location. **Parent company:** Atlas Copco Group.

READER'S WHOLESALE DISTRIBUTORS INC.
1201 Naylor, Houston TX 77002. 713/224-8300. **Contact:** Human Resources. **Description:** A wholesaler of flooring materials such as carpet, tile, and wood.

STRAUS-FRANK COMPANY
P.O. Box 600, San Antonio TX 78292-0600. 210/226-0101. **Contact:** Human Resources. **Description:** A wholesaler of automobile parts. Straus-Frank Company owns the retail chain automotive parts store Car Quest. **Corporate headquarters location:** This location.

SUMMIT ELECTRIC
2929 McKinney Drive, Houston TX 77003. 713/236-0971. **Contact:** Human Resources. **World Wide Web address:** http://www.summit. com. **Description:** A wholesale supplier of electrical apparatus and equipment.

WHOLESALE ELECTRIC SUPPLY CO., INC.
4040 Gulf Freeway, Houston TX 77004. 713/748-6100. **Contact:** Personnel Manager. **World Wide Web address:** http:// www.wholesaleelectric.com. **Description:** Distributes switches and

electrical equipment for the commercial, OEM, chemical, petrochemical, refining, and utility industries.

ACCOUNTING & MANAGEMENT CONSULTING

Deloitte & Touche/50
Ernst & Young LLP/50
KPMG/51
Paychex, Inc./51
PricewaterhouseCoopers/51

ADVERTISING, MARKETING, AND PUBLIC RELATIONS

Advo Inc./53
BRSG (Black Rogers Sullivan Goodnight)/53
Bates Southwest/53
Cable Time/53
Database Marketing Group Inc./53
Fogartykleinmonroe/54
Freeman Decorating Company/54
GSD&M Advertising/54
Greensheet/54
Harte-Hanks, Inc./54
KnowledgeBase Marketing/54
Robert Lamons and Associates/55
Mann & Mann Media Services, Inc./55
Nationwide Advertising Service Inc./55
Norwood Promotional Products, Inc./55
Print Mailers/56
Sachnowitz & Company/56
TL Marketing Inc./56
West Teleservices/56

AEROSPACE

The Boeing Company/57
CFAN Company/57
Continental Airlines/57
Delta Air Lines, Inc./58
Fairchild Dornier Corporation/58
GB Tech Inc./58
Goodrich Aerospace Aerostructures Group/59
Dee Howard Aircraft Maintenance, LP/59

Lockheed Martin Space Operations/59
New Systems/60

APPAREL, FASHION, AND TEXTILES

C C Creations/61
Custom Drapery, Blinds, & Carpet/61
Dilly Uniform Company/61
Houston Wiper & Mill Supply Company/61
Kast Fabrics/61
Tandy Brands Accessories/62
Tex Tan Western Leather Company/62
Texace Corporation/62
Williamson-Dickie Manufacturing Company/62

ARCHITECTURE/ CONSTRUCTION/ ENGINEERING (MISC.)

ABB Lummus Global/63
J.D. Abrams International Inc./63
American Homestar Corporation/63
APAC Texas, Inc./63
Associated Building Services Company/64
BS&B Process Systems, Inc./64
Beldon Roofing Company/64
The Bergaila Companies/64
Bernard Johnson Young, Inc./64
Cargill Steel & Wire/64
J.C. Evans Construction Company/65
Hernandez Engineering/65
Houston Wire and Cable Company/66
Jalco, Inc./66
Kellogg, Brown & Root/66
Lockwood, Andrews & Newnam, Inc./66
Lyda Company/67
Marek Brothers/67
Martin Marietta Materials/67
Mustang Engineering/67

BUSINESS SERVICES/ NON-SCIENTIFIC RESEARCH

Accenture/88
Analysts International Corporation (AiC)/88, 89
Aquent/89
BAE Systems/89
The Benchmark Company/89
Burns Pinkerton Security/89
Cirrus Logic, Inc./90
Dresser-Rand Company/90
Emerson Process Management/CSI/90
Exponent, Inc./91
Fugro Geosciences/91
Futron Corporation/91
GC Services/91
HVJ Associates/92
Hickam Industries, Inc./92
HydroChem Industrial Services/92
I-Sector Corporation/92
IKON Office Solutions/92
Initial Security/92
International Maintenance Corporation/93
Arthur D. Little, Inc./93
Loomis, Fargo & Company/93
Marsh USA, Inc./93
Modis, Inc./94
Philip Services Corporation/94
Pinkerton Security & Investigation Services/94
Bechtel Corporation/95
sai PeoplE solutions, Inc./95
TMP Worldwide Resourcing/95
Tabs Direct/95
TeamStaff/96
Telescan, Inc./96
Turner, Collie & Braden, Inc./96
Vignette Corporation/96
Xerox Corporation/97
Xerox Omnifax/97

CHARITIES/SOCIAL SERVICES

AIDS Services of Austin/98
American Red Cross/98
Baytown YMCA/98
Communities In School/99
Goodwill Industries/99
Houston Area Urban League/99
Lady Bird Johnson Wildflower Center/99
Life Resource/Spindle Top Mental Health & Mental Retardation/99
Lighthouse of Houston/99
Martin Luther Homes of Texas Inc./100
Neighborhood Centers Inc./100
The Ronald McDonald House of Galveston/100
Service Corporation International (SCI)/100
United Way of the Texas Gulf Coast/100

CHEMICALS/RUBBER AND PLASTICS

Albemarle Corporation/102
ATOFINA Chemical/102
ATOFINA Petrochemicals, Inc./102
BASF Corporation/102
BP Chemical Company/103
Baker Petrolite/103
BASELL Polyolefins/103
Celanese Corporation/103, 104
Continental Carbon Company/104
Continental Plastic Containers, Inc./104
DX Service Company/104
Dow Chemical Company/104
Engineered Carbons, Inc./104
Flint Hills Resources LP/105
GSE Lining Technology, Inc./105
Goodyear Chemical/105
Lubrizol Corporation/105
Lyondell Chemical Company/106
EQUISTAR CHEMICALS, LP/106
Maintenance Engineering Corporation/106
Merisol/106
NL Industries, Inc./106
Nova Chemical Corporation/107

HealthSouth/168
Hill County Memorial Hospital/168
Huntsville Memorial Hospital/168
IHS Hospital/168
IHS of Corpus Christi/169
KCI (Kinectic Concepts, Inc.)/169
Kerrville State Hospital/169
Kimberly-Clark Tecnol Inc./169
Matagorda General Hospital/169
McKenna Memorial Hospital/169
McNeil Consumer Health Care/170
Memorial Hermann/Memorial
  City/170
Merit Medical/170
Methodist Specialty and Transplant
  Hospital/170
Metropolitan Hospital/170
Mission Hospital, Inc./170
Misys Healthcare Systems/171
Nix Health Care System/171
North Austin Medical Center/171
Northeast Baptist MRI Center/171
Sid Peterson Memorial
  Hospital/171
Physicians Resource Group, Inc.
  (PRGI)/172
Prime Medical Services, Inc./172
The Methodist Hospital/172
Round Rock Medical Center/172
Polly Ryon Memorial Hospital/172
St. David's Medical Center/173
St. Luke's Episcopal Hospital/173
San Marcos Treatment Center/173
SETON Healthcare Network/174
Shriner's Hospital Burn
  Institute/174
South Austin Hospital/174
Southwest General Hospital/174
Southwest Texas Methodist
  Hospital/175
Methodist Women's & Children's
  Hospital/175
Starlite Recovery Center/175
Sulzer Carbomedics, Inc./175
Sulzer Orthopedics/175
Tenet Mid-Jefferson Hospital/176

Texas Center for Infectious
  Disease/176
Texas Department of Health/176
Texas Children's Hospital/176
Texas Medical Center/177
Texas Orthopedic Hospital/177
Tomball Regional Hospital/177
Twelve Oaks Medical Center/177
U.S. Department of Veterans
  Affairs/Houston Veterans
  Administration Medical
  Center/177
U.S. Department of Veterans
  Affairs/Veterans Administration
  Medical Center/178
Valley Baptist Medical Center/178
Valley Regional Medical
  Center/179
West Oaks Hospital/179

HOTELS AND RESTAURANTS

Alamo Café/180
Doubletree Guest Suites Hotel/180
Embassy Suites Hotel/180
Flagship Hotel Over the Water/180
Four Seasons Hotel Houston/180
Golden Corral/180
Hoffbrau Steaks/181
Holiday Inn Beaumont Plaza/181
Holiday Inn Express/181
Holiday Inn Midtown/181
Holiday Inn North/181
Hyatt Regency Hill Country
  Resort/182
Hyatt Regency Houston/182
Jack in the Box/182
La Quinta Inns, Inc./182
Quality Inn Baytown/183
Taco Cabana, Inc./183
Victorian Condo Hotel &
  Conference Center/183

INSURANCE

ACAP Group/184
American General Corporation/184

MINING/GAS/PETROLEUM/
ENERGY RELATED

PAPER AND WOOD PRODUCTS

PRINTING AND PUBLISHING

REAL ESTATE

RETAIL

STONE, CLAY, GLASS, AND CONCRETE PRODUCTS

American Flat Glass Distributors, Inc. (AFGD)/244
Dal-Tile International/245
Fordyce Company/245
Shepler's/245
Vulcan Materials/245

TRANSPORTATION/TRAVEL

Blue Whale Moving Company/246
Capital Metro/246
Central Freight Lines, Inc./246
Federal Express Corporation (FedEx)/246
Port of Houston Authority/247
RailAmerica, Inc/247
Thai Airways International Ltd./247
Tidewater/247
Via Metropolitan Transit/247

UTILITIES: ELECTRIC/GAS/WATER

Texas-New Mexico Power Company/248

MISC. WHOLESALING

ACR Group, Inc./249
AMC Industries/249
Conti Window Fashions/249
Ferguson Enterprises, Inc./249
Johnson Supply and Equipment/250
O&M Sales, Inc./250
Prime Service/250
Reader's Wholesale Distributors Inc./250
Straus-Frank Company/250
Summit Electric/250
Wholesale Electric Supply Co., Inc./250

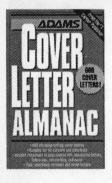

Adams Cover Letter Almanac

The *Adams Cover Letter Almanac* is the most detailed cover letter resource in print, containing 600 cover letters used by real people to win real jobs. It features complete information on all types of letters, including networking, "cold," broadcast, and follow-up. In addition to advice on how to avoid fatal cover letter mistakes, the book includes strategies for people changing careers, relocating, recovering from layoff, and more. 5½" x 8½", 738 pages, paperback, $12.95. ISBN: 1-55850-497-4.

Adams Cover Letter Almanac & Disk

Writing cover letters has never been easier! *FastLetter*™ software includes: a choice of dynamic opening sentences, effective following paragraphs, and sure-fire closings; a complete word processing program so you can customize your letter in any way you choose; and a tutorial that shows you how to make your cover letter terrific. Windows compatible. 5½" x 8½", 738 pages, *FastLetter*™ software included (one 3½" disk), trade paperback, $19.95. ISBN: 1-55850-619-5.

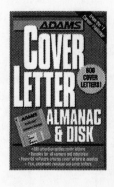

Adams Resume Almanac

This almanac features detailed information on resume development and layout, a review of the pros and cons of various formats, an exhaustive look at the strategies that will definitely get a resume noticed, and 600 sample resumes in dozens of career categories. *Adams Resume Almanac* is the most comprehensive, thoroughly researched resume guide ever published. 5½" x 8½", 770 pages, paperback, $12.95. ISBN: 1-55850-358-7.

Adams Resume Almanac and Disk

Create a powerful resume in minutes! *FastResume*™ software includes: a full range of resume styles and formats; ready-to-use action phrases that highlight your skills and experience; a tutorial that shows you how to make any resume terrific; and a full word processor with ready-made layout styles. Windows compatible. 5½" x 8½", 770 pages, *FastResume*™ software included (one 3½" disk), trade paperback, $19.95. ISBN: 1-55850-618-7.

Visit our Web site at adamsmedia.com

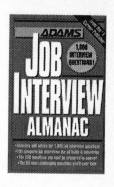